When Words Are Called For

When Words Are Called For

A Defense of Ordinary Language Philosophy

Avner Baz

HARVARD UNIVERSITY PRESS

Cambridge, Massachusetts

London, England

2012

Library of Congress Cataloging-in-Publication Data

Baz, Avner, 1964–
When words are called for : a defense of ordinary language philosophy /
Avner Baz.
p. cm.
Includes bibliographical references (p.) and index.
ISBN 978-0-674-05522-3 (alk. paper)
1. Ordinary-language philosophy.   2. Language and
languages—Philosophy.   I. Title.
B828.36.B39 2012
149'.94—dc23   2011039381

For Tal, Mishla, and Itamar

Contents

I know that the world I converse with in the city and in the farms is not the world I *think*. I observe that difference, and shall observe it. One day, I will know the value and law of this discrepance.

Ralph Waldo Emerson,
from 'Experience', *Essays*

We cannot learn philosophy; for where is it, who is in possession of it, and how shall we recognize it? We can only learn to philosophize—that is, to exercise the talent of reason, in accordance with its universal principles, on certain existing attempts at philosophy, though always with the reservation of the right of reason to investigate these attempts [or principles?!] themselves in their very sources, and to confirm or reject them.

Immanuel Kant, from
'The Transcendental Doctrine of Method',
Critique of Pure Reason

Preface

THE WORK OF PHILOSOPHY is full of surprises. The present book was nowhere in the offing when, in the fall of 2004, I joined the Philosophy Department at Tufts after spending four years at the University of Chicago as a Harper and Schmidt Fellow. I was at the time occupied with two variously related projects. The first, continuing on an earlier work of mine on Ludwig Wittgenstein's remarks on what he calls 'the seeing of aspects', was an attempt to articulate my understanding of his approach to the understanding and dissolution of philosophical difficulties. The second sought to express, from what I thought of as a Wittgensteinian perspective, my growing dissatisfaction with Kant's conception of judgment—empirical, moral, and aesthetic.

Once out of the University of Chicago, however, I became increasingly aware of the deep hostility and dismissive attitude within wide circles of mainstream analytic philosophy toward Wittgenstein's work, even if not toward some of his isolated 'results'.[1] I felt that I needed to go back and justify my general

---

1. I sometimes put single words or expressions in quotation marks, even though I am not quoting any particular text. I do this when presenting positions

philosophical approach—to myself first and foremost, but as far as possible in dialogue with those to whom that approach was alien.

I was quite confident, when I began working on this book, that the widespread hostility and dismissiveness toward Wittgenstein—more frequently encountered in the form of professional gossip than as the conclusion of serious engagement with his work—were suspect, and for two main reasons. First, I knew how hard it was to arrive at anything like a satisfying understanding of his work. Even if that work was fundamentally misguided in one way or another, successfully exposing it as such would not be a simple and straightforward matter. And second, the Wittgensteinian conceptual or grammatical investigation, as I understand it, while informed by a particular understanding of the nature of philosophical difficulty, is not *essentially* different from what competent speakers regularly do when they wish to become clearer about what they or others say or think. It would therefore be literally incredible if that form of investigation were somehow found to be illegitimate or misguided in some principled way.

But I did not know then, as I do now, how thoroughly reinforced by theoretical presuppositions the resistance to Wittgenstein's (later) work had become. As I wrote this book, I found myself again and again discovering, often with the help of colleagues and friends, yet another layer of theoretical bulwark set against the philosophical approach I was seeking to vindicate. The present book took shape in the wake of these discoveries.

---

or ideas that are not mine and that I do not (fully) endorse, and/or when the words in question are part of professional jargon. So there is a sense in which I *am* quoting in those moments. The quotation marks are meant to register this fact and the related fact that I myself may not be clear on what, if anything, the words in question mean, or could mean, in the particular philosophical context in which they appear. Here, for example, I mean to register the fact that what 'results' might mean in the context of discussing Wittgenstein's work is actually a difficult and important question.

The philosophical approach for which this book argues follows in the tradition commonly referred to as 'ordinary language philosophy' (or OLP). It also falls pretty squarely within the intended target range of the most common objections to that tradition. It is mainly for these reasons, as well as for the sake of convenience, that I chose 'ordinary language philosophy' as a label for the approach. However, I urge the reader to allow the book as a whole to clarify what, in it, is being designated by this rather vague and potentially misleading label. In presenting the approach, I make use of the works of others—in addition to Wittgenstein, I draw most heavily on the work of J. L. Austin and, to a lesser degree, on that of Peter Strawson. But my focus is not on exegesis. It does not matter to me in the end whether the philosophical approach articulated, exemplified, and defended in this book may aptly be attributed to any of these philosophers.

I wrote this book in response to what I saw as philosophical injustice, as well as a rather fateful philosophical mistake, and often felt embattled while writing it. This state of mind—exacerbated to be sure by the fact that the attacks on ordinary language philosophy, in any of its central historical forms, have often tended to be harsh, impatient, and heavily reliant on rhetoric—affected the tone of the book in ways that might sometimes work against my ambition of engaging seriously and fruitfully with those in contemporary analytic philosophy who would be inclined to dismiss the approach I seek to defend. I found, however, that conscious efforts to go back and alter the original tone of the book had only limited effect. I must therefore count on my readers to do some of the work themselves of separating passion from reason when assessing the case I make for a form of ordinary language philosophy.

Many people helped me write this book. My greatest debt is to Stanley Cavell. Years ago, when I was a graduate student of philosophy and continually worried that the world of professional philosophy was not one in which I could find myself, Cavell's work encouraged me to think that it could be and to look for ways of ensuring that it would be.

The friendly conglomerate of philosophical voices in the Tufts Philosophy Department created an ideal environment for working on this book. My colleague Jody Azzouni and my former colleague Mark Richard read early drafts of most of the chapters, and did what they could to help me accurately characterize the positions to which I was responding. They thereby saved me from any number of embarrassments. They are not, of course, responsible for those that have remained. Nancy Bauer and Dan Dennett share—to some extent at least, and each in their own way of course—some of my main reservations about contemporary philosophical theorizing in the analytic tradition, and they each provided me with much-needed advice and words of support at various stages of working on the book. George Smith read the epilogue and made helpful suggestions for how to deepen and make more precise my discussion of causation. Ray Jackendoff read an earlier version of the first two chapters and made some very useful and (mostly) encouraging comments from a linguist's point of view.

As I have mentioned, my four years at the University of Chicago did not quite prepare me for the conflict out of which this book grew. But numerous conversations with David Finkelstein, Michael Kremer, and especially Jim Conant, helped me to arrive at the philosophical approach for which it argues. More recently, a weeklong seminar at Åbo Academy in Finland in the fall of 2008 gave me an opportunity to discuss the main ideas of this book with a wonderful group of graduate students and faculty, and to test how well its different parts fit together to form a coherent whole. I benefited in particular during my time in Finland from long and spirited conversations with Lars Herzberg.

In addition to the people just mentioned, I received generous and valuable help from Stephen Affeldt, Reshef Agam-Segal, Laura Beeby, Pascal Brixel, Juliet Floyd, Warren Goldfarb, Robert Goodman, Martin Gustafsson, Jonah Horwitz, Peter

Hylton, Kelly Jolly, Gary Kemp, Kathrin Koslicki, Oskari Kuusela, Jean-Philippe Narboux, Tom Ricketts, Stephen Stich, Peter Sullivan, Charles Travis, and Molly Wilder. I thank them all. Versions of different portions of this book were advantageously shared with audiences at the University of Bordeaux, Boston University, Cambridge University, the University of Chicago, the University of East Anglia, the University of Glasgow, the 2008 Nordic Wittgenstein Workshop Meeting in Helsinki, the 2010 Annual Meeting of the North American Wittgenstein Society, and Tufts. Warm thanks are also due to Lindsay Waters at Harvard University Press for his support and assistance throughout the process of preparing this book for publication, and to three anonymous readers for deep and penetrating criticisms and suggestions without which the present book would have been significantly poorer.

During my time at Tufts I have been fortunate to be able to teach a number of courses and seminars that centered on the topics discussed in this book. I am deeply thankful to the graduate and undergraduate students who participated in those courses and seminars. Though this book strives to address itself to those who already think and work within the prevailing philosophical paradigm, it was written, in large part, with those just entering the world of professional philosophy in mind.

Throughout the time that I wrote the following pages, I was sustained—spiritually, emotionally, and bodily—by my family. Without my wife, Tal, and our two young philosophers, Mishla and Itamar, my work in philosophy, together with everything else that I do, would lose its reality for me, and its pleasures. This book is dedicated to the three of them with endless love.

When Words Are Called For

Introduction

THERE WAS A TIME, about midway through the twentieth century, when a new approach to understanding and
treating traditional philosophical difficulties seemed to hold the
promise of a fresh start, or turn, in philosophy. This approach
was thought to offer a way out of debates that, though typically
presenting themselves as in the business of making philosophical progress, had come to be seen, by some at least, as leading
nowhere. The new approach came to be known, generically, as
'ordinary language philosophy' (henceforth, 'OLP').

Within the mainstream of analytic philosophy, it is now
widely held that OLP has somehow been refuted or otherwise
seriously discredited, and that it may therefore philosophically
legitimately and safely be ignored. A central claim of this book
is that those who dismiss OLP have not entitled themselves to
that dismissal. The arguments and complaints commonly cited
against OLP, I will argue, do not succeed in undermining OLP's
general approach to the dissolution of philosophical difficulties. The other central claim of this book is that it is in the best
interests of present-day analytic philosophy to reopen the case
of OLP.

When 'ordinary language philosophy' is dismissed in contemporary analytic philosophy, what is actually being dismissed is something very broad, and only quite vaguely demarcated. What exactly *I* mean by 'OLP' and seek to defend in this book should become clearer as I go along. Very roughly, however, I refer to a particular form of critique of the tradition of Western philosophy—one that seeks to alleviate philosophical entanglements and obscurities by means of consideration of the ordinary and normal uses of philosophers' words, and the worldly conditions that make those uses possible and give them their specific significance.

I should emphasize at the outset that, in this book, 'use' will be used as I believe Wittgenstein uses it, to refer to a certain kind of human *achievement*, however humble and everyday—one that contrasts not with mentioning the words, but with letting them *idle*, or failing to do any (real) work with them.[1] One thing this means, and this is an important point to which I will return, is that whether certain uttered words are actually being *used* on the occasion of their utterance, inside or outside philosophy, and if so how, is never a straightforward empirical matter.[2]

---

1. The Austinian inflection of Wittgenstein's concern with what he calls 'use' is the emphasis on what we *do* with our words, and Austin's reminders to the effect that there are *conditions* for doing one thing or another with one's words. You can no more just decide, or bring it about just by willing, that your utterance will constitute, for example, a *claim*, than you could just decide or bring it about by willing that your saying 'I'm sorry' with no one to hear would constitute an *apology*.

2. Herein lies the most fundamental difference between the present book and Oswald Hanfling's (2000) admirable defense of OLP as he understands it. Hanfling and I share the general aim of reopening the case of OLP. We are also in agreement on any number of smaller points. Some of those points, as well as some points of local disagreement, will be noted in due course. The most important disagreement, however, is due to the fact that Hanfling follows Baker's and Hacker's (1992) influential reading of Wittgenstein—a reading from which Baker himself later distanced himself in Baker (2004). He therefore presents the appeal to ordinary language as, essentially, an *empirical* appeal to 'what we say', as opposed to an appeal to what it would *make sense* for us to say, and under what conditions; and he takes what we ordinarily say

Since the appeal in OLP to the ordinary and normal uses of words comes in response to traditional philosophical difficulties, understanding that notion of use goes hand in hand with understanding how OLP views those difficulties themselves. To put it simply, OLP rests on the claim that philosophical difficulties arise when we take our words to express thoughts, or to otherwise carry commitments or implications—of the sort, most importantly, that have been taken to generate traditional philosophical difficulties concerning truth, knowledge, meaning, or what have you—in virtue of something called 'their meaning', and irrespective of how we mean or may reasonably be found to mean them (which here just means irrespective of how we use or may reasonably be found to use them). In relying on the meaning of his words to identify his subject matter well enough and to ensure the sense or intelligibility of what he is saying about it, OLP argues, the traditional philosopher[3] expects

---

to provide a standard of 'correctness' (ibid., 109, 117). Accordingly, and again following Baker and Hacker, Hanfling's general complaint against traditional philosophers is that 'their claims . . . contravene the existing standards of correct use and inference' (ibid., 202). Elsewhere, Hanfling charges the traditional epistemologist, and particularly the skeptic, with 'redefining "knowledge" and changing the subject' (ibid.,125). I find the philosophical appeal to 'correct use' deeply problematic. It is bound not to impress the traditional philosopher, who knows as well as anyone that he is 'not speaking with the vulgar' but takes his extending (or 'subliming') of the ordinary meaning of words to be both called for and fully justified given his rather special interests. It also encourages a picture of language that is itself philosophically suspect—a picture according to which our words come with rules of correct use, as opposed to a history of use that endows them with powers or potentialities that constrain their future use, but do not foreclose more or less creative 'projections' of them into new contexts (see 'Excurses on Wittgenstein's Vision of Language' in Cavell [1979]). The philosophically pertinent distinction, I will propose, is not that between correct and incorrect uses of words but rather that between use and non- or merely apparent use, or else that between a use that serves the philosophical needs or purposes of the speaker and a use that undermines them.

3. The term 'traditional philosopher' is used here more or less technically to refer to whomever may be shown to have gotten herself into philosophical trouble by forming or otherwise committing herself to the above expectation. Later in the book the term will be used more narrowly to exclude

something of his words that—given the work we ordinarily and normally do by means of them and the conditions under which it may successfully be done—should not be expected of them. He thereby saddles himself with difficulties that derive whatever force they seem to have from that very expectation.

No less importantly, in disengaging the words of his theorizing from any of the needs, interests, and concerns that have given those words whatever powers they currently have, the philosopher risks having his theory lose contact with the world it is supposed to help us illuminate. OLP's unique value, and the main reason why I have found devoting a book to its defense worthwhile, is the way in which it enables us to bring our words back into contact with our world, while yet—and indeed *by way of*—acknowledging the philosophical pressures that have brought them apart. (One recurrent complaint against OLP that I will therefore want to challenge is that it is interested *only* in words. I will address this issue at the end of chapter 3.)

Upon encountering a stretch of philosophical discourse that she suspects of being ultimately nonsensical—that is, idling—or only fit for making sense in ways that would not sustain the philosophical concern supposedly under discussion, one thing the ordinary language philosopher characteristically does is to appeal to the ordinary and normal use of key words in that stretch of discourse. Against recurrent allegations to the contrary, I will argue that this appeal is not meant to *prove*, all by itself, that the stretch of discourse makes no sense. For, ultimately, the sense of words lies where people, including the traditional philosopher, are able to find it.[4] Rather, the appeal is meant to weaken the hold of the conviction that the philosophi-

---

contemporary 'contextualists', even though they still fit, as I shall argue, the description just given.

4. For the significance of this thought to an understanding of the later Wittgenstein, see Hertzberg (2001). Wittgenstein puts what I take to be the same point this way: 'I would like to say: "I must *begin* with the distinction between sense and nonsense. Nothing is possible prior to that. I can't give it a foundation"' (1978, pt. I, sec. 6: 81).

cal stretch of discourse does and indeed *must* make sense, simply because it consists of familiar words that are put together syntactically correctly. The appeal is also intended to invite those who take that stretch of philosophical discourse to make clear sense to ask themselves what that sense might be, and whether, given the sense or senses it could reasonably be found to have, it really does generate a genuine philosophical question or difficulty, or is otherwise fit to do the philosophical work that its author needs or wants it to do. OLP, as I understand it, is thus essentially *responsive:*[5] its 'reminders' are assembled for 'a particular purpose' (Wittgenstein 1963, remark 127), in an attempt to alleviate this or that particular philosophical difficulty or unclarity. OLP's reminders are assembled—when assembled well—not 'opportunistically', as Soames charges (2003, 216), but deliberately.

Even this rough characterization should make clear that much of what has gone in the last six decades or so under the title of 'ordinary language philosophy' is not what I will be referring to and seeking to defend. Furthermore, even though I will take my cues from a few exemplars, I do not intend to defend any one (or more) of them, or any one (or more) of their texts, in particular. My aim is to defend OLP at what I take to be its best, as a *general approach*, and to show that, persistent rumors to the contrary notwithstanding, it still has something viable to offer contemporary analytic philosophers.

Let me say a word about the overall structure of the argument of this book. OLP's approach, as I understand it, is better justified by the philosophical fruits it yields when applied to particular areas of philosophical difficulty than by any set of general arguments. In an important sense, therefore, the argument of this book only truly begins when, in chapter 3, I turn to the

---

5. This point has been most usefully emphasized at various junctures by Stanley Cavell.

contemporary debate concerning the reliance on 'intuitions' in philosophical theorizing. The argument continues in chapters 4 and 5, in which I discuss in detail the contemporary debate between 'contextualists' and 'anti-contextualists' with respect to the concept of propositional knowledge, and in the conclusion, where I propose an understanding of, and a response to, the form of skepticism to which both contextualists and anti-contextualists have responded. The epilogue, in which I compare and contrast OLP's approach to the dissolution of philosophical difficulties with Kant's proposed treatment of 'transcendental illusion', contains suggestions for how OLP might be applied in the case of other philosophically troublesome concepts, such as our concepts of causation and of the soul.

Ideally, I would have skipped chapters 1 and 2 altogether, and jumped straight to the argument of chapter 3, exemplifying from the very beginning my proposed approach rather than characterizing and defending it in the abstract, and hoping that it would, indeed, be vindicated by its fruits. Had I done that, I might not even have called the approach 'ordinary language philosophy'. Instead, I would have let the approach make a name for itself, so to speak, free of ancestral baggage.

However, when I began to make public early versions of chapters 3–5 and the conclusion of this book, it quickly became clear to me that I could not simply choose the philosophical context in which my argument would be encountered and evaluated. Thus, I would argue against Timothy Williamson that answers to the philosopher's question of whether some hypothetical case is a case of, say, knowledge, are importantly discontinuous with ordinary 'nonphilosophical' judgments, and that, therefore, the prevailing research program in analytic philosophy is even more deeply misguided than the common objections to it have suggested; and in response I would be told that if only one assumed the traditional distinction between semantics and pragmatics, the prevailing program could still be defended—even if not quite in the straightforward way that Williamson proposes. Or I would argue that the contemporary debate between 'contextualists' and 'anti-contextualists' with respect to propositional knowledge may not be settled in its current terms, and that the way out of the impasse is to recognize that the question to which both parties have been offering competing answers is itself misguided; and in response I would be charged with confusing 'meaning' and 'use', and referred to Peter Geach, Paul Grice, and John Searle for correction. Through these experiences I learned that the history of my argument had to be faced and shouldered, rather than set aside. I could not begin afresh.

This is how the first two chapters of this book came to be written. Their primary aim is not to defend any particular historical instance of what has been called 'ordinary language philosophy'—although I do believe that there is more in those instances that is defensible than is commonly acknowledged. Rather, the primary aim of these two chapters is to make clear that the argument of this book is not undermined by any of the common objections to previous attempts at OLP. Their aim, in other words, is to win a fair hearing for the argument of this book. For some readers, then, it would actually make more sense to skip the first two, ground-clearing chapters, and begin with chapter 3. They could then follow the argument all the way to the conclusion, and then return—or not—to the first two chapters as necessary.

CHAPTER I

The Basic Conflict—
An Initial Characterization

THIS CHAPTER PRESENTS, though necessarily provision-
ally, some of the main issues that will come into play in
subsequent chapters. Its main purpose is to set the stage for the
assessment, in chapter 2, of the main arguments against OLP. I
begin with the recurrent allegation against OLP that its practitioners tend to conflate the meaning of words and their use. As
I argue, the allegation presupposes one version or another of a
conception of meaning that OLP both questions in its own right
and, more importantly, sees as responsible for any number of
traditional philosophical difficulties. The upshot of my discussion in this first section will be that in the conflict between OLP
and its critics, each of the two sides is bound to seem to the other
to be begging a crucial question. This is a fact about the nature
of the conflict that the critics of OLP—and also many of its pur-
suers and advocates—have not properly appreciated. One thing
this fact means (assuming I am correct in calling it a fact) is that
a truly satisfying resolution of the conflict—which is, ultimately,
what this book seeks—is not going to be easy or straightforward
to attain. I conclude the section with a few words about how the
argument of this book is supposed to work.

I then turn to anchor my initial characterization of the conflict in two historical instances. In section 2, I discuss Strawson's 1949 and 1950 papers on truth—the first of which has often been held to exemplify OLP's conflation of meaning and use. In section 4, following a brief but rather important methodological remark about the nature of OLP's interest in the concept of meaning, I discuss Austin's 'Other Minds' (1979), paying special attention to his comparison of 'I know' and 'I promise', which also has drawn much fire from the critics of OLP. By the time we come to the end of this chapter, we should be ready for an informed assessment of the main arguments against OLP.

1. A Recurrent Charge against OLP, and a Prevailing Conception of Meaning

In one form or another, the most common objection to OLP, in any of its central historical forms, is that its practitioners are hopelessly confusing 'meaning' and 'use'. It is quite clear that those who put forth this objection take themselves to be disagreeing with Wittgenstein's suggestion that 'for a *large* class of cases—though not for all—in which we employ the word 'meaning', one could explain it thus: the meaning of a word is its use in the language' (1963, remark 43).[1] In most cases, however, the objection is more immediately directed at moments in which ordinary language philosophers allegedly confuse meaning and use *in their arguments*. Thus Grice announces—in introducing his theory of 'implicature', which was meant to serve in the rebuttal of what he took, erroneously as we shall see, to be a typical move on the part of ordinary language philosophers ('A-philosophers')—that 'the precept that one should be careful

---

1. I have slightly amended Anscombe's translation to bring out more clearly the theoretical un-ambitiousness of Wittgenstein's remark. To read into this remark the theory that the meaning of a word is its use is to do it violence. For an insightful discussion of this remark of Wittgenstein's, see Fox (2010).

not to confuse meaning and use is perhaps on the way toward being as handy a philosophical vade mecum as once was the precept that one should be careful to identify them' (1989, 4). In the same spirit, Searle argues that at the root of various fallacies that he attributes to OLP ('linguistic philosophy') lies the identification of meaning—which, similarly to Grice, he glosses over in terms of 'the applicability of concepts' (1999, 144)—and use (ibid., 146). As a result of that identification, Searle continues, 'the truth conditions of a proposition have been confused with the point or force of uttering a sentence' (ibid., 148).

In a more recent attack on what he calls 'ordinary language philosophy', Scott Soames describes its basic procedure as that of 'taking a given sentence' and trying to 'determine in what circumstances the sentence would ordinarily be used, as a more or less complete utterance' (2003, 129). Soames continues:

> If the [ordinary language] philosopher could not find such circumstances, he would be inclined to dismiss the sentence as meaningless, or as making only a pseudo-statement. If he could find circumstances in which the sentence would be used as a complete utterance, then he would look to see what speakers in such circumstances would normally be using the sentence to accomplish, or get across. When the philosopher had brought this out, he would take himself to have elucidated the meaning of the sentence. (Ibid.)

It is worth stating explicitly that the first part of this description does not accurately reflect the practice of any serious philosopher. As we shall see, it certainly fails to reflect Strawson's procedure in his 1949 paper on truth—the text that Soames is focusing upon in the part of his book from which the above quotation was taken. The ordinary language philosopher's question is not the one attributed to him by Soames: 'When or under what ordinary circumstances the philosophically troublesome or suspicious word (or combination of words) would—as a matter of empirical/statistical fact—be used?', where what is meant here by 'used' is, in effect, *uttered*. Rather, the ordinary language philosopher's question is, 'What are the ordinary and normal *uses* of this word (or combination of words), and what are their conditions?' The question, in other words, is when or under what ordinary circumstances utterances of this word would constitute genuine *uses* of it, and what uses those would be. Furthermore, the appeal to the ordinary and normal uses of some word or expression, and to their conditions, is not meant to *settle* the question of the sense or non-sense of some troublesome piece of philosophical discourse. Rather, it is meant to *raise* and to *press* that question against the assumption that the stretch of discourse does—and indeed must—make (clear) sense, simply by virtue of being composed of familiar words that are put together syntactically correctly; and to do so in the face of a philosophical difficulty that owes its apparent force to that very assumption.

The second part of Soames's description *might* have been true enough—of Strawson's early papers on truth, for example. Given how Soames and other detractors of OLP tend to conceive of the meaning of sentences and hence of what elucidating that meaning would require, however, there is reason to resist this part of his description as well. These issues will return in this and in subsequent chapters.

Following the lead of Grice and Searle, Soames then goes on to raise the following objection to the ordinary language philosopher's alleged approach:

> One shortcoming of this approach is that it overlooks the idea that the meaning of a sentence is only one factor in determining whether it will be used in a given situation. Other factors include what speakers and hearers take to be obviously true, and hence not worth saying, or obviously false, and hence incorrect to say, as well as things that are obviously irrelevant to the conversation. (2003, 129)

This is quite an incredible charge.[2] Can it really be believed that philosophers such as, for example, Wittgenstein, Austin, and Strawson, have simply *overlooked* the distinction between failing to say anything with one's words, or anything clear enough to be (for example) true or false, and saying something clear that is false, or trivial, or misleading, or impertinent, or otherwise 'conversationally inappropriate'? The accusation, as we will see, is false. And it stems from a failure to appreciate the philosophical significance of the first possibility—that of uttering a syntactically well-formed string of more or less familiar words and yet saying nothing, or nothing clear, or nothing that the utterer could reasonably be taken to have meant to say. But it is precisely this possibility that is at the heart of concern for the ordinary language philosopher.[3]

In terms of its effect, however, the above general line of objection to OLP has been very successful. One hears it recited, in one version or another, everywhere. The official line, or at least 'overarching agreement' within the mainstream of contemporary analytic philosophy, as Jason Stanley has recently summarized it in a text that presents OLP as a passing trend that analytic philosophy has thankfully managed to overcome, is that 'meaning and use should never be conflated, and that any

2. For an earlier version of the charge, see Searle (1999, 141). The charge is repeated, against Malcolm, in Hazlett (2009, 593–594). I agree that Malcolm is one of the so-called ordinary language philosophers who have made the life of detractors of OLP easier, by failing to appreciate the force of the prevailing conception of meaning and to address it head-on in their arguments. My claim, however, is that philosophers such as Soames and Hazlett have committed the mirror error, as it were, of failing to appreciate the distinction between understanding an utterance and merely *thinking* that one understands it. Thus, each of the two sides is bound to seem to the other to beg the main question—a fact about the nature of the dispute that Soames and Hazlett, unlike, for example, Grice (see 1989, 229), have failed to acknowledge. The argument of this book is an attempt to overcome this philosophical stalemate.

3. Compare Chomsky: 'Even if parsed and assigned an interpretation, [expressions of natural language] may be utterly incomprehensible' (1995, 3).

adequate account of meaning fundamentally employs the conceptions of reference and truth' (2008, 428).

The first thing to say about the accusation that ordinary language philosophers confuse meaning and use is that it presupposes one version or another of the very conception of (word) meaning that OLP, as I understand it, questions. This prevailing conception may *generically* be identified by means of three features. Not everybody who has opposed OLP, and not even everybody who I would regard as a proponent of the prevailing conception, is committed to all three features; but, as we shall see, each of those features has played a role in the dismissal of OLP, as well as in generating the traditional philosophical difficulties to which OLP has responded.

The first feature is the idea that for every word there is something that may be referred to as 'its meaning', which is theoretically separable from, and makes the word fit for, its ordinary and normal use(s). Wittgenstein identifies this first feature of the prevailing conception of meaning in the opening remark of his *Philosophical Investigations,* and it may be argued that his entire text is designed to combat this idea. Wittgenstein says that the idea has its roots in a picture and that the picture is found in Augustine's story of how he came to talk.

> In [Augustine's] words we get, it seems to me, a particular picture of the essence of human language. It is this: the individual words in language name objects—sentences are combinations of such names.—In this picture of Language we find the roots of the following idea: Every word has a meaning. This meaning is correlated with the word. It is the object for which the word stands. (1963, remark 1; see also 1958, 1)

The second defining feature of the prevailing conception of meaning is that sentences too are taken to have something that may be referred to as 'their meaning'. Generally speaking, the meaning of a sentence is thought of as what one would have to know in order to understand the sentence as it is in itself—that is, apart from any context of significant employment.[4] The meaning of a sentence is supposed to be theoretically separable from its possible uses, just as the meaning of a word is supposed to be theoretically separable from *its* possible uses.[5] Further, the meaning of a sentence is typically taken to somehow be combinatorially constructed from the meanings of the words that make up the sentence. Bach puts the basic, general idea thus: '[T]he meaning of a sentence [is] determined compositionally by the meanings of its constituents in a way that is predictable from how its constituents fit together syntactically' (2005, 16).[6]

It is commonly argued that this view of the relation between word-meaning and sentence-meaning must be true, for otherwise it would be impossible to explain our undeniable ability to use and understand indefinitely many combinations of words that we have never encountered before, and the *systematic* nature of how words may and may not be combined and used. In the third section of chapter 2, I will argue that what we might call the *systematic expandability* of language does not in any way undermine OLP's general approach and specific procedures. Compositionality as such carries no weight against OLP. It is only a very particular conception (or picture) of compositionality—one that presupposes versions of the first and third features of the prevailing conception of meaning—that clashes with OLP's understanding of and response to traditional philosophical difficulties. I will argue, however, that such a conception of compositionality is not required in order to account for linguistic phenomena and, in fact, tends to lead to distorted views of these phenomena.

4. See Dummett (1993, 107).

5. Davidson puts the basic idea this way: 'Literal meaning and literal truth conditions can be assigned to words and sentences apart from particular contexts of use' (2001, 247).

6. See also Dummett (1993, 108, 154). For a detailed characterization of the prevailing picture or set of assumptions at play here, see Jackendoff (1997, 48).

The third defining feature of the prevailing conception of meaning is that it takes the meaning of a word—at least in the majority of cases, and certainly when it comes to those 'singular substantives' that have given philosophers trouble for millennia ('knowledge', 'freedom', 'cause', 'meaning', etc.)—to be a matter of what it 'refers' to ('picks out', 'names', 'denotes').[7] And it takes the meaning of a sentence to be, or to determine, what the sentence 'says' or 'expresses', where *that* has often been called 'proposition' or 'thought' and taken to be cashable in terms of the conditions under which the sentence—either within some particular 'context' or as such—would be true.[8] This is why Stanley insists that 'any adequate account of meaning fundamentally employs the conceptions of reference and truth'. Timothy Williamson glosses over the prevailing conception in the

7. Of course, not very many people would take the meaning of 'and' or 'why', for example, to be a matter of its power to refer to some item or set of items in the world. But very many traditional philosophical difficulties may not be understood unless they are seen as rooted in the assumption that knowledge, for example, or free will, or causal relations, are in the world apart from any of the contexts in which we might felicitously speak of them, just waiting to be named and referred to by means of words. Much of this book will be devoted to demonstrating how this assumption controls contemporary debates concerning knowledge.

8. In chapters 4 and 5, I will argue that contemporary 'contextualism' does not represent a significant (enough) break with the prevailing conception. For the contextualist, the meaning of a sentence is still cashable in terms of truth conditions, albeit context-sensitive ones. Bach (1994, 2005) is another example of someone who insists on the second feature of the prevailing conception (and hence also on the first) but rejects the third. What Bach calls 'the semantic content' of sentences—while determined compositionally by the meanings of the words that make up the sentence (barring ambiguity, indexicality, etc.) and how the words are syntactically put together—often falls short of being a 'proposition', in the sense that it has no determinate 'truth conditions'. For all that, Bach insists that the semantic content of sentences is 'said' by these sentences, and by those who utter them. I find unclear Bach's notion of 'saying'—where the something that is said is presumably more than merely the string of words but less than what some utterer may be said to have asserted (stated, claimed, remarked, noted, or what have you) by means of it. But, in any case, deviations such as Bach's from the prevailing conception do not matter as far as the purposes of this book go.

following way: '[E]xpressions refer to items in the . . . world, the reference of a complex expression is a function of the reference of its constituents, and the reference of a sentence determines its truth value' (2007, 281). In some such way, words, or their meanings, are supposed to ensure the sense or intelligible content of human utterances.

The first feature of the prevailing conception is different from the third. That is, taking the meaning of a word to be theoretically separable from its ordinary and normal employment is different from taking the meaning of the word to be something like its power to 'refer to' some item or set of items—if not in the world, then in the speaker's mind, or in some Platonic heaven. These two features do, however, go hand in hand. Wittgenstein, as we just saw, speaks of the former as an 'idea' and of the latter as a 'picture', and says that the idea is rooted in the picture. At least when it comes to the philosophically troublesome singular substantives, it is very difficult to give any substance or plausibility to the idea without relying on the picture.[9] As we will see in the next section, where philosophers have given up on finding a reference for some philosophically troublesome word—'true', in this case—they have thereby rendered problematic the idea of a clear separation between the meaning of that word and its use. It is no accident therefore that Grice, one of the champions of the idea of meaning as separable from use, when he tries to come up with an analysis of the meaning of 'true' (1989, 55–57), and equally of 'saying' (86–138), and of 'seeing' (224–247), is looking for some worldly-cum-mental constellation in which the truth of

9. One could try to distinguish between essential and inessential aspects of the use of a word (see Wittgenstein 1963, 562–564). One could then propose that the meaning of the word consists of the former. But the distinction between what's essential and what's inessential to the ordinary and normal use of a word, however exactly one draws it, will not substantiate the common complaints against OLP's procedures.

an utterance, or the saying or seeing of something, would consist. He is looking for what x consists in in order to find out the 'conventional meaning' of 'x', and thereby to find out what someone who uttered a well-formed combination of words featuring 'x' would be saying.

Proponents of the prevailing conception of meaning will typically have a more sophisticated story to tell than that of, say, Locke or Hume, about *how* words come to refer to items in the world. Even so, however, in populating the world with nameable items—mental states, processes, and powers, relations, properties, etc.—that are simply waiting to be referred to or picked out by words such as 'know', 'cause', 'understand(ing)', and 'mean(ing)', and that are not dependent upon the actual practice of using those words for their identity or presence, these philosophers continue to participate in the basic empiricist picture of how our words and our world relate to each other.

The prevailing conception of meaning is, importantly, *representational,* or as it has sometimes been put, 'descriptivist'. Those who adhere to it would not deny, of course, that we do any number of things with words other than *describing, asserting, stating,* or otherwise representing things as being one way or another. Nonetheless, they would insist (and presuppose in their theories and arguments) that the representational function of language is somehow primary and fundamental to it, and that there is in every (philosophically interesting) case a representational ('semantic') element to speech and thought—an 'indicative core', as Davidson puts it (2001, 121)—that may, and should, theoretically be separated from the rest of what is involved in speaking or thinking.[10]

In Searle, for example, every speech-act is said to include 'a propositional act' that consists of 'referring' to an object and

---

10. For a recent break from the representationalist conception of language, see Kukla and Lance (2009).

'predicating' some property of it (1999, 22ff.).[11] This basic idea is subsequently developed into the idea that in every speech-act—at least every speech-act that features a 'subject expression' and a 'predicate expression'—'the question of the truth of the predicate expression is raised vis-à-vis the object referred to by the subject expression' (ibid., 122). The illocutionary force of the speech-act affects only 'the mode in which the question of truth is raised' (ibid.). As we shall see, Geach (1960, 1965) insists on similar ideas, taking the basic point to originate in Frege's distinction between, on the one hand, entertaining or considering a thought and, on the other hand, asserting it, or judging it to be true.[12]

The idea that language is first and foremost an instrument for the formation of representations, or for the expression of truth-evaluable thoughts or propositions, has led to a rather flat vision of the functioning of language and, consequently, of the meanings of our words. As a result of this flattened vision of language, differences that may be philosophically important between different words and the ways they function are either ignored, or else relegated to the realm of '(mere) pragmatics' and taken to be inessential to their meaning. The prevailing assumption is that our words, and hence their meanings, ought first and foremost

---

11. For a recent expression of the idea that every indicative sentence has a single proposition that is 'semantically expressed' by that sentence, see Cappelen and Lepore (C&L) (2005). If you ask C&L, '*What* proposition?', they'll invariably just repeat the sentence (modulo adjustments for indexicals, demonstratives, etc.). If you point out to them that the sentence contains words whose meaning has befuddled philosophers for millennia, they'll tell you that this is a problem for the metaphysician, not the semanticist (ibid., 155–175). One implication of this is that C&L's semanticist is no help to us when we wish to become clearer about what we mean or say, or to find our way out of conceptual entanglements. But from the perspective of OLP, this is not the deepest problem with C&L's position. The deepest problem is that C&L, in insisting that, say, 'know(s)' means *know(s),* and that it is now the metaphysician's job to tell us what *knowing* is, are presupposing the very picture of language that got us into trouble in the first place.

12. See also Dummett (1993, 153ff.).

to enable us to form representations of things and the ways they stand—to 'capture the world', as Horwich tellingly puts it (2005, v)[13]—and only *as such* may be usable for doing things other than, or beyond, representing. This is taken to be true not just of words such as 'Gödel', 'cat', 'water', and 'red', but also of philosophically troublesome words such as 'know', 'think', 'believe', 'see', 'seems', 'looks', 'good', 'reason', 'will', 'world', 'part', 'cause', 'free', 'voluntary', 'intention', 'soul', 'mind', 'pain', 'meaning', and so on.[14] (Expressivist accounts of 'moral' predicates are here an important exception that proves the general tendency.) Thus it is presupposed, as we shall see in great detail in subsequent chapters, that the basic function of 'know' and its cognates is to enable us to 'ascribe' knowledge or, in other words, to describe potential knowers as knowing this or that. What makes these words fit for this function, it is further presupposed, is their power to 'refer to' or 'denote' or 'pick out' some particular relation that sometimes holds between knowers and facts, or propositions— namely, the relation of *knowing*. To find out what 'know' means, the thinking goes, we need to find out what knowledge, or knowing something, is. The competent employment of these words is accordingly taken to require a capacity for identifying cases of knowledge (or absence of knowledge)—cases to which these words may in turn be 'applied' (if not positively then negatively) apart from any context of significant employment.

OLP challenges the prevailing conception of meaning and the conception of language of which it is a part. In particular, it sees them as the root of at least very many philosophical difficulties. In contrast to the prevailing idea that each of our philosophically

13. Thus, Horwich's *'use* theory of meaning' (2005) is still very much representationalist. Horwich takes himself to be following Wittgenstein, but his notion of 'use', unlike Wittgenstein's, is essentially representational.

14. I do not mean to imply that we can know in advance which of our words is liable to give us philosophical trouble. It seems to me empirically undeniable, however, that some words are more liable to do so than others.

troublesome words *first* refers to some item or set of items in the world, and only *thereby* becomes suitable for its various uses, OLP proposes that the way out of philosophical difficulties is to consider things in the reverse order: that is, to take the ordinary and normal use(s) of a philosophically troublesome word as primary, and as the best guide to what, if anything, it refers to, or picks out—in general, or on a particular occasion.[15] OLP further proposes that the ordinary and normal use of a word is normative for its future employment, including its philosophical employment, not in the sense that it is governed by or embodies rules that determine how the word may and may not be used, but just in the sense that it makes the word fit—within suitable contexts, and always ultimately depending on human judgment— for some uses and not others. For this reason, OLP proposes, when the worry arises that the philosopher might be failing to make clear sense with his words, or might be failing to make the sense he evidently wants or needs to make, a consideration of the ordinary and normal uses of his words is the best way to find out what sense, if any, he *could* be making.

What these proposals come to is a matter of what they come to *in practice;* and this is something that should become clearer as I go along. One potential misunderstanding may already be averted, however, by noting what should probably be obvious by now, which is that 'using *x*' as used in this book is not in general interchangeable with 'referring by means of *x* (or "applying" it)

---

15. Brandom puts the basic proposal helpfully, albeit still 'descriptively', this way: 'Don't look, to begin with, to the relation between representings and representeds, but look to the nature of the doing, of the process, that institutes that relation' (2008, 177–178). See also Williams (2004, 109). And compare Chomsky, who urges that we 'drop the empirical assumption that words pick out things, apart from particular usages' (1995, 23). Chomsky is here thinking of words like 'house', 'door', 'London', and 'water'; and he offers compelling evidence that what a word picks out, on occasion, is a function of the 'interests and concerns' that inform the particular usage (ibid., 22). My own proposal will be that when it comes to philosophically troublesome words such as 'know', we should drop the assumption that they are always, or even primarily, in the business of picking out things.

to some item or set of items in the world'. The reason why a philosopher such as Grice could have thought of himself as an ordinary language philosopher who was explicating in his proposed 'analyses' the ordinary 'use' of philosophically troublesome words, and equally the reason why I would question Grice's self-characterization, is that these two expressions, as *he* means them, *are* interchangeable (see, especially, Grice 1989, 174–175).

I have characterized the conflict between OLP and its detractors as being rooted in two different ways of thinking about the meaning of words and how it relates to what may be said by means of them. This initial characterization must be taken with a grain of salt, however, and not merely because it is extremely schematic. For, as I will emphasize later on, the conflict, at its core, is better seen as concerning not the nature of linguistic meaning, but the nature of traditional philosophical difficulties and the response for which they call. As I have said, OLP sees at least very many traditional philosophical difficulties as rooted in the key assumption that our words by themselves—irrespective of how, if at all, we are using them on some particular occasion—may express thoughts and thereby carry commitments sufficient for generating and sustaining precisely such difficulties. What I referred to as the 'prevailing conception of meaning' is one way of spelling out this widespread assumption, but it is surely not the only way. One may, for example, following Davidson, deny that there is anything to usefully refer to as 'the meaning' or, for that matter, 'the reference', of a word and still be committed to the assumption by taking the assessment of sentences in terms of truth and falsity as key to the understanding of human discourse, and by taking words to make systematic and stable contributions to the truth-conditions of (an individual's or a community's) sentences.[16] As long as one

---

16. See, for example, Davidson (2001, 18–22, 221). Whether or not Davidson himself was ultimately committed to the assumption that words alone may

continues to embrace the assumption that words may somehow ensure by themselves the sense of what is said by means of
them, however exactly one spells out this assumption, one will
find OLP's general approach to the understanding and treatment of traditional philosophical difficulties misguided. I will
therefore be variously concerned with this assumption throughout the book.

What I mean the argument of this book to accomplish is not
to *refute* the assumption in any of the ways in which it might
be spelled out—whatever refuting a fundamental philosophical
commitment might mean—but to show that, and how exactly,
it leads us to seemingly intractable philosophical difficulties;
and also to show that it is noncompulsory—that it has a viable
alternative: a perspective from which those difficulties lose their
apparent force. This argument, if sound, would show that the
traditional difficulties, however naturally generated, are ultimately self-inflicted and optional. But mostly I hope to vindicate OLP, as I understand it, by practicing it.

2. Exhibit 1: Strawson on Truth

In this section, I will consider Strawson's early pair of articles
on truth (1949, 1950) in order to illustrate how the prevailing
conception of meaning guides and informs objections to OLP
and to begin to challenge this conception. Of the two articles,
the second, which has been mostly ignored by Strawson's critics, better exemplifies OLP's approach as I understand it. But
my main reason for focusing on these two texts is that the *first*
has often been taken to exemplify the alleged failure of OLP to
distinguish meaning from use.[17]

---

ensure the sense of what is said by means of them is a complex issue that I
cannot go into here. Some of his later writings suggest that he was not (see, for
example, Davidson 2005), though not quite for the same reasons that lead OLP
to question the assumption.

17. Austin (1979, 133), by the way, also accuses Strawson of committing
some such mistake in that article.

I should note outright that Strawson's early broadly 'deflationist' approach to truth has a significant number of adherents
within the mainstream of contemporary analytic philosophy.
In this respect, its fate has been markedly different from that
of what may be called Austin's deflationist approach to knowledge, which, as we shall see in the second part of this book,
goes against the grain of contemporary theorizing about knowledge. The idea that 'true' is best thought of as a tool—whose
meaning is not first and foremost a matter of what in the world
it refers to but rather of what work may be done with it, and
how, and under what conditions—would not seem nearly as
foreign to contemporary analytic philosophers as the equivalent
idea about 'know'. There are two reasons why it would nonetheless be worth our while to consider Strawson's discussion of
truth. First, the discussion exemplifies a general approach to the
dissolution of philosophical difficulties that has not itself been
assimilated by the mainstream of analytic philosophy. And second, doing so will allow us to begin pressing the question of
what, if anything, those who accuse OLP of conflating meaning
and use could possibly mean.

Strawson's first article on truth is written in response to what
he refers to as 'the Semantic or Meta-linguistic Theory of Truth'
(1949, 83). Strawson does not identify his target by reference to
any particular text. It is quite clear, however, that he is responding to theories that derive from Tarski's semantic theory of truth
(1944), insofar as they purport to capture—as Tarski's theory
itself did not—the meaning of the ordinary predicate 'true'.
Strawson emphasizes that he has no problem with theories of
truth that confine themselves to artificially constructed 'languages' and only propose to define 'true' as a technical term that
applies within, or to, such languages. His quarrel is only with
those who believe that *our* 'true', like its technical namesake, is
a 'meta-linguistic' or 'second level' predicate (1949, 94) whose
function is to ascribe a property to sentences in our language.
Strawson recognizes that our 'true' is syntactically a predicate
and a 'singular substantive'. Even so, however, he argues that

it is neither apt nor philosophically useful to think of it as in the business of ascribing the property of *being true*—whatever it might be—to anything, be it sentences, the statements they might be used for making, the thoughts (or propositions) they might be used for expressing, or what have you.[18]

Strawson sees the theory of truth he targets as deriving at least part of its appeal from the thesis, originally put forward by Ramsey (1927), that in 'stating', 'It is true that such and such', we at least normally are not stating anything other than what could be stated by means of 'such and such' alone. In other words, 'is true' does not add to what is being *stated*. The mistaken theory of truth—taking it, after Ramsey, that 'is true' is not a first-order predicate that is used for making first-order statements about the world, but at the same time driven by the 'desire that the phrase "is true" should be some kind of a descriptive phrase' (Strawson 1949, 94), which is in turn encouraged by 'the fact that "true" occurs as a grammatical predicate' (1950, 147)—has made 'is true' out to be a second-order predicate that is used for making statements about declarative ('first-order') sentences of our language.

Now, about Ramsey's thesis, Strawson says that it is 'right in what it asserts, and wrong in what it suggests' (84).[19] It is right in asserting that to say that a statement is true is not to make a further statement—i.e., a statement about a statement. It is wrong in suggesting that the addition of 'is true' makes *no* difference. According to Strawson, the difference is not in what

18. The older Strawson came to retract this (see Strawson 1998, 402–404). And of course, if one understands 'ascribing (or predicating) the property of being true' as meant to do no more than to describe the ordinary and normal functioning of 'is true' *without* commitment to the existence of some linguistic (or mental)-cum-worldly constellation that is identifiable apart from that functioning and in which truth consists, then there may be no harm in saying that 'is true' is ordinarily and normally used for ascribing the property of being true to statements (claims, thoughts, beliefs . . .).

19. Notice, by the way, that Strawson has no problem making use of the distinction between what is said and what is 'implicated'—the distinction that lies at the heart of Grice's theory of 'implicature'.

we state, but in what we *do:* in uttering 'It is true that such and such', we at least commonly *affirm, agree with,* and in other contexts *concede,* the statement (contention, claim . . .) that such and such—where 'statement' here refers not to a speech-act or 'episode' of some particular type, but to what may be expressed in such an act (see Strawson 1950, 129–130). The mistaken theory of truth derives another part of its appeal, according to Strawson, from our sense that 'It is true that' *does* make a difference when placed before 'such and such'—a difference that Ramsey's thesis does not register, but that the theory under criticism mistakenly presents as a difference in the *representational* or 'descriptive' content of our utterance.

Strawson pays special attention to sentences of the form 'S is true if and only if S', where S is some syntactically well-formed sentence of a declarative form. In taking ourselves to understand such sentences, we presumably take them to speak of some relation that holds between the sentence S and a worldly constellation that *makes* sentence S, when true, *true.* Some have considered such 'T-sentences' to give us the meaning of S, taking it that the meaning of a (declarative) sentence is equivalent to its 'truth conditions' (Strawson 1949, 85). Others have taken such sentences to tell us something about truth, or about the meaning of 'true' (ibid., 88). Partly because he takes it that our 'true' does not normally apply to sentences, but rather to what may be said or expressed by means of sentences, and partly because he takes the 'correspondence' theory of truth to collapse upon reflection for lack of suitable correspondents,[20] the young Strawson maintains that these sentences are fit to do neither of those things. Of such sentences, he says that they make 'pseudo-statements' (1949, 87). *Pace* Soames (2003, 129), however, Strawson nowhere supports this proposal by arguing that he cannot think of circumstances in which such sentences would ordinarily be used (though his basic point *could* be made by saying that he cannot think of a genuine *use* for these sen-

20. Showing this is the main burden of Strawson's 1950 paper.

tences). Rather, he contrasts sentences of this form with sentences of the form 'S is true if and only if R', where R is a sentence different from S (belonging either to the same language or to a different one). Sentences of the latter form, he proposes, *may* be put to use—even if quite awkwardly, and only once it is stipulated that 'is true if and only if' is to be understood as equivalent to 'means that'.[21] Sentences of this form may be used to explain S, Strawson says, or to state a contingent matter— namely, that S means something rather than nothing, and that it means what it means rather than something else (1949, 86). Strawson further suggests that sentences of the first form are best thought of as 'degenerate cases' of sentences of the second form. The former, he says, may be gotten from the latter by 'a quite legitimate process of translation, inference, and retranslation' (1949, 86), but he thinks it is clear that they can be used neither for giving the meaning of S nor for stating a contingent fact about it. By contrasting the two forms of sentences, Strawson both invites his readers to ask themselves what contingent matter sentences of the first form could possibly state (1949, 86) and suggests why we might be tempted to suppose that there is something they state. He questions the widespread assumption that, simply because they seem to be syntactically well-constructed sentences of declarative form, there *must* be something (clear) they state.

Simply to assert in response to Strawson that T-sentences 'are perfectly meaningful by virtue of the meaningfulness of their parts' (Soames 2003, 132) is either empty or begs the question against Strawson. It is empty if calling part of a sentence 'meaningful' is a way of saying that we can see what work it does, or could do, *as part of that sentence,* for then the meaningfulness

---

21. I should say that Strawson is not sufficiently careful when it comes to what he expects of 'means that'. '"The monarch is deceased" means that the king is dead' (1949, 85) is awkward; and, as Travis shows convincingly in response to Grice (Travis 1991, 250ff.), there is no simple way of alleviating the awkwardness and having 'means that' do the sort of work that Strawson, like Grice, supposes it to do.

of the parts is no more ensured than the meaningfulness of the sentence.[22] And it is question-begging if 'meaningful', when applied to words, is supposed to mean something like 'has a meaning'—in the sense of 'is part of the language, is not mere noise, etc.'—and 'meaningful' when applied to sentences is supposed to mean something like 'says something clear' or 'expresses a truth-evaluable proposition', as it does in Soames (cf. 2003, 127). For it is clear that Strawson does not take the meaningfulness of a sentence, thus understood, to be ensured by the meaningfulness of its parts, thus understood.

I have only provided the gist of Strawson's response to the theory of truth he targets in his 1949 article, but this should suffice for now. Further pertinent details will come up as we go along. My aim, remember, is not to defend this particular article of Strawson's, nor to contribute to the vast philosophical literature on truth, but to explicate and defend an approach to the dissolution of traditional philosophical difficulties. What should be noted is that Strawson's appeal in that early article to what we ordinarily and normally *do* with 'true', or with expressions containing it, is not, or anyway need not be taken as, aiming to support a theory of truth.[23] Rather, as I have indicated, the appeal is *diagnostic* in nature: an attempt to account for our sense that the word does make a difference to stretches of discourse of which it is a part, and thereby to disarm that sense as a source of theoretical confusion and difficulty. It seems to me, therefore, that a charitable reading of the 1949 article would find in it not a 'performative theory of truth', but rather only a description of certain common uses of 'true' and their conditions—a description that is meant to weaken the hold of a prevailing conception of truth.

Searle brands Strawson's early essay on truth an instance of 'the speech-act fallacy', of which he accuses 'the linguistic

---

22. This is a version of Frege's famous 'context principle' (1999, x).

23. Strawson's own later description of himself as proposing a theory of truth in that early article notwithstanding (1998, 8).

philosophers' (1999, 136ff.). To succumb to the fallacy is to mistake a particular speech-act that may be performed with some
word or expression for the meaning of that word or expression.
Having attributed to these philosophers—quite misleadingly,
as we shall shortly see—the ambition of coming up with an
'analysis' of the meaning of philosophically troublesome words,
he goes on to articulate the following requirement for any successful analysis:

> Any analysis of the meaning of a word (or morpheme) must
> be consistent with the *fact* [my emphasis] that the same word
> (or morpheme) can *mean the same thing* [my emphasis] in
> all the grammatically different kinds of sentence in which it
> can occur. (1999, 137; see also 138–139)

Since any particular speech-act that may be performed with
sentences of one type that contain the word in question will not
be performable with sentences of other types that also contain
that word—this is just what 'different types of sentences' means
here—and since presumably the word nonetheless means or at
least can mean *the same thing* in all of those different sentences,
it follows, according to Searle, that the meaning of a word is
theoretically separable from the various speech-acts that may
be performed with sentences containing it. The 'analyses' allegedly proposed by ordinary language philosophers ignore this
basic 'fact', according to Searle. I will come back, in chapter 2,
to Searle's attempt to establish this 'fact'.

Along similar lines, Grice argues that 'on the assumption that
it was intended to give an account of the meaning of "true"',
Strawson's 'theory' has 'two unattractive features'. The first
feature—originally put forward by Geach (1960) and Searle
(1962)—is that 'it gives no account, or no satisfactory account,
of the meaning of the word "true" when it occurs in unasserted
subsentences (e.g., "He thinks it is true that . . ." or "If it is true
that . . .")' (1989, 55). The second is that it does not 'provide for'

the occurrences of 'true' in sentences in which the content of the statement said to be true is not specified (e.g., 'The policeman's statement was true') (ibid.). Grice goes on to propose that 'true' does refer to a property (though of utterances, not of sentences), and he attempts to define that property along Tarskian lines (ibid., 56–57).

Soames too attributes to Strawson the ambition of coming up with a 'theory' or 'analysis' of truth, and argues against him that his theory 'fails to properly distinguish meaning from use' (2003, 123). He then explains:

> It is correct to observe that the sentence *The proposition that S is true* is often used, when uttered assertively, to endorse, confirm, or concede the proposition expressed by S.[24] However, it is a mistake to think that this observation provides an analysis of the meaning of *true*, or of sentences containing it. To suppose otherwise is to ignore a crucial requirement on analyses of meaning—namely, that an adequate analysis of meaning of an expression must specify the contribution made by the expression to the meanings of larger sentences or discourses in which the expression may be embedded. (Ibid., 123–124).

Now, it certainly is true that Strawson does not provide an analysis (or theory) of the meaning of 'true' as Searle, Grice, and Soames appear to conceive of such an analysis. He does not, in other words, offer an account of the form 'Truth is . . .' or '"true" means . . .', from which one would be able to derive,

---

24. It is worth noting that Strawson actually says nothing in his essay about how 'The proposition that *S* is true' is often used, and for the simple reason that sentences of this form most likely are never used outside of philosophy. In fact, he doesn't even talk about how sentences of the form 'That such and such is true' are used, for even sentences of this form are hardly ever used outside of philosophy (and certain literary occasions). He mainly talks about how 'It is true that such and such' and 'That's true' are used.

perhaps with the aid of a general theory of speech-acts, all of the possible uses of 'true'.[25] But he also never claims to be providing such an analysis. In the sequel to his early essay on truth, he makes it abundantly clear that he regards any attempt to come up with such an analysis of the meaning of 'true' or theory of truth as hopeless. In that second article, Strawson's main target is the 'correspondence' theory of truth; but it would be a mistake to take him to be offering a competing theory. A major obstacle to understanding him is the assumption that he must be.

To the extent that Strawson may aptly be said to offer, not a theory of truth, but something like a philosophical position with respect to truth, that position is probably best expressed in passages such as the following: 'Better than asking "What is the criterion of truth?" is to ask: "What are the grounds for agreement?"—for those we see to be not less various than the subjects on which an agreed opinion can be reached' (1949, 94).[26] Such passages, I think, should not be read as expressing a general theory of truth—antirealism, say, or pluralism, or what have you. Rather, they are best read as aiming to reorient our philosophical attention away from general questions about the nature or essence of truth, and toward questions that are typically fairly easy to answer about the uses of 'true' and their conditions. For this reason, Searle's insinuation that Strawson's invocation of some common uses of 'is true' is supposed to 'tell us the solution to the philosophical problem of truth' (Searle 1999, 154) is misguided. For the invocation is rather part of an effort to get us to stop supposing that we already know what *the* philosophical problem of truth is and what form an adequate solution to it would need to take.

Strawson speaks of the attempt to offer an analysis of 'true' or a theory of truth of the sort envisioned by his critics as the

25. Here I am not so much interpreting Searle, Grice, and Soames, as—to borrow a phrase from Quine (1991, 272)—taking their word ('analysis' or 'theory') and handing it back to them.

26. Compare Kant (1998, A 58–59/B 83, A 820–821/B 848–849).

attempt to take a word whose normal employment is *within* a discourse of a certain type—Strawson refers to it as the 'fact-stating' or 'empirically informative' type of discourse (1950, 142, 156)—and try to use it for saying something general about that particular 'frame of discourse' from a point of view altogether external to it (142).[27] He argues that such an attempt is doomed to frustration. According to Strawson, what we inevitably do when we attempt to give an analysis of the sort envisioned by his critics is rely on other words whose primary (relevant) employment is also within the discourse that we seek to ground metaphysically—words such as 'fact', 'state of affairs', 'statement', and, one might add, 'assert(ion)', 'exist(ence)', 'real(ity)', 'thought', 'belief', 'objective', 'evidence', 'proof', 'being right', 'being mistaken', and so on. The result is that we are idly going in circles. The words used in our proposed analysis presuppose, or incorporate in *their* meaning, the very 'problem' we were looking to solve by means of analysis (141).[28] It is futile, Strawson contends, to try to use 'fact' or 'statement' in an analysis of the meaning of 'true', because you cannot understand (know the meaning of) 'fact' and 'statement' unless you *already* also understand 'true' (ibid.).[29] If we wish to become clearer about

27. John McDowell would say that in such moments we wish to be able to assess 'from sideways-on' the relation between a particular region of discourse and reality.

28. One is reminded here of Hartry Field's (1972) well-known contention that Tarski does not succeed in defining 'true' in 'non-semantic' terms. And compare Wittgenstein's saying that 'the proposition that only a *proposition* can be true can say no more than that we only predicate "true" and "false" of what we call a proposition' (1963, remark 136). Compare also Brandom's saying that 'one cannot properly understand any of the concepts <u>assertion</u>, <u>sentence</u>, and <u>proposition</u> apart from their relation to each other' (2008, 117); and Williams's saying that 'With such concepts as belief, truth, and meaning, none can be defined. But all can be illuminated by tracing their relations with each other' (1999, 552). Grice's failed attempts over the years to develop and improve upon analyses of 'saying' and 'meaning' seem to me to illustrate particularly well the problematic Strawson has in mind.

29. Witness here Kölbel's recent proposal to define a substantive notion of 'truth' by means of a deflationary notion of 'truth' plus a notion of 'factuality',

the meaning of 'true', Strawson says, we should consider 'how this word fits into that frame of discourse?' (143), or ask 'How do we use the word "true"?' (145), instead of looking for general conditions—the truth-conditions of 'is true', as it were—that would enable us to 'apply' the word from outside of that discourse. Following Wittgenstein, we might say that what Strawson regards as doomed to frustration is the attempt to establish, or discover, 'a *super*-order' between '*super*-concepts'—between concepts, that is, that do not depend for their identities and mutual relations on the 'humble' uses of the words that express them within the very discourse that their super-order was supposed to ground (see Wittgenstein 1963, 97).

If Strawson, as I read him, is right that no truly satisfying analysis of the meaning of 'true', or theory of truth, of the sort envisioned by those who accuse him of conflating meaning and use, is forthcoming (and the history of the philosophical quest for such an analysis or theory gives us no reason to suppose otherwise); and if there are good reasons to take the *demand* for such an analysis or theory to be not only ill-founded, but also responsible for much philosophical difficulty (I will argue in subsequent chapters that there are); then humble and tailored-to-this-or-that-particular-difficulty elucidations of the use(s) of 'true', of the sort found in Strawson's early pair of articles on truth, may well be not only the best we could reasonably expect, but also all that we really need, as far as dissolving philosophical difficulties with the concept of truth is concerned.

Soames, as we saw, insists—against Strawson—that an analysis of the meaning of 'true' should specify the contribution made by the word to 'sentences or discourses in which it

---

which he in turn proposes to define in terms of the notion of 'objectivity', where an objective proposition, according to Kölbel, is any proposition, *p*, such that 'it is a priori that when one thinker believes *p* and another thinker believes not-*p*, one of them must be mistaken' (2008, 376). I suspect that if Kölbel were to try to explicate the notion of 'being mistaken', he would ultimately find himself relying on the notion of 'truth', or anyway on notions no less treacherous, philosophically speaking.

is embedded'. But surely, Strawson *does* specify, albeit not in the way Soames has in mind, the contribution made by 'true' or by expressions containing it, not to sentences *per se,* but to certain kinds of utterances or stretches of discourse. Not only does Strawson emphasize the use of this word in confirming or agreeing with a statement already made, or in conceding a point, for example, but he also argues that this is all that it, or an expression containing it, contributes *in such contexts.* Substitute 'Yes' or 'Ditto', or 'I agree', for 'That's true' and, in certain contexts, nothing will be lost, he claims (1949, 89). Similarly, substitute 'Although . . .' or 'I concede that . . .' for 'It's true that . . .' and again, in certain contexts, nothing will be lost (ibid., 95). The expressions that, according to Strawson, may, in certain contexts, replace 'is true' (or expressions containing it) without loss cannot plausibly be thought of as being used for ascribing a property to some entity, and this should discourage us from presupposing that 'is true', at least in these contexts, is used for representing something (a statement, a sentence, a proposition, or what have you) as having some particular property (being true) (ibid., 95–96; 1950, 146).[30] Now, doesn't this tell us something about the contribution made by 'true', or by expressions containing it, to certain stretches of discourse? And doesn't it thereby tell us, not everything, to be sure, but nonetheless something about the meaning of 'true'—something, moreover, that one would have to know, if one were to count, by ordinary criteria, as knowing its meaning?[31]

---

30. Strawson's method of "translating" sentences in which 'is true' (or 'is false') appears to be used descriptively by sentences in which there is no expression that may plausibly be taken to perform *that* descriptive function is yet another important respect in which he anticipates later deflationists. See Azzouni (2007), for example, for a far more systematic method of such 'translations' of sentences featuring 'true' by sentences—of a language Azzouni calls 'Anaphorish'—that feature no expression that does the 'predicative' work one might be tempted to attribute to 'true'.

31. This question is pressed quite powerfully, and to my mind compellingly, by Glock (1996). See also in this connection Hare's (1970) defense of his (1952) account of the meaning of 'good'. Part of the reason why Hare and his critics

The only reason for insisting that Strawson has not told us anything about the meaning of 'true' is the presupposition that the meaning of 'true' ought to be specifiable apart from any specification of the ways in which it is ordinarily and normally used, and that it ought to be something that 'true' brings with it to each and every one of its uses. Drop the presupposition, and it will not be clear why reminders such as Strawson's are not revelatory of (aspects of) the meaning of 'true', and why their deliberate assembling may not be the best method for becoming clearer about that meaning.

Nor will it be clear how pointing to uses of 'true' that Strawson does not discuss—as Searle, Grice, and Soames do—is supposed to undermine his argument. Strawson is happy to admit that he has not described all of the 'functions' or 'jobs' of 'true' (1949, 96; 1950, 147). Why can't the philosophical elucidation of a concept, or of the meaning of a word, take its cue from the philosophical difficulty or confusion at hand, and focus just on those uses of a word that are deemed pertinent to it? Strawson says at the outset that he is confining himself to the truth of empirical statements (1949, 83), and he makes clear that he is focusing just on that use of 'true' that seems to him pertinent to showing what's wrong with the theory he targets (1949, 90). I am *not* saying that Strawson has correctly identified all of the uses of 'true' that might be pertinent to an assessment of the theory he criticizes.[32] Nor am I saying that his description of the

---

seem to be talking past each other is that it simply does not occur to him, and for quite good reason I believe, that the meaning of 'good' may be anything less than what an otherwise competent speaker would have to know in order to employ it competently and to understand other people's competent employment of it, in a variety of different contexts. This is why Hare insists that the word's (context-dependent) descriptive powers do not exhaust its meaning, and why he further insists that the 'performative' dimension of this word's function is essential to its meaning.

32. The use of 'true' in *generalizations* ('Everything [much of what, none of what] he says is true'), for example, may be pertinent for an assessment of the theory Strawson targets, but it is not hard to see how Strawson's deflationist account could be expanded to accommodate it. The same goes for the

uses on which he does focus is everywhere accurate and sufficiently complete. He himself acknowledges in his second article on truth that he 'over-emphasized' the performatory dimension of our use of 'true' in his earlier article (1950, 150).[33] The point remains, however, that we have not yet seen any reason for taking Strawson's *general approach* to be misguided in the way that his detractors claim it is.

It is one thing to complain against Strawson that he has only given a partial account of the use of 'true'. Given Soames's general deflationist position with respect to truth,[34] *this* seems to me the complaint he should have leveled against Strawson; but, again, only if that partialness could be shown to undermine Strawson's basic point in his 1949 article. At any rate, to accuse Strawson of conflating *meaning* and use—as opposed to getting the use wrong or not entirely or quite right—muddles the issues. It also encourages the prevailing conception of meaning, which has *not* been vindicated in any way by the shortcomings of Strawson's account.

Those who accuse Strawson of conflating the meaning of 'true' and its use evidently assume that the word has a meaning such that we could *first* come up with an account of that meaning—without any reference to its ordinary and normal uses— and then see how a word with *that* meaning is usable in all of the ways that this word is usable. And it is this assumption that OLP, as I understand it, both questions in its own right and sees as responsible for at least very many of the difficulties that have exercised philosophers for millennia and which conceptual

---

'embedded' uses that Searle and Grice accuse Strawson of having missed. I'll return to the 'argument from the possibility of embedding' in chapter 2.

33. This seems to me to suggest that something like the 'prosentential' account of 'true' might better have captured the deflationary (though not the diagnostic) point that Strawson was trying to make in his first article. For the prosentential account of 'true', see Grover, Camp, and Belnap (1975). For a proposed dissolution in light of that account of the liar's paradox, which acknowledges its indebtedness to Strawson, see Grover (1977).

34. As presented, for example, in Soames (2003b).

analysis was supposed to bring to an end. In assuming meanings for our words that are theoretically separable from their various uses and carry commitments for their utterer regardless of how, if at all, she uses them, OLP proposes, *we have created problems for ourselves*—problems for which not the meanings of our words, but a deeply entrenched conception of what they must be and do, is responsible.[35]

3. A Methodological Remark: OLP and the Meaning of 'Meaning'

As we have just seen, Strawson suggests that if we wish to become clearer about the meaning of 'true', and about truth, we should consider 'how this word fits into' the 'fact-stating' discourse (1950, 143) or ask 'How do we use the word "true"?' (ibid., 145). Wittgenstein likens words to instruments (*Werkzeuge;* literally, 'work things', things to do work with), and suggests that in many cases, 'the meaning of a word' would best be explained by saying that the meaning of a word is its use in the language. And I will later propose that we think of the meaning of a word as its suitability or potentiality for being put to various uses (under suitable conditions). It would be a mistake to take any of this as putting forward a theory of meaning, or an analysis of the meaning of 'meaning'. If the ordinary language philosopher were to try to provide *that,* he would be guilty of the grossest self-contradiction. To understand the ordinary language philosopher's 'meaning' is, ultimately, to see what work he does with it. I do believe that where that work is not diagnostic—an attempt to characterize and shake the hold of the prevailing conception of meaning—it is not essentially different from the work that we ordinarily and normally do with this word outside of philosophy. The basic disagreement between OLP and

35. The famous 'liar paradox', which Strawson briefly discusses in the earlier article, is a case in point. Fully developing an OLP response to the paradox is a task that I leave for another occasion.

the philosophical tradition it responds to, at any rate, is not about the meaning of 'meaning', or even about what meanings are; rather, it is about the nature of philosophical difficulty, and the response for which it calls. But for my reluctance to concede the humble and everyday concept of meaning to the theoretician, I might have tried to avert potential misunderstandings by following Quine's and Davidson's 'meaning deflationism' and saying: in appealing to the ordinary and normal uses of a philosophically troublesome word, the ordinary language philosopher is seeking to elucidate not its meaning, but rather the particular philosophical puzzlement or difficulty at hand.

In many cases, it does not matter very much whether we say that the difficulties we run into in our attempts to come up with a philosophical theory of x—truth, knowledge, freedom, causation, or what have you—are difficulties with (our understanding of) the meaning of 'x', our concept of x, or x itself. At least in very many cases, we can say what we will, as long as we do not confuse ourselves or others. What does matter for OLP is that—notwithstanding the traditional philosopher's tendency to think of himself as investigating x, as contrasted with the meaning of 'x' or our concept of x—the difficulty all too often takes the form of, or is ultimately rooted in, our being unclear about what we mean, or say, or think; our 'not knowing our way about', as Wittgenstein puts it (1963, remark 123). This is in contrast with a widespread conception of philosophy, according to which the worst that could befall one in philosophy is saying or thinking something false, or otherwise incorrect, about x.[36]

The ordinary language philosopher's appeal to ordinary and normal discourse would typically need to be more systematic

---

36. A recurrent motif of OLP is the suggestion that the question to which philosophers have been offering competing answers is somehow out of order. See Wittgenstein (1958, 169); Austin (1964, 1–5); Ryle (2000, 22); and Strawson (1974). In this, as in other respects, OLP was anticipated by Kant, especially in the 'Transcendental Dialectic' part of the *Critique of Pure Reason* (1998). I will return to this Kantian motif at various points in this book and more systematically and in detail in the epilogue.

and deliberate than anything called for outside of philosophy (and certain branches of linguistics—but in linguistics the examination of ordinary and normal discourse is guided by different interests, and therefore tends to take a different form). It is also informed by a particular understanding of what leads us to philosophical trouble. At the same time, however, it is not essentially different from what we do when, outside philosophy, we try to figure out or make clearer to ourselves what, if anything, someone is saying with her words, or how her words ought to be understood. This is an important point that has not been adequately appreciated by opponents of OLP. In both philosophy and ordinary life, a consideration of the ordinary and normal use(s) of someone's words serves to make clearer what, if anything, she *could* reasonably be taken to say with her words, and whether what she could reasonably be taken to say is what she apparently has wanted to say, or needs to (be able to) say given her situation and purposes.

If I am right in claiming that the practice of OLP is a natural extension of perfectly ordinary and everyday attempts to become clearer about what we or others are saying or thinking, then no plausible theory of language could entail the illegitimacy of this practice. I will come back to the topic of OLP's relation to philosophical theories of language in the third section of chapter 2.

4. Exhibit 2: Austin's 'Other Minds'

Before I turn to examine, in the next chapter, the main arguments put forward in support of the prevailing conception of meaning and against OLP, I want to consider Austin's 'Other Minds'— another text that has been said to exemplify OLP's alleged conflation of meaning and use. Unlike Strawson's early papers on truth, which were used purely heuristically in this chapter and which will not play any significant role in subsequent developments of the argument of this book, Austin's paper will prove pertinent throughout the book, all the way to its conclusion.

The critics of OLP have tended to focus exclusively on very few pages of 'Other Minds'. In those pages, Austin argues that what 'I know that . . .' adds to 'such and such' is not a description of some further purported fact—a fact about the speaker's epistemic relation to such and such, or about some particular mental state of his—but rather is to be understood on the model of what 'I promise . . .' adds to 'I will do such and such'. To say 'I know that such and such', according to Austin, is not to describe ourselves at all, but rather to perform the speech-act of 'giving others our word' and 'giving them our authority' for saying that such and such (1979, 99ff.). Just as Strawson urges that we not be misled by the fact that 'is true' is grammatically 'a singular substantive' into thinking that it is used to 'refer to something' (1950, 130), or is 'a descriptive phrase' (1949, 94), so Austin urges us not to suppose that 'I know' is 'a descriptive phrase' (1979, 103).

I should say outright—and this is a point that in subsequent chapters I will further develop and press—that Austin's account is importantly incomplete; and since it does not present itself as such, it may simply be said to be false. The use of 'I know (that such and such)' Austin discusses is in fact *very* rare. Normally, we simply say (claim, assert, inform the other . . .) that such and such, and then give the other our *basis* for taking it, and for saying, that such and such, often upon being asked 'How do you know?'—the question on which Austin focuses in 'Other Minds'. In the majority of cases, the other person would be just as competent to assess our basis as we are, and there would therefore be no special authority for us to claim for ourselves, or give. If I have a good basis for my claim, and one, moreover, that I think you would be able to properly appreciate, it would make no sense for me to urge you to trust *me*. Normally, I will in such a case simply tell you what my basis is, and *thereby* seek to alleviate your doubts. In subsequent chapters I will argue that in situations of this common sort, the question of whether I *know,* as pressed by philosophers—whatever exactly it might be thought to come to—is beside the point, or idle, as far as those involved in the situation are concerned.

The use of 'I know (that such and such)' on which Austin focuses would be natural only in situations where the claim that such and such is grounded in some sort of *expertise,* as for example when the claimer is an expert in identifying birds, or perhaps in identifying some particular person's moods. More generally, this use would be in place where the other is for some reason not in a position to assess one's basis.[37]

'I know that such and such' is far more commonly used in situations in which the obtaining of such and such is *not* in question and no one is in need of being assured of it. Think, for example, of the 'I know' of sharing a reaction to a piece of purported news,[38] or the 'I know' of acknowledging a significant fact.[39] Austin—taking his cue from the tradition's obsession with knowledge as that which supposedly puts one in a position to give assurance (first and foremost to oneself)—ignores such situations. Clearly, the normal use of 'I know' in such situations is not analogous to the normal use of 'I promise' in the way Austin suggests.

Of course, from the tradition's perspective, both Austin's observations and my reservations would seem beside the point, as far as the meaning of 'know' is concerned, since what may be done—and what ordinarily and normally is done—with 'know' and cognates is taken to be inessential to what 'know' means and to what knowledge is. As the tradition understands it, there is one and the same thing that 'I know that such and such', when uttered literally and seriously, says of the speaker—namely, that he *knows;* that he stands in the relation of *knowing* to such

37. According to John Hardwig (1991), contemporary scientific research relies essentially on expertise and on the collaboration of individuals—none of whom knowing, or even able to know, the full basis for claims collectively put forward by the research group. If so, then contemporary science may provide occasions for the use of 'I know' that Austin discusses.

38. 'Jack and Jill are getting married!'

'I know!' (with a tone of excitement, or, alternatively, with a sigh).

39. 'I know he is angry with me; I just haven't had the time to speak with him about what happened'.

and such. What things we ordinarily and normally illocution-arily do in uttering these words in different contexts, what the significance or point might be of doing them, when it would be appropriate or possible to use the words in some particular way, how they might appropriately be responded to when thus used and so forth—all of this is taken to presuppose the mean-ing of 'know' and what is said ('expressed') in saying 'I know'.

As I read it, 'Other Minds' challenges the tradition's perspec-tive at the most fundamental level. It invites us to take the sorts of questions just enumerated not as secondary or derivative, but as primary, and as the sorts of questions on which we should focus if we wish to find our way out of the difficulties that have plagued the tradition. This basic idea—of the primacy of use over reference, if you will—will recur in subsequent chapters.

Searle says of Austin that he is 'rather cagey about whether his analysis is supposed to give the meaning of "know"' (1999, 137). But Austin is not cagey at all about this. He *nowhere* claims to be, nor does he present himself as, offering what Searle would call an analysis of the meaning of 'know'. He makes clear at the opening of his paper what his aim is: to remind us of 'What we should say if asked "How do you know?"', as a way of dispelling the pervasive idea that how we know that another person is, for example, angry is fundamentally differ-ent from how we know that there's a goldfinch in the garden, for example (1979, 76–77).

By comparing coming to know what bird is in the garden to coming to know what another is feeling, Austin, quite inge-niously to my mind, aims to transform the traditional way of thinking about knowing other minds: he invites us to consider that coming to know that someone else is, for example, angry is not a matter of drawing an inference from one thing ('behav-ior') to another ('the anger itself'), but rather is a matter of *recognizing* what the other feels and manifests in her behavior to be anger—*telling* that it is anger she feels. One thing this suggests is that the essential difference between our relation to our own feelings and emotions and our relation to the other's feelings and emotions is better seen as metaphysical, and ethical, as opposed to epistemological. The other's anger is hers all right—to express in one way or another, or else try to suppress—and not ours. What is for us to do is respond to it, in one way or another.[40] But, epistemologically speaking, both she and we need to (be able to) recognize what she feels to be anger; and both she and we may fail to recognize it correctly. Her anger is not a private sensation but rather is a context-sensitive 'pattern' to which no particular sensation or set of sensations is either necessary or sufficient (see Austin 1979, 110).

Again, the details of Austin's response to 'other minds skepticism' do not matter for our present purposes. What does matter is that his comparison of 'I know' and 'I promise', which has drawn so much fire from critics of OLP, occurs within a context that has been completely ignored by these critics. Once we are clear on what Austin is trying to do in 'Other Minds', we may well find what he says about the force of 'I know that such and such'—in those (rare) situations in which the other is in need of an assurance that such and such, and we have no basis to offer her that she could reasonably be expected to be able to appreciate—to be philosophically quite illuminating. In particular, it can be quite illuminating as a response to the long-standing skeptical worry that knowledge is supposed to be infallible ('If I (you) know, I (you) can't be wrong'), and that it would therefore appear that we fallible creatures can at best know very little—whether about other minds or about anything else—and are speaking falsely (almost) whenever we say that we or others know something (see Austin 1979, 98ff). The basic idea, as I understand it, is that we should give up the assumption that it must be possible just to apply 'know' or one of its cognates to any pair of potential knower and fact or proposition without doing anything else, illocutionarily speaking, in doing *that*—the assumption, if you will, that it must be possible to apply the

---

40. This is one of the main lessons of Cavell's 'Knowing and Acknowledging' (in Cavell 1969).

word without (yet) doing any work with it.[41] And we should also give up the companion assumption that all 'serious and literal' utterances of indicative sentences featuring 'know' are in principle assessable in terms of truth and falsity.

Once we give up these assumptions—and I am not saying that it is easy to give them up, for they are deeply entrenched—the question of how we fallible creatures can ever be entitled to say 'I know' becomes no more bewildering and threatening than the question of how we fallible creatures can ever be entitled to say 'Trust me' or 'Why don't you trust me?' or 'I assure you' or 'I'm not just saying this' or, alternatively, 'I heard!' or 'You don't need to tell me' or 'I share your frustration'. This is, or anyway ought to have been, Austin's main point.

For Austin, as I read him, the truth of 'If I (you) know, I (you) can't be wrong' is a truth about what competently employing 'know' and cognates, against the inescapable and undeniable background of human fallibility, involves and requires (see 1979, 98); it is not, for him, a truth about some relation—the relation of *knowing*—which sometimes simply holds between potential knowers and propositions, irrespective of whatever might lead us to (wish to) put it into words. In the conclusion of this book, I will come back to Austin's unique way of acknowledging the 'infallibility' and 'factivity' of knowledge while yet avoiding the skeptical conclusion.

As I have said, there are important uses of 'I know' that Austin does not discuss. There are also, of course, other inflections of the verb. Austin acknowledges that he hasn't discussed all forms of indicative sentences featuring 'know' and cognates. He claims, however, that other inflections of the verb are not 'worrying' in the way that 'I know . . .' is (1979, 98n1). Here, as

---

41. Putting the point this way may be misleading, since, normally, to *apply* something is to make some use of it—do some work with it—whereas the philosopher's 'application' of a word is precisely *not* a use of the word. 'Applying (a word)', as used in contemporary analytic philosophy, is a technical term *par excellence*.

elsewhere, Austin seems to me too quick. He does not pursue clearly, patiently, and far enough his own insights and philosophical instincts.[42] For surely, there *are* uses of 'know' and cognates that may aptly be called 'descriptive'; these uses are not peripheral to the meaning of these words, or to our concept of knowledge; and the traditional philosopher is likely to insist, against Austin, that *she,* in any case, is interested in the descriptive or representational dimension of the concept. She is interested, that is, in the question of when and under what conditions 'know that' or one of its cognates (truly) applies to some pair of person and fact, regardless of what else might be done with these words beyond sheer application to the pair.

The main lesson of 'Other Minds' as a whole—a lesson that is at once dramatized and obscured by the comparison of 'I know' and 'I promise'—is that 'know' and its cognates are simply not fit for the philosopher's 'application', the sheer attachment of word to item or case. (What exactly I mean by 'the philosopher's "application" of a term' will become clearer as I go along, especially in chapters 3–5.) The ordinary and normal application of words, *both* when aptly describable as 'descriptive' and when aptly describable as 'nondescriptive', is too tightly connected to the point of the application—to what Austin refers to as the 'intents and purposes' that guide and inform the application and to which it is ultimately answerable (1979, 84). *This* could be shown to hold generally, and not just in the case of 'I know' when used to claim, or to give, authority. In fact, this is precisely what I am going to argue in the following chapters. I will also argue that, appearance to the contrary notwithstanding, the position known in contemporary analytic philosophy as 'contextualism', when viewed from the Austinian perspective just sketched, still ends up too close to the traditional way of

42. And, incidentally, he is also going against his own dictum that '[it is always fatal] to embark on explaining the use of a word without seriously considering more than a tiny fraction of the contexts in which it is actually used' (1964, 83).

thinking. It therefore does not quite succeed in showing us the way out of the traditional problem of skepticism.

At the root of all of the apparently interminable debates between skeptics and anti-skeptics, fallibilists and anti-fallibilists, externalists and internalists, contextualists and anti-contextualists, and so on, is the adoption by all parties of the assumption that it ought, in principle, to be possible for us simply to apply 'know' and cognates to any pair of person and fact; not, perhaps, apart from any specific 'context', but apart from any specific context of *significant use*.[43] As I read it, Austin's essay invites us to consider that there is no better way out of the above debates than to give up that assumption and concern ourselves precisely with what it has led us to regard as inessential to the meaning of 'know', or to our concept of knowledge. We should concern ourselves, that is, with the different uses of 'know' and its cognates, and with the human needs, interests, and concerns that give those uses their specific point and to which, ultimately, they are answerable. Put in Wittgensteinian terms, the assumption that ought to be given up is that by reflecting on words on holiday, we may discover something that is essential to them when they are being employed, and which suffices for sustaining fruitful and significant philosophical inquiry.

43. It should become clearer later in the book, and especially in chapters 4 (notes 4 and 5) and 5 (note 18), why I find much of the contemporary invocation of the notion of 'context' vague and problematic.

CHAPTER 2

The Main Arguments against Ordinary Language Philosophy

O F THE MAIN LINES of argument against OLP and its procedures that have appeared in the literature, one, I think, may
already be rejected. *Simply* to point to uses of the word under
investigation that the ordinary language philosopher has not
considered, as Searle, Grice, and Soames do, would only appear
to undermine OLP and its procedures to someone who assumed
two things: First, that the ordinary language philosopher was
after what the opponents of OLP would call 'an analysis (or theory)' of the meaning of the word in question, or of the concept
it embodies; and second, that the meaning of the word or the
concept it embodies is theoretically separable from its ordinary
and normal use and capturable in some such analysis (or theory).
Given what the opponents of OLP seem to mean by 'analysis' or
'theory', the first assumption is both false and baseless, at least
when it comes to Strawson's 1950 paper on truth and Austin's
'Other Minds'. I do not see how the authors of these two papers
may plausibly, let alone charitably, be taken to be attempting to
provide anything of that sort.[1]

---

1. Searle moves seamlessly from attributing to the 'linguistic philosopher'
the ambition of offering 'at least partial explication' of the meaning of some

The second assumption is precisely the one that OLP as defended in this book questions and takes to be responsible for any number of philosophical impasses and puzzlements. Furthermore, since two and a half millennia of Western philosophy and a century or so of analytic philosophy have produced numerous impasses and puzzlements but no truly satisfying analysis or theory of the envisioned sort for any of our philosophically troublesome words or concepts, it seems to me that the opponents of OLP owe us a good argument in support of that assumption. Put another way, the opponents of OLP owe us an argument for why the meaning of a philosophically troublesome word, or the concept it expresses, is not best elucidated, in the face of some particular philosophical difficulty, through a consideration of the ordinary and normal use(s) of the word. The demand for such an argument from opponents of OLP is all the more pressing where taking the use of the word as primary has the tendency, as I will argue in detail in subsequent chapters, of dissolving the difficulty at hand.

I will discuss three arguments that seem to me representative of all of the basic arguments for the prevailing conception of meaning and thereby against OLP. The first argument is offered by Searle and I will call it 'the argument from the possibility of conversation'. Though historically earlier, the second argument is, in a way, a sophisticated version of the first. It is offered by Geach and is known in the literature as the 'Frege-Geach' argument. The third argument is offered by Soames and I will call it 'the argument from our ability to employ and understand new sentences'. It is a version of the argument from 'compositionality' alluded to in the first section of chapter 1.

As we turn to assess these three arguments, keep in mind that my aim is not to defend this or that particular claim of

---

philosophically troublesome word to attributing to him the ambition of offering 'an analysis' of that meaning (cf. 1999, 137, 139–140). But only prior commitment to the prevailing conception of meaning would lead one to assume that the former ambition, on the most natural understanding of it, commits one to the latter ambition, as Searle thinks of it.

either Strawson's or Austin's. My aim, once again, is to defend an *approach* that I find exemplified in, or at any rate derivable from, their work, and what I am going to argue is that none of the above arguments succeeds in undermining that approach.

Had Strawson claimed that the role 'is true' plays in expressing agreement, say, or in affirming or conceding statements, *exhausts* its meaning and potential philosophical interest, then the sorts of considerations put forth by Searle, Geach, and Soames would have undermined his claim. And to the extent that Austin appears to suggest that the role 'I know' plays in the speech-act of assuring others that such and such exhausts *its* meaning and potential philosophical interest, his apparent suggestion is undermined by such considerations. But then, in order to undermine some such claim or suggestion, one would need no fancy argument. A couple of counterexamples would do.

Strawson, as we saw, may not charitably be charged with making the above claim. Austin arguably does unwittingly appear to make the above suggestion, but without ever purporting to offer an analysis of the meaning of '(I) know' and while making it abundantly clear that his comparison of 'I know' and 'I promise' does not exhaust his response to skepticism. The important thing, in any case, is that both Strawson and Austin exemplify in their essays a general approach to understanding and treating traditional philosophical difficulties that does not depend for its validity or viability on the truth of any such claim or suggestion. That approach will be further articulated, defended, and applied in the second part of this book.

The arguments to which we now turn have widely been taken to establish the correctness of the prevailing conception of meaning and thereby to undermine not merely this or that specific claim or suggestion of this or that ordinary language philosopher, but OLP's general understanding of the nature of philosophical difficulty and the response for which it calls. As such, they have been instrumental in bringing about and encouraging the widespread dismissal of OLP. My aim is to show that all three arguments *presuppose* one version or another of the prevailing conception of meaning rather than establish it, and that none of them succeeds in undermining OLP's general approach.

Before I turn to consider each of the arguments, I want to point out an important feature that they all share. They all have the effect of shifting the focus away from the particular concept and conceptual difficulty on which the ordinary language philosopher focuses, and toward general questions about what meanings are, or must be. As I have said, the ordinary language philosopher *begins* with some perceived conceptual difficulty or unclarity. Her appeal to how the words in question function in ordinary and normal discourse comes in response to that difficulty or unclarity and is meant to alleviate it. None of the arguments against OLP even purports to point to an alternative way of removing that difficulty or unclarity. On something like the contrary, they are all arguments in support of the very conception of meaning apart from which those difficulties would not have arisen and gripped us in the first place, at least not in their traditional form.

1. Searle's Argument from the Possibility of Conversation

Searle begins by attributing to ordinary language philosophers such as Austin and Strawson the ambition of providing an 'analysis' of the word whose meaning they seek to elucidate. He then claims, as we saw, that their reminders of what is normally done in uttering 'indicative' sentences featuring the word are ill suited for the purpose of constructing such an analysis, since 'any analysis of the meaning of a word must be consistent with the fact that the same word can mean the same thing in all the grammatically different kinds of sentences in which it can occur'. Searle goes on to offer the following brief argument in support of his claim:

> The word 'true' means or can mean the same *thing* [my emphasis] in interrogatives, indicatives, conditionals, negations, disjunctions, operatives, etc. If it didn't, conversation

would be impossible, for 'It is true' would not be an answer
to the question 'Is it true?' if 'true' changed its meaning
from interrogatives to indicative sentences. (1999, 137)

Since the same word can be used in the performance of any
number of very different speech-acts, and since the possibility of conversation presumably requires that what the word
means—or, as Searle rather revealingly puts it, *the thing it
means*—remain the same, or at least can remain the same, in
different speech-acts, it follows, according to Searle, that what
is ordinarily and normally done with the word can at best only
indirectly reveal something about its meaning. The meaning
itself is assumed by Searle to be theoretically separable from,
and logically prior to, the different things we (may) do with
the word—illocutionarily and more broadly. But of course, this
is precisely the assumption that his argument was supposed to
support, and *must* support if it is to carry any weight against
OLP. And it seems clear to me that it does not do that.

The first thing to note about the little exchange Searle imagines for us is that it actually lends support to the main point
Strawson is trying to establish about 'true'. For while it is true
that 'It is true' may be used to competently answer the question
'Is it true?', the question *might* also be expressed by means of,
say, 'Did you do it?', or, more naturally perhaps, 'Did you *really*
do it?'—where 'really' would be in the business of expressing
disbelief or shock, not in the business of predicating a property
(reality) of the proposition that the other person did the deed.
The question might then fully competently be answered by 'I'm
afraid I did', or simply by 'Yes'—so again without predicating
the alleged property of truth of anything. Whatever the imagined
exchange is supposed to show about 'true', then, it does *not* show
that the word's primary function is to predicate some property
of something. Nor does it show that the meaning of 'true' may
aptly and philosophically usefully be thought of in terms of the
'conditions of applicability' of the concept of truth or in terms of
the word's 'truth conditions' (Searle 1999, 144, 155).

More pertinently, given the main purpose of this book, Searle's example simply does not show that there is some one thing of the sort he envisions that the word means in both the question and the answer. Yes, it would normally be at least very misleading to say that 'true' *changed* its meaning from the question to the answer, but this does not even tend to show that its meaning is not best thought of as a matter of how it normally and ordinarily functions or may function in different contexts—including contexts of the sort Searle invokes here.[2] And yes, if what either the person asking the question or the person answering it meant by his 'true' were special or idiosyncratic—if, for example, he meant by it what we normally would mean by 'what everybody says'—they would be talking past each other. But the question 'What does so and so mean (here) by "*x*"?' itself must have a point. It would make no sense if raised for no specific reason,[3] and competent answers to it will not normally take the form of anything like an analysis of '*x*' or a theory of *x*, as the opponents of OLP envision it. What someone may aptly be said to *mean by* '*x*' on a given occasion is not *the meaning of* '*x*'.

What someone may aptly be said to mean by '*x*' *might* innocuously be thought of as something for which his '*x*', on that occasion, stands. But the meaning of '*x*' may not plausibly be thought of in this way. To know what so and so means (here) by '*x*' is to know that he means by it *y* rather than *z*, where knowing *that* makes a difference to how we (ought to) understand *him*. By contrast, to know the meaning of '*x*' is—by ordinary and normal criteria—to be able to competently employ

2. Compare Hare: 'It is natural to suppose that if [the word] has a common meaning [in different contexts of employment], there is a common property to which it refers . . .' (1952, 97). Hare is, of course, questioning that natural supposition, and says that efforts to find such a property in the case of 'good' are 'doomed to failure' (ibid.).

3. Compare Wittgenstein: 'The question "What do I mean by that?" is one of the most misleading ways of talking *(Redeweisen)*. In most cases one might answer: "Nothing at all—I *say* . . ."' (1981, remark 4. I have slightly amended Anscombe's translation).

it in indefinitely many different situations and to competently respond to other people's employment of it.[4] To know the meaning of 'true', for example, is to know, among other things, when raising a question by means of 'Is it true?' would be in place and when answering such a question by means of 'It is true' would be correct. Why suppose that there is more to our knowledge of the meaning of 'true' than our knowledge of how to use it competently, in different ways in different sorts of contexts? Searle's argument, at any rate, gives us no reason for supposing this.

It is true that in English (and certain other languages),[5] we can ask for the meaning of an unfamiliar word, 'x'—typically a word of a foreign language—by means of 'What does "x" mean?' (or one of its equivalents in certain other languages). And it is also true that a proper answer to that question might take the form '"x" means y', where 'y' is a word whose meaning is already familiar to the person who asked the question. (It is commonly recognized that 'y' is neither merely mentioned nor exactly used either when serving in this way in an explanation of the meaning of 'x'.) Thus someone who does not know the German word may ask 'What does "wahr" mean?', to which the correct answer—at least in most cases—would be 'It means true', and this might aptly be said to be a way of teaching that person the meaning of 'wahr'. We might even say, in English (and by means of equivalent expressions in certain other lan-

---

4. See Williamson (2003, 253; 2005a, 11–12; 2007, 89ff., 216) for expressions of the same basic point.

5. It should be noted that it is merely a contingent fact about English (and some other languages) that we can ask for the meaning of a word by asking what that word *means*. In Hebrew, for example, words may be said to 'have meaning', and one can of course ask for the meaning of an unfamiliar word, but there is no proper way of describing words as *meaning* their meaning. (This, of course, has not prevented philosophers who think and express themselves in Hebrew from thinking of the meaning of a word as an object-like something that it carries with it into each and every one of its uses; they just have not had a ready and natural expression with which to express that picture. The forcing of concepts has therefore had to be made manifest in a forcing of language, whereas in English it has disguised itself with seemingly natural expressions.)

guages), that '*wahr*' and 'true' mean the same thing. But to draw metaphysical conclusions about (the essence of) meaning from these familiar facts about usage would be both unwarranted and deeply misleading. In particular, there is no reason to suppose that there is a something—something that is commonly supposed to be referable to (by those writing in English) by means of 'TRUE' or '<u>true</u>'—such that both 'true' and '*wahr*' mean *it*. That the two words have (more or less) the same meaning—or, if you will, mean the same thing—*may* just be a matter of their having (more or less) the same function in their respective languages.

'"True" means TRUE'—if it is not a way of saying, emphatically, something like 'I meant what I said'[6]—is metaphysically loaded philosophers' talk, not a (contingent) truism. And while there is nothing necessarily wrong with stretching language for theoretical purposes (and sometimes great value in doing so), one must be careful not to base metaphysical theories solely on (the possibility of) such expansions. That we can speak in English of what 'true' means does not mean that there is something such that 'true' means it.[7] 'True', it might be helpful to say here, no more means its meaning than an action or event or institution signifies its significance.

Searle's example does not show that it should be possible for us to specify the meaning of 'true' without specifying its ordinary and normal uses. Nor does it show that the meaning of 'true' may not best be explicated, and that philosophical entanglements cannot truly and effectively be removed, by means of reminders of the sort given by Strawson. Searle, I think it is fair to say, has assumed from the outset the conception of meaning

6. 'I asked you whether it was true; and "true" means TRUE, not more or less or partly true!'

7. One is reminded here of Quine's objections over the years to the talk of word-meaning as if it were a something that the word means. And compare Wittgenstein: 'When we say: "Every word in a language signifies something" we have so far said *nothing whatever;* unless we have explained *what* distinction we wish to make' (1963, remark 13).

that his argument was supposed to support. But apart from rhetorically encouraging us to think of the meaning of a word as *a something* that it means, he has not done anything to support that conception.

2. The 'Frege-Geach' Argument

The declared target of Geach's argument is 'anti-descriptive theorists'. The argument has often been discussed as an argument against 'expressivist' or 'non-cognitivist' accounts of moral discourse.[8] Originally, however, it was presented by Geach as an argument against anti-descriptive theories of the meaning of this or that *word,* not against anti-descriptive theories of this or that *region of discourse.* Among the anti-descriptive theories he says he means to 'refute' is Strawson's 'theory' that 'to say a proposition is true is not to describe it but to confirm or concede it' (1965, 462), and Austin's 'theory' that 'to say "I know that *p*" is no statement about my own mental capacities, but is an act of warranting my hearer that *p*' (ibid.).

As we turn to discuss Geach's argument, I must once again remind the reader that my aim here is not to defend any particular claim made by Strawson or Austin concerning either 'true' or 'know'. My aim is to defend a general approach to the dissolution of philosophical difficulties that is exemplified in, or at any rate derivable from, their work. As I said at the opening of this chapter, if anyone described just one thing or set of

8. On the face of it, Geach's argument is better designed to give trouble to accounts such as Hare's (1952) account of 'good', in which something like an analysis of the meaning of a word *is* on offer, than to give trouble to accounts such as Austin's account of 'I know', which do not purport to give anything like an analysis of the word or expression in question but only to point out and clarify aspects of its use that bear on some particular philosophical difficulty or set of difficulties. I believe, however, though I will not here attempt to show, that Geach's much-cited example of a 'piece of moral reasoning' (1965: 463) is no less problematic, and no more establishes the correctness of the prevailing conception of meaning, than his example of the inference featuring 'know'.

things that may illocutionarily be done with simple declarative sentences that contain some philosophically troublesome word (or expression), and went on to claim that that description tells us *all* we need to know about the meaning of that word, then she would indeed be committing the 'speech-act fallacy' (Searle 1999,136–141). Simply providing a few examples showing that the word may be part of sentences of different kinds that are unfit for that illocutionary act or set of acts would be enough to refute her. Invoking Geach's argument from the possibility of inference would be overkill in such a case. However, if the idea is that the particular contribution the word makes to the sense of some utterance depends on the point of the utterance and so may not be known just by knowing the meaning of the word— an idea that amounts to denying that we can tell what, if any, Fregean 'thought' is expressed by (means of) some sentence just by knowing the meaning of its words—then Geach's argument does not succeed in undermining it. Or so I will try to show in this section.

Geach begins his argument by noting that sentences of the form 'It is true that such and such' or 'I know that such and such' may be embedded in longer sentences—for example, in 'If. . . , then . . .' constructions (1965, 462). Recall that Strawson says in his 1949 paper that 'It is true that such and such', at least as ordinarily and normally used, is not in the business of predicating the property of *being true* (whatever it might be thought to come to) of something (whether 'such and such' itself, the statement it may be used to make, or the 'proposition' it may be used to express). Rather, Strawson says, the sentence may be used, for example, *simply* to agree or concede or acknowledge that such and such. Similarly, Austin argues that 'I know that such and such' is not normally used for predicating a relation— the relation of knowing (that)—of the speaker and such and such, but rather for *assuring* the other that such and such, giving him our authority, for example, to tell others that such and such. It is clear, however, that whatever work may be done by 'It is true that such and such' or 'I know that such and such' when embedded in an 'If. . . , then . . .' construction, it isn't the work that the unembedded sentences are normally or commonly used to perform, according to Strawson and Austin.

Geach anticipates the response that he simply has pointed to *another* use of 'is true' or 'I know'—one in which Strawson or Austin was, for reasons good or bad, not interested (1965, 463). And indeed, if OLP is right in its general way of thinking about how the meaning of a word relates to what may and may not be said and done by means of it, then effective elucidations of the meaning of this or that philosophically troublesome word will have to take their cue from this or that particular philosophical difficulty and so will be, in this innocuous sense, partial. Again, I am not saying that Strawson's account of 'is true' and Austin's account of 'I know' are full and accurate enough by the lights of *their* philosophical purposes. The point remains, however, that Strawson's specific point in comparing as he does the work sometimes done by 'This is true' with the work normally done by 'Ditto' (say), and Austin's specific point in comparing as he does the work sometimes done by 'I know' and the work normally done by 'I promise', are not undermined merely by the fact that these expressions may be embedded in longer stretches of discourse in which they do different kinds of work.

Geach, as I said, appears to be aware of this, and he moves on to what he clearly regards as weightier considerations. However, since there are many who believe that the mere possibility of 'embedding' poses a very serious problem for accounts such as Strawson's account of 'is true' or Austin's account of 'I know', let me say a word about that alleged problem.

There is a very good reason why Austin and Strawson focus on simple 'declarative' sentences in which the word under consideration is being 'applied' to or 'predicated' of someone or something. They focus on these particular forms of sentences because they are responding to the tradition. The difficulties encountered by the tradition in trying to give an account of *x*—knowledge, truth, or what have you—have to do with the application of '*x*' to cases. *When is something (a sentence, a statement, a belief, a proposition, or what have you)* true? *What makes something* true? *When and under what conditions does anyone* know *something? Do we* know *this or that? Can we?* These are the sorts of questions that the tradition has taken as basic and that have haunted it. How, the tradition's perspective would incline us to ask, can we reasonably hope to understand a sentence such as 'If I know Smith's painting is a forgery (and I am no art expert), then the forgery is clumsy' (Geach 1965, 463)—which presumably is to be used for asserting that the relation of 'natural (factive) meaning' holds between the speaker's *knowing* that the painting is forged and the forgery being clumsy—if we do not know when, if ever, someone counts or ought to count as knowing that a painting is forged?

This is why Austin and Strawson invite us to look more closely and without prejudice at precisely those speech-acts in which the word in question is being applied to a particular case—in which, so it would seem, we say *of* something *that* it is true (or untrue), or *of* someone *that* he knows (or does not know) something. Their basic aim, as I have interpreted it, is to get us to see that, outside of philosophy, the competent application of the relevant words has *a point,* and its competent assessment is guided and informed by that point. Outside of philosophical theorizing, we simply do not apply our words in the philosopher's sense of 'apply'. Rather, we put them to use. This is a good reason for suspecting that the philosophically troublesome words may not be fit for the philosopher's sheer application. And that, in turn, would explain the fact that when we theorize on the basis of the assumption that they must be, we run into seemingly inescapable and insurmountable difficulties (as we shall see in detail in the following chapters). The embedding possibility in no way undermines this general point about what we ought and ought not to expect of our words and the approach to the alleviation of philosophical difficulties that is informed by this general point. The sheer possibility of embedding the sort of sentences Strawson and Austin focus on in longer stretches of discourse, in which the words under investigation do work Strawson and

Austin do not discuss, would only seem to undermine their argument to someone who failed to see and appreciate its philosophical point and who presupposed the prevailing conception of meaning.[9]

Geach himself, as I said, while nowhere asking himself what philosophical work Strawson and Austin were trying to do with their words, does not put much stock in the sheer 'embedding problem', at least not in his later (1965) paper. His 'refutation' of Austin and other 'anti-descriptive theorists' proceeds rather from the (presumed) fact that, for example, both 'I know that such and such' and 'If I know that such and such, then . . .' can be used as *different premises in one and the same formally valid inference*. '[The] possibility of varying use . . .', he contends, 'cannot be appealed to in cases where an ostensibly assertoric

9. Consider in this connection Soames's argument against the thought originally put forward by Austin that performative utterances are 'quite plainly *not* utterances which could be "true" or "false"' (Austin 1999: 12). Soames writes:

> Although, in the right circumstances, uttering ['I promise to return the book'] on its own may count as making a promise to return the book, to utter 'If I promise to return the book, then you can be confident that it will be returned' is not itself to promise, but rather to make a straightforward assertion. This is relevant because, presumably, the sentence 'I promise to return the book' *has the same meaning* when it occurs on its own as it does when it occurs as the antecedent of a conditional. Since in the latter environment it expresses a normal (descriptive) proposition that contributes to the proposition expressed by the conditional as a whole, *it must also do so* when it occurs on its own. (Soames 2003a, 127, my emphases)

This is simply to *assert* the prevailing conception of meaning, not to argue for it, and thus to beg the question against Austin and OLP more generally. Insofar as it makes sense at all to speak in general of (indicative) sentences as 'having a meaning', and as 'having the same meaning' in all of their different uses, why assume that that 'meaning' may be cashed in terms of a something—some 'proposition'—that each of these sentences 'expresses' every time it is uttered? Why assume that there is *anything* associated with every syntactically well-formed indicative sentence that fulfills Soames's expectations? If the meaning of a sentence is whatever it brings with it to its different uses and which makes it fit for those uses, why can't it allow for both 'descriptive' and non-'descriptive' uses—uses in which it may aptly be said to serve to 'express thoughts (or propositions)', and uses in which it may not aptly thus be described?

utterance "*p*" and "If *p*, then *q*" can be teamed up as premises for a *modus ponens* [for "p" read 'It is true that such and such" or "I know that such and such"]. Here, the two occurrences of "p," by itself and in the "if" clause, must have the same sense if the *modus ponens* is not to be vitiated by equivocation' (1965, 463). Geach continues:

> For example, Austin would maintain that if I say assertorically, 'I know Smith's Vermeer is a forgery,' this is not an asserted proposition about me, but an act of warranting my hearers that the picture is a forgery. Austin never observed that this alleged nonproposition could function as a premise obeying ordinary logical rules, in inferences, like this:
>
> I know Smith's Vermeer is a forgery.
> I am no art expert.
> If I know Smith's Vermeer is a forgery, and I am no art
>   expert, then Smith's Vermeer is a very clumsy forgery.
> *Ergo,* Smith's Vermeer is a very clumsy forgery.
>
> Still less did Austin discuss *how* a nonproposition could be a premise. But failing such discussion, Austin's account of 'I know' is valueless. (Ibid.)

Presumably, Austin's whole point was to show that (the unembedded) 'I know that such and such' *never* functions 'descriptively'—what Geach would call 'propositionally'. For even if it only *sometimes* functioned descriptively, and therefore manifestly *could* so function, this would seem to validate the philosopher's worry about knowledge's infallibility and the skepticism it seems to entail. That is, it would seem to validate precisely the worry that Austin meant to dispel. According to Geach, however, premises are essentially descriptive, or 'propositional'. So, by Geach's lights, if 'I know that such and such' *could* function as a premise, this would be enough to undermine Austin's account (1965, 463).

What is supposed to be even more problematic for Austin is the (presumed) fact that 'I know that such and such' functions, in Geach's example, both as a separate premise and as part of an 'If. . . , then . . .' sentence in another premise, in a single *valid inference*. Valid inferences, as Geach thinks of them, are supposed to abstract from the Austinian question of what's being done with the words or how the words 'function in discourse'. Validity, as Geach views it, is supposed to be a function of ('descriptive') meaning abstracted from use in just the way that according to Austin (as I read him) the meaning of 'know' may not be. If 'know' and its cognates may be employed unproblematically in logically valid inferences of the sort imagined by Geach, this by itself would seem to give us reason for thinking that these words have a meaning of the sort assumed for them by the critics of OLP. But of course, that these words may thus unproblematically be employed is what Geach's example ought to have established. Has it?

The mere fact that we can plug a sentence of the form 'I know that such and such' in the place of '*p*' in the schema for *modus ponens* does not prove Geach's point. For his point to be established, the result must not merely be a string of familiar words making up sentences that are organized in the form of *modus ponens*. Geach, I think, knows this. He takes himself to be presenting us with a stretch of discourse that we clearly and unproblematically *understand*. Do we?

I note first that, while sounding remotely *like* something that someone might naturally say under suitable circumstances, the *modus ponens* argument Geach imagines for us is not something that someone might naturally utter outside philosophy circles. Geach's imagined argument would be awkward in an everyday conversation in a way that something like, for example, 'What a clumsy forgery; even I can tell that this is not a real Vermeer' would not be. It would be extremely odd for anyone (who was not trying to prove a philosophical point about 'know') to actually utter Geach's imagined argument.

But of course, since Geach wrote his article, Grice came up with his theory of 'implicature' (1989), Searle purportedly exposed the 'assertion fallacy' (1999, 141ff.), and we have all been trained to explain away the oddness or gross unnaturalness of certain stretches of philosophical discourse by attributing their oddness or unnaturalness to 'pragmatic' or otherwise '*extra*-semantic' factors. We are supposed to reason thus: *Geach's imagined argument is clear and makes perfect sense. It is only the speech-act of expressing it that would be odd or unnatural. What we need to explain is precisely why coming out with a stretch of discourse that makes perfect sense, semantically speaking, would be odd or unnatural. And there are any number of possible explanations: the argument is just too formal for everyday use; the argument, or anyway some parts of it, would be so obviously true as to not be worth expressing; in actually uttering the argument, or some parts of it, we would imply false things or things that for some other reason we might not wish to imply; there might be various more or less complex but merely psychological causes for our not being inclined to come out with just this form of words, or for our finding them odd or unnatural.*[10]

This line of reasoning, which one hears everywhere in one version or another, misconstrues OLP and begs the question against it. Both Grice and Searle give a false and misleading account of the point of departure of OLP. Both suggest that the ordinary language philosopher *begins* by 'noticing' or 'observing' that a particular form of words that the philosopher has produced would be 'odd' or 'inappropriate' or 'bizarre' to utter under normal circumstances, or apart from some special circumstances (Grice 1989, 3, 235; Searle 1999, 141–142). Grice and Searle would have us think that what would and would

10. Throughout the book, I use italics to mark passages in which I anticipate objections to my argument or, more generally, articulate positions which are not mine.

not be appropriate to say under, or apart from, this or that set of circumstances is *all* the ordinary language philosopher has got to go on in her criticism of the philosopher's words. And then they offer their counterexplanation for the ordinary language philosopher's alleged data: what the philosopher says is perfectly clear and, in particular, is either true or false (valid or invalid, sound or unsound); it's just that actually saying it apart from the appropriate circumstances—where, again, it is assumed that there is no question about the identity of the *it* that would be said, the 'proposition' or 'thought' that would be 'expressed'—would somehow be inappropriate or misleading or otherwise conversationally infelicitous.[11] To support their counterexplanation, they remind us that *any* English sentence—even a sentence as simple and (presumably) impossible not to understand as 'This pillar-box is red' (Grice 1989, 235) or 'He has five fingers on his left hand' (Searle 1999: 143)—would strike us as utterly odd if uttered in circumstances in which we could find no point for it. Even so, they insist, it would still be clear *what* the utterer was saying, even if not *why* he said it; and what he would say could very well still be *true*. In fact, its being obviously or trivially true may be precisely the reason why we find the speaker's saying it odd.

All of this might have been philosophically pertinent if the ordinary language philosopher really began where Grice and Searle say she begins. But she doesn't. She doesn't find the philosopher's utterance merely odd, or bizarre, or out of place in ordinary contexts, and she certainly does not find it obviously or trivially true. She finds it lacking in sense or only fit for making sense in ways that would actually undermine the philosopher's project.[12]

11. See Conant (1998) for an argument on behalf of Wittgenstein against the prevailing assumption that (barring indexicality, ambiguity, etc.) every declarative sentence has a determinate and truth-evaluable something that it, as such, says.

12. This point is pressed especially clearly and compellingly, in response to Grice, by Travis. 'The issue', Travis argues against Grice, 'is one of *making sense;* not one of what we wouldn't say' (1991, 241).

Moreover, the stretch of philosophical discourse in question would typically be problematic by the traditional philosopher's own lights. This philosopher, recall, typically takes 'I know Smith's Vermeer is a forgery', for example, to attribute *knowledge* of some fact or proposition to its utterer, but he would also typically acknowledge as a philosophically open question what knowledge *is* and under what conditions it may truly be said to be present. It is therefore problematic for this philosopher to insist, as against the ordinary language philosopher, that any 'serious and literal' utterance of 'I know Smith's Vermeer is a forgery', whatever its point might be, says, or expresses the proposition, *that the utterer knows Smith's Vermeer is a forgery,* purporting thereby to have identified a clear something that is said or expressed by means of these words.[13] If, with Geach, one understands 'proposition' as 'a form of words in which something is propounded, put forward for consideration' (1965, 449), then it is important that one also realize, or acknowledge, that at least some utterances of strings of words with an indicative form may fail to put anything forward for consideration, and therefore may fail to be utterances of propositions in Geach's sense.

'The moral of Grice's work', Stanley writes, 'is that the facts of linguistic use are the product of two factors, meaning and conversational norms. Failure to absorb this fact', he continues, 'undermines many of the main theses of ordinary language

---

13. This sort of insistence, moreover, sometimes ends up biting the philosopher in the back, so to speak. Searle, for example, argues in response to certain moments in Austin and Ryle that the only reason why it would be odd to say of some perfectly normal and unremarkable action that it was 'voluntary' or that the agent acted 'of his own free will' is that the proposition thereby expressed would be *obviously* true (1999, 141, 149). There are two options: either Searle presumes to have already resolved, by 1969, the traditional 'problem of free will'—the very problem to which Austin and Ryle are responding and in which Searle still seems to be entangled three decades later (see Searle 2007); or he takes 'free will' to mean something entirely different in the 'odd because obviously true' utterances he imagines from what it means in the metaphysician's mouth. If the latter, then he is opening himself to the weighty objections to prevailing philosophical practice with which chapter 3 opens.

philosophy' (2008, 412). But the moral of Grice's work was presupposed by him from the start, and is beside the point as a response to OLP; and the fact which according to Stanley the ordinary language philosopher is failing to absorb is not a fact, but a theoretical construction that might perhaps be useful for explaining *certain* facts, but which has all too often had the tendency of obscuring the facts. Like Grice, Stanley relies on an understanding of 'meaning' that OLP finds both questionable in itself and responsible for any number of philosophical difficulties. And the 'facts of linguistic use' that Grice's theory of 'implicature' is suited to explain are in turn mostly irrelevant to an assessment of OLP. For what concerns OLP is not the conditions under which it would be conversationally appropriate to say something that is otherwise perfectly clear. Rather, OLP is concerned with the conditions under which uttering a string of words would so much as amount to saying something (clear)—something, for example, that may felicitously be assessed in terms of truth and falsity, or validity and invalidity, and which we might choose, for whatever reason, to keep to ourselves.

It is true that the ordinary language philosopher, upon encountering a stretch of philosophical discourse that he suspects of being ultimately nonsensical or only fit for making sense in ways that would actually undermine the philosophical purposes for which it was produced, characteristically appeals to the ordinary and normal use of key words in that stretch of discourse. But *pace* Searle, Grice, Soames, and others, this appeal is not meant to prove, all by itself, that the stretch of discourse makes no sense. As I said in the introduction, it is meant to weaken the hold of the conviction that the stretch of discourse does, and indeed must, make sense, simply by virtue of the meaning of its words and how they are put together, and to force upon those who take it to make clear sense the question of what that sense might be, and whether, given the sense or senses it could have—the way(s) in which it may aptly or genuinely be *understood*—it is fit to do the philosophical work that its author needs or wants it to do.

Go back to Geach's imagined argument. The argument's hypothetical author says, 'I know Smith's Vermeer is a forgery'. What does, or could, he mean? What (work) is he, or might he be, doing with his words? Geach would have us suppose that these questions are beside the point, and of course they are beside the point as far as the *formal* validity of the argument goes. But then, as far as *that* goes, we could have stayed with '*p*' and '*q*', or could have replaced the two tokens of 'I know Smith's Vermeer is a forgery' in Geach's imagined argument with two 'I Φ's. If Geach's example is to show that '(I) know' has a *meaning* separable from its use(s), and that, therefore, any utterance of 'I know that such and such' expresses a Fregean 'thought' regardless of what (work) is done with the words or how they are meant, it must at least be possible for us to *understand* the example, and to understand it as an example of an intelligible stretch of human discourse—an inference, for example—in which 'I know' functions meaningfully. And insofar as we are looking for *this* kind of understanding, how the utterer of Geach's *modus ponens* argument could mean his words, or use them, is very much to the point.

I note first that the utterer of Geach's imagined argument *need not* mean the 'I know' of the first 'premise' 'descriptively'. One 'nondescriptive' way of meaning 'I know' is the one on which Austin focuses in his comparison of 'I know' and 'I promise'. Another far more common one would be this: in uttering the first sentence of Geach's imagined argument, the speaker could express—not *report*—conviction ('I just *know* it's a forgery!'). If he meant his words that way, it would be forced and misleading to say that he expressed a *premise* with his first sentence, and it would not be clear how he meant, or could mean, the third sentence of the 'argument'. Overall, the 'argument' would clearly be flawed. One might say, with Geach, that 'the argument would be vitiated by equivocation', but this would be to force Geach's 'descriptivist' conception of meaning upon the case, for the speaker would not be referring to two different things in his two utterances of 'know'. Rather, he would be *doing* one thing with that word in the first 'premise', and *doing* nothing clear with it in uttering the third 'premise'. The overall result would be incomprehensible. It would not be clear what the speaker said, or meant to be saying, in uttering the 'argument'. There would simply be the uttering of a syntactically well-constructed string of familiar words.

Suppose, on the other hand, that in uttering the first sentence in Geach's imagined argument, the speaker meant simply to *inform* the other—simply to let her know—that *this* (the painting's being a forgery) is something he happens to know, perhaps in response to the proposal or insinuation that he had no idea whether or not the painting was a forgery. This, it seems to me, is as descriptive a use of 'I know' as Geach could plausibly be granted here. In subsequent chapters, I will argue that even when put to such descriptive uses, what 'know' means—what *knowing* that such and such comes to in such contexts, if you will—depends in part on the point of the utterance and may not be known apart from knowledge of that point.

For now, I simply note that if Geach's speaker put his 'I know' to some such descriptive use, there would still be the question that Austin makes so much of in 'Other Minds' of *how* the purported knower purportedly knew—what his basis was for saying he knew. And that question is crucial here precisely because we are trying to imagine a context in which knowledge is not *merely claimed,* but is, or can at least fairly easily become, something like a foregone conclusion. Simply to claim that Smith's Vermeer is a clumsy forgery is one thing. But in order to felicitously *infer* that it is, *from the fact that one knows* it is a forgery, one's knowledge—whatever exactly it might be thought to come to[14]—had better be more than merely claimed.[15]

---

14. The aim of this clause is to remind the reader that after two and a half millennia of Western philosophy, we still have no satisfying answer to the metaphysician's question of what knowledge is, and therefore also no satisfying answer to the 'classical' semanticist's question of what 'know' means.

15. Compare Wittgenstein: 'It needs to be *shown* (proven, *erwiesen*) that no mistake was possible. Giving the assurance "I know" doesn't suffice. For it is

Consider now what would become of Geach's imagined argument if the speaker's basis for asserting the first premise were that Smith himself, or an expert who had examined the painting, told him so; or that he was there, hiding behind a curtain, when Smith commissioned the forgery; or that he could tell by the twitch in Smith's nose that he was lying when he said the painting was an original. At least in many ordinary contexts these kinds of bases would, or at least could, settle the question of whether the speaker knew—not somehow absolutely, but 'for present intents and purposes'. I think it is clear, however, that *something* would be wrong with the argument (or 'argument') in that case. An even more extreme case of infelicity would be that of asserting the first premise on the force of *one* basis and then having a *different* basis in mind when asserting the third premise.

The prevailing conception of meaning would lead one to insist that in none of those cases would the validity of Geach's imagined argument be affected. It would be insisted, along Gricean-Searlean lines, that the argument would still be valid, 'semantically' speaking, even if utterly incoherent 'pragmatically' as a speech-*act*. It would be maintained that the speaker's first 'I know Smith's Vermeer is a forgery' refers to *knowledge*—a particular kind of relation that sometimes holds between potential knowers and propositions (or facts)—and attributes *it* to the speaker and the proposition that the painting is a forgery, regardless of how it is meant and what basis the speaker has for claiming to know; and the third premise in Geach's imagined argument simply says that if a nonexpert has come to stand in the relation of knowing to the proposition that Smith's painting is a forgery, this factively ('naturally') means that the forgery is clumsy.

Chapters 3–5 will present an extended argument against this way of thinking about the meaning of 'know' and its cognates. Here I focus just on Geach's argument, and I note what should

---

after all only an assurance that I can't be wrong; and it needs to be *objectively* established that I am not wrong about *that*' (1969, remark 15).

have become clear by now: namely, that the traditional semanticist's insistence on there being a strict separation between
what is said by means of 'I know that such and such' and what
might entitle one to say it, commits her to maintaining that the
third premise in Geach's imagined argument is simply false,
regardless of the basis or bases the speaker might have, or
have in mind. *Just* from the fact that a nonexpert *knows* that a
painting is a forgery, whatever knowing this might be thought
to come to, it simply does not follow that the forgery is clumsy.
And now I think we should want to know how two genera-
tions of readers have missed this seemingly glaring fact about
Geach's imagined argument.

As competent speakers, we are generally quite good at hearing
the words of others so as to make the most sense of them—seeing through them, as it were, to their intended point. My proposal is that Geach's readers have done the same: knowing quite
well what Geach meant his imagined speaker to be trying to say,
they have managed to hear it in, or through, the imagined speaker's words. When we engage in everyday discourse, our ability
to see the speaker's intended point in, through, and sometimes
even despite his words, is essential. It can become detrimental,
however, when, doing philosophy, we reflect upon what purports
to be an example of a perfectly intelligible and unproblematic
stretch of human discourse—an example, moreover, that is supposed to teach us something important about '(I) know'.

Geach would have us assume that it does not matter what the
argument's utterer does with his 'I know', or how he means or
uses it. But I think it is clear that he actually wants and needs the
speaker's two utterances of 'I know' to be heard in a *very* particular way. He wants and needs the speaker's 'I know' to be heard
as something like 'I can tell (or see)' or, better yet, 'even *I* can
tell (or see)'. (Note that here 'tell' means something like 'discern'
or 'distinguish', not 'give an account' or 'relate'.) And indeed, if
you replace the two occurrences of 'I know' in Geach's imagined
argument with 'even *I* can tell', you get a stretch of discourse
that, while probably too formal to naturally be used by anyone in

an everyday situation, would nonetheless *make sense* if uttered in the appropriate context. Informal versions of similar arguments have most likely occurred in the course of human history.

Our question therefore ought to be whether 'I know' *may* be used as Geach wants and needs it to be used—whether it may competently be meant and heard as he wants and needs it to be meant and heard. I believe that the correct answer to this question is no. Before I say why, however, let me point out that even if the correct answer were yes, this would not show that the meaning of 'I know' is such that it may simply and unproblematically be plugged into a valid, and possibly sound, argument of (for example) the *modus ponens* form. Rather, it would show that the meaning of 'I know' is such that, *when used in an appropriate context in some very particular way,* it may contribute to a valid and possibly also sound *modus ponens* argument. This might show that Austin's account is incomplete even in terms of his own purposes—which, as I said, I believe it is—but it would *not* undermine Austin's *approach*. Nor would it in any way validate the conception of (word) meaning that OLP questions and that Geach wishes to validate.

Let me say why I think 'I know' and 'I can tell (or see)' are not interchangeable in the way Geach needs them to be. For Geach's imagined argument to make the sense he wants and needs it to make, 'I know' would need to be interchangeable with 'I can tell (or see)' when both are used descriptively. When used descriptively, however, they are not normally interchangeable. And this is due not merely to the fact that 'knowing that' is more general than 'telling (by looking) that'. Rather, it is a fact of what Wittgenstein calls 'grammar' that, normally, telling by looking, or seeing (with one's own eyes), that such and such is not a way of knowing but a way of *coming to know;* and this actually makes a big difference to how, or whether, Geach's imagined argument may reasonably be understood.

This connects with a potentially significant inaccuracy in Williamson's (2000) account of knowledge. Williamson says that *seeing that, recognizing that, remembering that,* etc., are all 'factive stative attitudes' and argues that *knowing that* is 'the most general factive stative attitude' (ibid., 34). Accordingly, he says that 'if one knows that A, then there is a specific way in which one knows; one can see or remember or . . . that A' (ibid.). But seeing—with one's own eyes—that such and such is not a way of knowing that such and such. It is a way of coming to know that such and such.[16] Thus we sometimes ask, 'When did you see that such and such?', but not, or anyway not in the same sense, 'When did you know that such and such?'. Similarly, we sometimes ask, 'How long have you known that such and such?', but not, or anyway not in the same sense, 'How long have you seen that such and such?'. If one wants to follow Williamson in calling seeing (by looking) that such and such a mental *state,* then one must keep in mind that, unlike knowledge, it is conceptually ('grammatically') a momentary state.

'Being able to tell (or see)' would accordingly mean something like 'being able to come to know (in some particular way)', which under no plausible understanding is equivalent to 'knowing'. Saying of myself that I know—in order, say, to inform the other—is therefore under no plausible or natural understanding the same as saying of myself that I can tell or see. What entails, 'factively' or 'naturally' means, that a forgery is clumsy is not the fact that a nonexpert has come to stand in the philosophically elusive relation of *knowing* to the painting's being a forgery—whatever standing in that relation to a fact might be thought to come to. What entails it, rather, is the fairly straightforwardly establishable *empirical* fact that even a nonexpert can tell (or see), just by looking at or examining the painting, that it is a forgery.

What makes the oddness—and ultimate incomprehensibility—of Geach's imagined 'argument' easier to overlook is the

16. 'Remember' poses complexities of its own. Like seeing (with one's own eyes) that such and such, remembering that such and such may not plausibly be said to be a way of knowing that such and such. I set this issue aside here, since it has no bearing on our present concerns.

fact that under appropriate circumstances, 'I know' and 'I can tell' *may* be used more or less interchangeably. They may thus be used, however, precisely when both are used to express conviction. We can imagine the person standing in front of the picture and exclaiming either 'I (just) know it's a forgery!' or 'I can (just) tell it's a forgery!', and it would not matter much which of the two she used. In such a context and when thus used, either expression would also be replaceable without loss by 'I'm sure it's a forgery!'[17] As I already noted, however, if we hear the first 'premise' in Geach's imagined argument as the expression of conviction, it becomes extremely difficult, to say the least, to make sense of the 'argument' as a whole, not to mention making sense of it as an *argument,* or *inference.*

Geach's imagined example of a (purported) piece of human discourse is supposed to be an example of a valid inference featuring 'I know', and as such is supposed to show that '(I) know' has a descriptive meaning separable from its use(s). But the example ultimately makes no clear sense—in the simple sense that it is just not clear how a competent speaker could mean it, or how *it* (as opposed to its utterer) might reasonably be understood. As far as I can tell, the example only shows that you can take a sentence of the 'I know that such and such' form and plug it twice into the schema for a *modus ponens* argument, which is hardly news. It does nothing to show that '(I) know' has something that may be referred to as 'its meaning', which is theoretically separable from how it functions in discourse, and which makes it suitable for the expression of Fregean 'thoughts' that may be equated with the senses of declarative sentences considered apart from any contexts of significant employment.[18] Nor does it show that Austin's general approach is wrongheaded,

17. Compare Wittgenstein: 'The difference between the concept of "knowing" and the concept of "being certain" isn't of any great importance at all, except where "I know" is meant to mean: I *can't* be wrong. In a law-court, for example, "I am certain" could replace "I know" in every piece of testimony. We might even imagine its being forbidden to say "I know" there' (1969, remark 8).

18. See Frege (1977).

or that his account is 'valueless' (Geach 1965, 463). But then it seems that Geach never truly asked himself what value Austin's account was designed, and supposed by its author, to have.

It might be objected: *Granted, Geach chose a bad example. The third premise in his imagined argument is false, and it would (therefore?) be odd for a competent employer of 'know' to come out with such an 'argument'. But why make such heavy weather of this, instead of simply looking for a better example that would illustrate the* point *Geach was trying to establish? For example:*

> *1. I know he was married before.*
> *2. I'm not one of his close friends.*
> *3. If I know he was married before, and I'm not one of his close friends, then it's not much of a secret that he was married before.*
> *Therefore,*
> *It's not much of a secret that he was married before.*[19]

Surely, there is nothing wrong with this argument.

In response to this objection, let me say, first, that it was important for me to discuss Geach's actual example rather than a 'better' one, because Geach and any number of other competent employers of 'know' who have read his article have taken his imagined 'argument' to make sense as a piece of human speech when, in fact, it doesn't. Geach and his readers only *thought*

---

19. I thank Jodi Azzouni for pressing me to consider examples that might appear to better serve Geach's purposes. Another form of inference featuring 'know' would be practical syllogisms, in which someone's knowing something is not supposed to naturally (factively) entail some other fact, as it was supposed to do in Geach's example, but rather is presented as committing the knower to doing or not doing something. I focus on the use of 'know' and its cognates in such contexts in chapter 4, and argue that it does not lend support to the assumption that 'know' and its cognates have a (descriptive) meaning separable from their different uses.

the argument made sense; they only *thought* they understood it. And if such a hallucination of sense, as we might call it, can happen to us even with what presents itself as a stretch of ordinary discourse, how much greater must be the danger that this could happen to us with a stretch of philosophical discourse?[20] The practice of OLP, as I understand it, is largely meant to help us identify and overcome such hallucinations of sense, the possibility and significance of which Geach and other detractors of OLP have failed to adequately appreciate.

The second thing to say in response to the above objection is that the alternative example offered on Geach's behalf does not show that 'I know (he was married before)' has a meaning that, all by itself and irrespective of the use made of the words, determines what someone would say in uttering it ('literally and seriously')—what Fregean 'thought' he would be expressing or putting forth for consideration. Rather, we can understand the example as an intelligible stretch of human discourse, and so understand the first premise, precisely because, or to the extent that, we can see what point would be made by means of the words in a suitable context. It is not that we are able to understand the first premise just by virtue of knowing what it is to *know* that your friend was married before, or what 'knowing that your friend was married before' *means*. (Nor are we able to understand the second premise just by virtue of knowing the meaning of 'being someone's close friend' or to understand the conclusion just by virtue of knowing the meaning of 'it being much of a secret that someone was married before'.) Rather, we understand the premises and the inference as a whole and would be able to respond to them competently—challenge them, for example—only because, or to the extent that, we can see what overall point the utterer of the words is making (on the most natural hearing of his words).[21]

---

20. On this, see Conant (1998, 246–247).

21. Compare Recanati: '[The] meaning of the whole is *not* constructed in a purely bottom-up manner from the meanings of the parts. The meaning of the

And once we do see that point, we ought to also see that this use of 'I know' does not undermine Austin's basic point as presented in the fourth section of chapter 1. For this use is only in place, or possible, in a context in which what's said to be known is not in question (among the participants). Hanfling calls this general type of context 'the commenting situation' (2000, 96). Here the context is one in which no one has doubted that such and such, and 'I know that such and such' means something like 'I (too) have come to possess the information, have learned that such and such'. What shows that it's not much of a secret that the speaker's friend was married before is not the fact that the speaker *knows*—in the (philosopher's favorite) sense of 'has conclusive evidence' or 'can prove'—that he was married before. It is rather the fact that (even) *the speaker* knows (has heard, has found out). The context invoked in this example, on the most natural hearing of it, is accordingly precisely *not* of the sort that concerns Austin in the relevant passages from 'Other Minds'—the sort of context in which more or less ordinary skeptical worries have become salient in one way or another. No one who did not *already* assume that 'I know', however used, always says of the speaker the same thing—*that he knows,* that he stands in the relation of *knowing* to some fact or proposition, where knowing is presumed to always come to essentially the same thing—would take the example just offered on Geach's behalf to undermine Austin's philosophical point. But, again, it is precisely this prevalent assumption that Geach's argument was supposed to validate.

---

whole is influenced by top-down pragmatic factors, and through the meaning of the whole the meanings of the parts are also affected' (2004, 132; see also 155 for a rejection of Geach's argument against contextualism). This seems to me just right, as far as it goes. In subsequent chapters, I will argue that the contextualist position Recanati advocates is still subject to the 'descriptive fallacy', and therefore does not go far enough toward pointing the way out of traditional philosophical difficulties.

3. Soames's Argument from our Ability to Employ and Understand New Sentences

So far, we have seen no reason to suppose that words such as 'know' and its cognates or 'true' have something associated with them that may aptly be called 'their meaning' and meets the expectations, or requirements, of those who accuse OLP of conflating meaning and use. In particular, neither the competent employment of such words in the back and forth of conversation nor the ways in which they may felicitously be employed in the drawing and expressing of inferences shows their meaning to be what the critics of OLP claim it must be. For all we have seen so far, these words may have nothing that could be referred to as 'their meaning' that is theoretically separable from their ordinary and normal employment in the way presupposed by these critics and has the sorts of (descriptive) powers these critics expect of meanings.

Soames's argument for why words must have meanings of the sort presupposed by the critics of OLP is different in nature from the first two arguments we have considered. It is essentially empirical:[22] a claim about what the meanings of words must be if we are to be able to explain our undeniable ability to understand and employ sentences that we have never previously encountered.

> Linguistic meaning is systematic. Standardly, the meaning of a complex expression is determined by the meanings of its parts. If this were not so, we *could not explain* [my emphasis] how language users are routinely able to understand new sentences that they have never previously encountered. In order to account for this fact, we need a theory of

---

22. Searle's and Geach's arguments may also be given an empirical reading. However, it is quite clear that they were not originally intended or presented that way.

meaning of an individual expression that makes clear how it is able to systematically contribute to the meanings of larger linguistic compounds that contain it. Strawson's performative analysis of the truth predicate doesn't do this. (2003a, 129; see also 147)

As I argued, Strawson may not charitably be read as offering an analysis or theory of meaning of the truth predicate—not, at any rate, if by 'analysis' or 'theory of meaning' one means what Soames evidently means by it here. He therefore may not charitably be criticized for having offered a faulty analysis or theory of meaning. But again, my aim here is not to defend Strawson. My aim is to examine arguments that have been taken to support the prevailing conception of meaning and thereby to speak against the practice of OLP. *Taken this way,* I will now argue, arguments from 'compositionality' are both off-target and empirically implausible. They are off-target because what 'meaning' is supposed to refer to in them has no clear connection to what OLP seeks to elucidate in the face of philosophical difficulty. They are empirically implausible because what they in effect purport to establish, or anyway must establish if they are to reveal the practice of OLP as misguided in principle, is the impossibility of failing to make (clear) sense with one's words— at least as long as they are syntactically correctly put together and do not suffer from some *obvious* failure (such as a 'referring term' lacking a referent or a clearly ambiguous term uttered in a context that does not disambiguate it). It seems to me an undeniable empirical fact, however, that we can and do sometimes get lost with our words—in both obvious and far from obvious ways. Neither our words' meanings nor their familiarity to us ensures their sense in our mouths.[23] And this is part of what any plausible theory of language would need to explain.

---

23. I assume that no one who has ever graded students' papers for an introductory philosophy course would deny this fact. It might be imagined that philosophical training somehow immunizes us against getting lost with our words.

What Soames presents as a standard—understood as it must be understood if it is to so much as even seem to carry weight against the practice of OLP[24]—is indeed what is standardly *assumed* by many in contemporary analytic philosophy. What is standardly assumed—namely, one version or another of the prevailing conception of meaning—is presented by Soames as what we *must* assume, if we are to be able to explain empirically the undeniable fact that competent speakers are able to use and understand combinations of words they have never encountered before. And this means, first of all, that Soames's meanings are *theoretical posits*: they are what an empirical explanation of a certain fact is taken by him to require.[25] It is therefore not clear what, if anything, they have to do with *our* 'meaning (of a word)'—with what we ask for when we ask for the meaning of a word, what we explain when we explain the meaning of a word, what we may be said to (mis)understand when we (mis)understand a word, and so forth. But since it is precisely our humble 'meaning' that Wittgenstein suggests may in many cases be explained by saying that the meaning of a word is its use in the language, and since what he and other ordinary language philosophers wish to elucidate in their appeals to the ordinary and normal use(s) of the word or expression under consideration may in many cases usefully and aptly be called 'its meaning', it is not clear how arguments from 'compositionality' such as Soames's are supposed to engage with, let alone undermine, the ordinary language philosopher's general approach.

But it seems to me that the history of Western philosophy rather suggests that it only makes us better at getting lost in ways that are harder to detect and make perspicuous.

24. As I note later in the text, the idea that the meaning of a complex expression is determined by the meanings of the words that make it up may be understood in a way that makes it innocuous. Understood that way, however, the idea is perfectly compatible with the practice of OLP as defended in this book.

25. Compare Davidson: 'I suggest that words, meanings of words, reference, and satisfaction are posits we need to implement a theory of truth' (2001, 222).

Furthermore, it is bad scientific practice to take oneself to know what form the explanation of a certain empirical phenomenon *must* take. Empirical theories are underdetermined by their data. It *may* turn out that the best or most plausible or compelling or useful explanation of the fact that we can understand and use combinations of words we have never previously encountered or used will make no use—at least not in every case—of Soames's meanings. It *may*, for example, turn out that the best explanation will only appeal to a combination of our knowledge of syntax, our familiarity with and mastery of enough of the ordinary and normal uses of the word, and a more or less shared sense of what, given its ordinary and normal uses, may be done with it, more or less creatively, in more or less novel contexts.[26] The best explanation of my ability to competently employ, or understand someone else's competent employment of, for example, 'I know Smith's Vermeer is a forgery', where I have never previously 'encountered' that particular sentence, may turn out to proceed along the following line: I know the syntax of English in general and of 'know' in particular; I am familiar with and have mastered, among other things, the use of 'I know' to express conviction; and I am capable of recognizing some particular situation as suitable, or calling, for that particular use of these words.

An explanation along these lines of our ability to use and understand 'know' and its cognates in hitherto unencountered constructions would not attribute to competent employers of these words the ability simply to apply them to cases, apart from any particular context of significant use. It would, on the contrary, take these words to be unfit for such applications, for reasons that will emerge in subsequent chapters. But it would

26. Compare Chomsky: 'It is possible that natural language has only syntax and pragmatics; it has "semantics" only in the sense of "the study of how this instrument, whose formal structure and potentialities of expression are the subject of syntactic investigation, is actually put to use in a speech community"' (1995, 26).

nonetheless be perfectly compatible with the idea that, *in some sense,* the meaning of 'know', together with the meanings of the other words that make up the sentence, determines the meaning of 'I know Smith's Vermeer is a forgery'. Apart from a particular picture of what the meanings of words are, and what the meanings of sentences are, and how the former determine the latter, the talk of meanings of words determining the meanings of the sentences they make up may be perfectly innocuous.[27] But apart from that picture, such talk does nothing to undermine OLP's general approach and specific procedures.

Thinking of the meaning of a word not in terms of its applicability to cases even apart from any context of significant use, but rather as something like its potentiality for being put to use—a potentiality with which the history of its use has endowed it—and of knowing the meaning of a word as a matter of the ability to actualize this potentiality in one way or another under suitable conditions, leaves open the possibility of uttering a word without saying or meaning anything clear by it. Furthermore, if this alternative way of thinking of meanings and what should be expected of them is on the right track, then we are more likely to speak confusedly or emptily when we utter our words apart from any of the contexts in which they would ordinarily and normally be employed, and rely on their meanings alone to ensure the sense of what we are saying. This suggests that, and why, we may be especially prone to getting lost with our words 'when we do philosophy', as Wittgenstein tends to put it.

At least in the case of 'know' and its cognates, an explanation along the lines just sketched of our ability to carry on with them and to use and understand them in novel constructions does not, on the face of it, seem to me empirically less promising than an explanation along the lines of the prevailing conception

27. See Horwich (2005, 202ff.) for this innocuous, or 'deflationary', 'principle of compositionality'. A similar point is made by Brandom (2008, 136) against Fodor and Lepore.

of meaning, which presumably would go roughly like this: *First I must come to know what the relation of knowing (that) is and how to tell it is present, and to know that 'know' and cognates refer to that relation and are (to be) used first and foremost for attributing it to pairs of knower and fact (or proposition). Knowing that, I may additionally come to know that one thing one may do with 'I know', beyond of course predicating the relation of knowing of the speaker and some fact, is to express conviction—for example, the conviction that Smith's Vermeer is a forgery. Never mind that conviction, by most philosophical and nonphilosophical accounts, is very different from knowledge. Or I may come to know that in certain contexts 'I know!' means something like—carries no more and no less commitment than—'I heard!'. Never mind, again, that knowing that such and such is, of course, very different from having heard that such and such. Or I may come to know that in certain contexts 'I know' may be used interchangeably with 'You can trust me (on this one)' or 'I'm not just saying this'. Never mind . . . , etc.*

But it is not my aim here to argue for any particular theory of meaning. As I will emphasize shortly, the practice of OLP as defended in this book presupposes no such theory. My aim has only been to bring out a fact about arguments from compositionality for the prevailing conception of meaning (and thereby against OLP): namely, that while they present themselves as justified on empirical grounds, they tend to be dogmatic in a way that empirical theories ought not to be. These arguments take what Recanati aptly describes as 'a stipulating and question begging stance on empirical matters' (2004, 160).

Should it turn out that the best explanation of our ability to employ and understand previously unencountered combinations of words has no use for meanings as Soames and other opponents of OLP conceive of them, their fate would not be unlike that of phlogiston. However, unlike 'phlogiston', '(word) meaning' has plenty of uses for us outside of empirical theorizing. Therefore, the empirical discovery that there is no need or justification for positing meanings as Soames conceives of them[28]—we may even come to say that *there are no such meanings,* just as we now say there is no phlogiston—would *not* be the discovery that there is nothing for us to learn, understand, explain, become confused about, and so on, and to which we may with full right continue to refer as the meaning of this or that word. This is yet another way of seeing why Soames's argument does not so much as even come into contact with the philosophical work it is meant to undermine.

I have sketched two different ways of thinking about the meanings of words and how they relate to what may be said by means of them. The first is not only compatible with the practice of OLP but makes clear why it should sometimes be called for. It is vitally important to see, however, that OLP's approach to the dissolution of philosophical difficulties presupposes no *theory* of meaning in any significant sense of that term. It only "presupposes" that to know the meaning of a word is to know how to use it competently and how to respond competently to other people's use or attempted use of it in a wide enough range of contexts. And this is no theory of meaning. It is just our common and everyday criterion for 'knowing the meaning of a word'.[29] What the use of some philosophically troublesome word normally involves and requires—hence, in particular, what it is that the word may aptly be said to carry with it to particular instances of its employment, call it 'its meaning'—is in turn left open by this criterion. It is something, as Wittgenstein puts it, to 'look and see' in each particular case, not something knowable in advance.

28. Compare the 'concept eliminativism' that Machery (2009) proposes for psychology and cognitive science.

29. See Williamson (2003, 250; 2005a, 11–12; 2007, 216). In chapter 3, we will see how this innocent piece of Wittgensteinian grammar gets Williamson into trouble when he attempts to respond to criticisms of the reliance on 'intuitions' in analytic philosophy.

The second, prevailing way of thinking about meaning, by contrast, proceeds from an *assumption* of what speakers *must* know in knowing the meaning of a word, at least when it comes to 'singular substantives': namely, how to 'apply' the word to cases, how to refer to (denote, name, classify, pick out) cases or items by means of it, apart from any context of significant use. If contemporary 'contextualists' such as Travis and Recanati are correct, this assumption is untrue even of such philosophically innocent predicates as 'weighs 79 kilos' or 'is green'. Not even such predicates, contextualists have argued, are fit for (either true or false) application to cases apart from contexts of significant use. Much of the rest of this book will be devoted to arguing that when it comes to 'know' and its cognates, the above assumption is once again unsupported by what we see when we look with eyes unprejudiced by theory, except that in this case not even 'contextualist' amendments would save it. Furthermore, we will see that this assumption is also responsible for deep and seemingly insurmountable philosophical difficulties. Thus, while OLP's way of thinking about meaning is as weak or unambitious as can be, theoretically speaking, philosophically it may prove powerful—as powerful as the philosophical difficulties it will enable us to put to rest.

I do not know whether we will ever have a comprehensive and truly satisfying empirical explanation of our ability to expand indefinitely our linguistic resources—systematically, but also more or less creatively. Nor do I know what form such an explanation would take. I do not think anyone does.[30] Should such an explanation be found, however, I cannot see how it *could* undermine OLP's attempts to attain clarity in the face of conceptual difficulties. For those attempts, after all, are an extension and refinement of something that we speakers have always been called upon to do in the face of conceptual confusion or

---

30. According to Pietroski, a truly satisfying theory of meaning 'may still be undreamt of' (2005, 271).

lack of clarity.[31] That the practice of OLP is possible, and sometimes called for, far from being incompatible with an empirical theory of language use and acquisition, is therefore part of what any truly satisfying such theory would need to explain.

4. Concluding Remarks

In accusing ordinary language philosophers of conflating meaning and use, the critics of OLP have relied on a conception of meaning that is at least open to dispute and that is not well supported by their arguments. Rather than succeeding in undermining OLP, the three arguments we have considered have turned out to call, each in its own way, for an OLP intervention. This much I hope to have shown in this chapter. Much of the rest of this book will be devoted to showing that, and how, the prevailing conception of meaning has led to entanglements and impasses in philosophical theorizing about knowledge.

Echoing many others, Soames argues that the ordinary language philosophers 'suffered from the lack of systematic theory of meaning and language use' (2003a, xiv, 3, 286, 292; see also Searle 1999, 131, 151, and Burge 1992, 13). Though it certainly is true that ordinary language philosophers do not proceed on the basis of a systematic theory of meaning and language use of the sort envisioned by Soames, I do not see that they have *suffered* from this. Their arguments may well have been confused, incomplete, inaccurate, or otherwise faulty in any number of ways. But I do not see that the best remedy for such failures would have been a systematic theory of the sort envisioned by Soames and others.

It had better not be. For, according to Soames, Davidson-inspired truth-conditional semantics is the best we have done by

31. Of course, getting lost with our words, and consequently getting entangled in conceptual difficulties, is also something that, as speakers, we have always been prone to do.

way of coming up with a systematic theory of meaning. And even if we set aside for the moment all of the weighty difficulties theories of this type have faced in accommodating linguistic data,[32] it seems clear that they simply are not what we masters of our own language need when we come to wonder whether we perceive material objects or only sense-data, say, or whether we can know what other people think or feel, or whether water is *necessarily* H20, or whether we have free will, or how we ought to think of the meaning of words. If we competent speakers of English (or any other natural language) find ourselves unclear about these and other matters, and get entangled even when we think or talk about them in our native language, how could a theory of meaning and language use of the sort envisioned by Davidson possibly help us? As Davidson himself readily acknowledges, it could not. A theory of the kind he proposes, he says, 'leaves the whole matter of what individual words mean exactly where it was' (Davidson 2001, 32–33); the most it can do is 'transfer the mystery', 'without gain or loss', from the troublesome word in the object language to its translation in the meta-language (ibid., 30–31). And this means that, at best, such a theory leaves conceptual entanglements and unclarities exactly where they are.[33]

Soames himself nowhere tells us how a systematic theory of meaning and language use might help resolve traditional

32. For a helpful and compelling review of some of those difficulties, see Pietroski (2005). 'The evidence', he argues, 'now suggests that theories of meaning/understanding are *not* plausibly viewed as theories of truth' (ibid., 272).

33. I say 'at best', because some entanglements and unclarities may in fact be generated by the theory itself. The talk of 'translation' covers up important issues here. For of course, we can *translate* stretches of human discourse from one language to another—for example, stretches of discourse featuring 'true' or 'know'—without resolving conceptual difficulties, and it is true that a good translation will simply preserve existing difficulties, not create new ones. But a Davidsonian theory of meaning for a language is no mere translation. It is a translation that is guided by a set of substantive and challengeable assumptions about language. And as we will see in subsequent chapters, those assumptions sometimes encourage distorted views of linguistic phenomena and thereby create conceptual difficulties.

philosophical difficulties, nor does he anywhere *illustrate* the usefulness of such a theory to the resolution of such difficulties. When, having presented his arguments against OLP, he turns to consider, following Kripke, the relation between the concepts of 'necessary truth' and 'a priori truth', for example, he seems to suppose that he could do this just fine without any theory of meaning—Davidsonian or otherwise. Like Kripke, he seems content to rely on his intuitions in this case.

Soames is not unaware of this fact and of the difficulty it seems to pose for the grand story he wishes to tell about analytic philosophy in the twentieth century and its overcoming of OLP. His resolution of the difficulty seems to go something like this: the ordinary language philosophers maintained that all philosophical problems were linguistic problems, or problems of meaning (cf. 2003a, 186, 192); this is why *they* needed a systematic theory of meaning. Kripke, by contrast, has shown us that not all philosophical problems are problems of meaning; and this is why he, and those who follow him, can proceed in good faith without a theory of meaning (see 2003a, xv).

I find this line of reasoning doubly problematic. First, as I've said, I do not know of any case in which an ordinary language philosopher suffered from the lack of systematic theory of meaning. And second, I cannot see how Kripke's claims concerning the relation between necessity and apioricity, for example, are any less claims about meaning than Austin's claims about knowledge or Strawson's claims about truth. The questions addressed by Kripke are no less *conceptual* than those addressed by Austin or Strawson.[34] The difference lies in their respective

---

34. Inspired by Kripke, Melnyk (2008) has recently argued that philosophers would do well to forego 'conceptual analysis' altogether and focus instead on the discovery of a posteriori necessary identity truths such as that water = H2O. I'll make just one brief comment about Melnyk's proposal. Neither water, nor our concept of water, has befuddled philosophers for millennia, or is likely to have ever driven one to philosophy. Philosophers became concerned with 'water = H2O' only when they became concerned with *the nature of the claim/truth* it (supposedly) makes/expresses, and in particular with the *conceptual* possibility

methods of inquiry and argumentation. Whereas Strawson and Austin take the ordinary and normal practice of employing the words in question as primary, Kripke mostly relies on what he himself is happy to call 'intuitions' about the truth (conditions) of sentences (1980, 12, 14, 42).[35]

In recent years, however, analytic philosophers have been hard-pressed to acknowledge that it is far from clear what justifies the reliance on intuitions in philosophical theorizing. In the next chapter, I will argue that the philosophical reliance on intuitive 'applications' of terms to cases is even more deeply problematic than has hitherto been recognized. OLP, I will then propose, offers us a way of becoming clearer about our concepts and the phenomena they delineate, without relying on intuitions.

---

of what they have called 'a posteriori necessary truths'. Does Melnyk propose that we attempt to resolve the issues raised by Kripke's *Naming and Necessity* by searching for an a posteriori necessary truth of the form 'a posteriori necessary truth = x'? And how, taking another example, could philosophers even begin to look for an a posteriori identity truth of the form 'knowledge = x' (Melnyk 2008: 284), if they can't even agree among themselves about whether passenger Smith, in Cohen's (1999) 'Airport' example, knows or does not know that the flight has a layover in Chicago, or whether *that* question is or is not 'context-sensitive'? I find it striking, and a little ironic, that Kripke's intuitions about our concepts of *necessary truth* and *contingent truth* and their relation to our concepts of *a priori truth* and *a posteriori truth* have encouraged philosophers to think that philosophy could do altogether without reflection on our concepts.

35. Kripke's case, I should note, is a bit more interesting, because there are moments in which he does appeal, à la Wittgenstein and Austin, to 'what we would (or should) say'. However, Kripke regards what we should say when as 'secondary phenomena' (cf. 1980, 14, 113).

CHAPTER 3

Must Philosophers Rely

on Intuitions?

For several decades now, philosophers in the mainstream of analytic philosophy pursuing a theory of some subject x (knowledge, necessary truth, causation, intentional action, and so on) have centrally relied on what they themselves have been happy to describe as their own and other people's 'intuitions' of whether or not our concept of x, or the word 'x', applies to this or that particular case, real or imagined.[1] I will call the question of whether or not our concept of x, or 'x', applies to some real or imaginary case when it is raised as part of an attempt to develop or test a philosophical theory of x, 'the theorist's question'; and I will call the research program that takes answers to the theorist's question as its primary data 'the prevailing program'.

In recent years, the prevailing program has come under serious pressure. Two general lines of objection to the philosophical reliance on intuitions have appeared in the literature. First, it

---

1. Of course, appeals to 'intuitions' in philosophy have taken other forms. In this chapter I focus on this particular form, partly because I focus on Williamson who focuses on that form, and partly because it is central and, to my mind, representative of the other forms.

has been argued that the intuitions on which philosophers rely are merely *their* intuitions and, given that others could, and as a matter of empirical fact sometimes do, have different intuitions, it is not clear what weight, if any, philosophers should give to their own. This line of criticism was originally broached by Stich (1988)[2] and more recently was claimed to have acquired empirical support (Weinberg, Nichols, and Stich [hereafter WNS] 2001). Following Stich, I will call this line of objection to the prevailing program 'the cognitive diversity objection'. Second, the question was raised of how, if at all, we can tell whether our intuitions successfully (reliably) track whatever it is—knowledge, say, or our concept of knowledge—that they are supposed to track. This second objection was originally raised by Cummins (1998) and, following his way of putting it, has come to be called 'the calibration objection'. The two objections are not unrelated. Both concern the fundamental question of what it is we are after or ought to be after in philosophy, and how it might best be pursued. Both objections have also been invaluable in forcing analytic philosophers to address questions of philosophical method that for many years have largely been ignored. Neither objection, however, goes quite to the heart of what is wrong with the prevailing research program. Or so, focusing on our concept of propositional knowledge—*knowing that* such and such—I will argue in this chapter.

In a series of articles that have recently been incorporated into a book entitled *The Philosophy of Philosophy,* Timothy Williamson attempts to defend the prevailing research program against the above lines of criticism.[3] All of the talk about philosophers relying on intuitions, Williamson argues, has been

2. See also Weinberg and Stich (2001).

3. In the book, Williamson seems more focused on bringing about an improved shared understanding of the prevailing program among those already committed to it than he is on defending it against those skeptical of it. My interest in this chapter, however, is in Williamson's account as containing a line of response—to my mind the best available line of response—to the cognitive diversity objection and to the calibration objection.

wrongheaded:[4] what philosophers have relied upon is simply our everyday capacity to judge (2007, 3)—that is, to 'apply' our terms, or concepts, to 'empirically encountered cases' (2005a, 12). The talk of intuitions, Williamson contends, denies, and for no very good reason he thinks, 'the continuity between philosophical thinking and the rest of our thinking' (2004, 152; see also 2007, 192ff.). After all, no one would say that I'm relying on intuition when, in the course of my everyday life, I find or say that someone knows or does not know this or that. So why should we talk about intuition when I do what is, presumably, essentially the same thing when invited by the theorist to say whether the protagonist of some example knows or does not know?

For the purposes of the argument of this chapter, it will be useful to think of Williamson's defense of the prevailing research program as proceeding in two steps.[5] The first step, which he develops in great detail, aims to establish that it should not matter, as far as the purposes of the prevailing research program go, that its practitioners have tended to apply, and to invite their audience to apply, the concept of x, or 'x', to imagined, *hypothetical* cases. After all, Williamson contends, the cases that figure in philosophers' examples have tended, for the most part at least, to be ones that *could* very well have been actual. In fact, he continues, cases that are in all philosophically relevant respects the same as the ones that figure in philosophers'

---

4. This is in contrast with Sosa (1998, 2007a, 2007b) and Bealer (1998), who concede that philosophers have indeed been centrally relying on intuitions and go on to defend what they call intuitions as a special source of philosophical knowledge. Since, with Williamson (2007, 136), I do not find the attempts to defend philosophical intuitions as products of some *special* faculty or capacity compelling, I take Williamson's approach of trying to defend the prevailing program to be its best shot.

5. There is actually a further step that's meant to give us reason to think that everyday judgments 'tend to be true' (2004, 139–152; 2007, 247–277). But since my aim is to show that Williamson's second step is unsound—to show, more specifically, that what holds for everyday judgments does not hold for responses to the theorist's question—I will not consider the step that follows it.

examples most likely *have* occurred; or, if not, they could easily be brought about. Williamson reports that he himself brought about a Gettier case by telling the audience of a lecture he gave that he had been to Algiers, which was false but which they had no reason not to believe and so 'justifiably' believed; he then 'made sure they inferred' from their false but justified belief that he had been to Algiers the proposition that he had been to North Africa, which happened to be true. He thus put his audience in a Gettier-type relation to that proposition (2005a, 12; see also 2007, 192).[6] This first step of Williamson's defense of the prevailing program is not in itself beyond dispute.[7] But my main objection to it here is that it draws attention away from where the real problem lies.

The real problem lies with Williamson's second step, and I find it both striking and telling that he does not really argue for this step. Having argued that we could have encountered, or anyway could fairly easily imagine ourselves encountering, cases essentially similar to those featured in philosophers' examples, Williamson simply goes on to claim that what we are invited to do when we are invited (or invite ourselves) to answer the theorist's question is not essentially different from what we do outside philosophy when we judge that, for example, someone knows or does not know this or that (2005a, 12; 2007, 188). Why should answering the theorist's question counterfactually in the face of, say, an imaginary Gettier case, Williamson in effect asks, be different in any philosophically significant

6. A Gettier case is one in which someone believes something on seemingly solid grounds (so that her 'belief' is 'justified'); what she believes is, moreover, true. And yet the connection between her grounds for belief and the truth of her belief is such that she is actually lucky, so to speak, to believe what's true. Examples of such cases were originally constructed by Edmund Gettier (1963), who expected his readers to find, as many of them have indeed found, that the subject's true and justified belief in such cases does not amount to *knowledge*. This finding has widely been taken to show that knowledge is not simply justified true belief.

7. I doubt that anyone will ever encounter, let alone have to apply his concepts to, cases of the sort found in Williamson (2000, 69–70), for example.

respect from answering it in the face of an actual Gettier case? And why should *that* require anything other than 'the same capacity to classify empirically encountered cases with respect to knowledge as we use when, for example, we classify a politician as not knowing the truth of his claims about terrorists' (2004, 112; see also 2005a, 12)? Williamson concludes that the philosopher's armchair theorizing on the basis of made-up examples presupposes, for its philosophical relevance and methodological soundness, nothing but our 'ordinary capacities for making judgments about what we encounter, and a further capacity to evaluate counterfactuals by running those capacities "offline"' (2005a, 15; see also 2007, 188, 216).

However, it is one thing to show that we could have encountered, or anyway could fairly easily imagine ourselves encountering, outside philosophy, the cases that figure in philosophers' examples or ones philosophically relevantly like them, and quite another thing to show that the question that we are invited by the theorist to answer in the face of his examples is philosophically relevantly no different from questions that we normally and ordinarily answer in our everyday, 'nonphilosophical' judgments. I will argue that at least when it comes to 'know that' and its cognates, the theorist's question, whatever exactly it might come to,[8] is *fundamentally* different from any question we might need to consider as part of our everyday employment of these expressions, and that this difference renders the prevailing program misguided. Moreover, it is misguided in a way that the objections put forth by Stich and Cummins do not capture, and in effect help cover up. Williamson's defense of the prevailing program therefore fails. In failing, it gives us an opportunity to rethink some of the deep-

---

8. The qualification is meant to register the fact that the theorist's question has so far only been identified by means of some particular form of words ('Is this or is this not a case of *x*?', or, more particularly, 'Does so and so know that such and such, or doesn't she?'). That it is none too clear what the question comes to, or how it is to be understood, is part of what I aim to show in this and in the following chapters.

est assumptions that underlie this program and points us in the direction of OLP.

The argument of this chapter also bears on the new trend of 'experimental philosophy' that seeks to eliminate various philosophical biases by conducting experiments in which ordinary subjects—i.e., subjects who are not professional philosophers—are invited to answer different versions of the theorist's question.[9] If my argument is on the right track, then the new approach partakes of what is most deeply problematic about the prevailing 'armchair' program. The new approach promises, among other things, to shake the hold of certain philosophical dogmas concerning particular concepts. A more fundamental dogma, however, and one that proponents of the new experimental program share with their 'armchair' opponents, is a conception of language that leads both parties to assume that answers to the theorist's question—be they the philosopher's or the layman's; those of the few or those of the many—are our indispensable and best guide when we seek to elucidate our concepts and the phenomena they pick out.[10] OLP, I will finally

9. Experimental philosophy is now a thriving, if also contestable, industry. In addition to Weinberg, Nichols, and Stich. (2001), see also Knobe (2003, 2006). Knobe's attitude toward the prevailing program is corrective and constructive, as opposed to the mostly critical attitude of WNS. For a collection of papers representative of either of these two attitudes, see Knobe and Nichols (2008). For a helpful survey and further references, see Alexander and Weinberg (2007). Williamson argues against the new trend in 2007 (7, 191).

10. In their 'Experimental Philosophy Manifesto', their introduction to Knobe and Nichols (2008), Knobe and Nichols deny that experimental philosophers are mostly concerned with conceptual analysis and attempt to sketch a more complex and pluralistic picture of the movement. They nonetheless are still happy to say, with Williamson and other 'armchair' philosophers, that in answering the theorist's questions we are simply 'applying concepts' (cf. 5), and that our intuitive answers express 'beliefs' that may be 'right' or 'wrong' (10), 'warranted' or 'unwarranted' (8). They thus also seem to share the traditional philosopher's assumption, which is insisted on by Williamson and which I will question in this chapter, that there is no philosophically important difference or discontinuity between our everyday judgments and whatever it is that we do when we answer the theorist's question. To the question of what we may

propose, constitutes an approach to the elucidation of our concepts that does not rely on answers to the theorist's question and does not rely on intuitions (in the relevant sense).

1. Stage Setting: The Prevailing Conception and the Intuitions Dialectic

Why doesn't Williamson feel the need to argue *from* the fact that at least many of the cases that feature in philosophers' examples are ones that we could fairly easily imagine ourselves encountering outside philosophy *to* the conclusion that the question that we are invited by the philosopher to answer in the face of those examples is not philosophically relevantly different from questions that we address, and answer, in our 'non-philosophical' judgments? Williamson, I propose, is here taking for granted a deeply ingrained conception of what the everyday employment of our words involves and requires, and how that employment relates to what encounters us in our everyday experience. As will become apparent shortly, this prevailing conception of language is intimately connected to the prevailing conception of meaning sketched and discussed in chapters 1 and 2. Accordingly, I will sometimes simply use 'the prevailing conception'

---

be right or wrong *about* when we answer the theorist's question—whether it is the case under consideration or the concept we are invited to apply to it (or perhaps both?)—Knobe and Nichols give no clear answer. Mostly they suggest, and the work of experimental philosophers for the most part seems to presuppose, that what gets revealed in our answers to the theorist's questions, and what the experimental philosopher studies, are 'people's concepts' (cf. 12); but, if so, it is not clear on what basis they would count someone as right, or wrong, about his concept. At other times, Knobe and Nichols describe experimental philosophers as interested more generally in 'how the mind works' or 'how people think' (12), and it does seem undeniable that our answers to the theorist's question may be revelatory, in one way or another, of *that*. But then, this would be true of any set of human responses to anything. Overall, my sense is that what Wittgenstein says about the experimental science of psychology is also true of the new philosophical movement—that it is armed with 'experimental methods' but suffers from 'conceptual confusion' (Wittgenstein 1963, pt. II, sec. xiv). And it is hard to see how further experiments could help with that.

to refer to the set of theoretical commitments that underlie the prevailing program and Williamson's defense of it.

According to the prevailing conception of language, an essential element or dimension of everyday speech and thinking is something we might call pure judgment—the sheer 'application' of terms, or concepts, to cases.[11] As we have just seen, Williamson very tellingly describes this presumed element or dimension as 'classifying empirically encountered cases' with respect to some term or concept.[12] The philosopher who holds this conception does not deny that there are any number of other things that we do with words *beyond* this act of sheer application or classification. She insists, however, that there is this fundamental element or dimension and that it underlies all other elements or dimensions of speech and thought. And she further insists that our concepts reveal themselves in *it,* whereas the rest of what we do with our words tends to obscure them. The basic picture, as we saw in chapter 1, is that expressions 'refer', first and foremost and independently from the uses to which we might put them, 'to items in the . . . world' (Williamson 2007, 281) and *thereby* become fit for their different uses. The philosopher's invitation to apply our words to different cases is then thought of as part of an attempt to *isolate* that purely referential or 'semantic' element of speech and thought, precisely so as to come to see more clearly the concepts 'expressed' by our words (and hence the 'items' to which they refer) without the obstruction of all of the rest of what normally goes on when we speak or think.

---

11. As I've already noted, the notion of 'applying a word (or a concept)' that features centrally in contemporary analytic philosophy has no straightforward connection with anything that we might naturally describe, outside of philosophy, as 'applying a word (or a concept)'. It is a philosophical term of art that is meant to capture that element of pure judgment—the sheer attaching of word to object or case—that is supposed to underlie human discourse. Outside philosophy, to apply a word, or anything else for that matter, is to put it to this or that use.

12. See also Jackson (1998, 36–37), who speaks of conceptual analysis as 'concerned to elucidate what governs our classificatory practice'.

In the case of 'know that' and its cognates, this representationalist conception of language is expressed in the view that their basic role is to 'refer to' or 'pick out' or 'denote' some particular 'relation' that may hold between potential knowers and facts (or true propositions)—namely, the relation of knowing that. It is accordingly assumed that, as competent employers of 'know that' and its cognates, we should be reliable detectors of that relation, which either holds or does not hold between any subject and any fact.[13] And it is therefore further assumed that, given enough information, we ought, in principle, to be able to simply 'apply' 'know that' or one of its cognates, either positively or negatively, to any given pair of person and fact (or true proposition). In fact, it is assumed that *this* is essentially what we do when we 'assertively' utter indicative sentences featuring these words in everyday discourse, whatever *else* we do with the words—illocutionarily and, more broadly, 'pragmatically' speaking. The theorist's invitation to ask ourselves, in the face of various examples, whether one of the protagonists knows or does not know that such and such, is accordingly taken to be methodologically sound precisely because it is taken to ask us to do, albeit in a theoretically controlled manner, what we do ordinarily, and presumably (mostly) correctly. This, I take it, is what underlies Williamson's contention that philosophical thinking, as he thinks of it, is continuous with the rest of our thinking.

Williamson nowhere directly addresses the calibration objection to the prevailing program. However, some proponents of that program who also assume the prevailing conception of language have suggested the following line of response to that objection (a line of response that, I suspect, Williamson

---

13. I am setting aside here the possibility of vagueness. An appeal to the vagueness of *knowing* might save the prevailing conception, but only by *undermining the prevailing program,* since the latter presupposes that there is one clear-cut and correct yes or no answer to the theorist's question, at least when it comes to the sorts of cases to which theorists have invited us to apply 'know that' and its cognates.

himself would reject as overly 'psychologistic'[14]): *A way of putting the calibration objection is that there is no way for us to certify our answers to the theorist's question of, for example, whether some protagonist knows or does not know the proposition in question—no reason to think that these answers in fact track our concept of propositional knowledge, or propositional knowledge.*[15] *This, however, is confused, for it supposes that our answers to the theorist's question are meant to track something that is external to and independent from whatever it is that guides and informs our everyday applications of 'know that' and cognates. But they're not. They are meant to track precisely that which guides and informs our everyday applications of these words. What certifies our answers to the theorist's questions is therefore the simple fact that they come from competent speakers who are asked to do something that, in their competent employment of 'know that' and cognates, they do all the time, in the face of cases not essentially different from the ones that appear in philosophers' examples.*[16] *The*

14. On this point, see next note (n15).

15. I confess not to know what tracking propositional knowledge, philosophically, could be, if it is not at the same time a tracking of our concept of propositional knowledge. I suspect, however, that Williamson would have reservations about my assuming here, as I'm assuming throughout, that what we are looking for in philosophy is a clarification of our concepts. Historically, he would say, philosophers have thought of themselves as investigating things, not just our concepts of them (cf. 2005a, 2 and 2007, 10–22; see also Sosa 2007b). Williamson would be likely to say that my proposed response to Cummins reflects a 'psychologizing [of] the subject matter of philosophy' (2007, 211). I will return to this issue in the final section of this chapter. For now I will only say that, at least when it comes to phenomena such as knowledge, I doubt that it makes sense to distinguish the attempt to become clearer about our concepts from the attempt to become clearer about the phenomena they pick out. Williamson's identification of the conceptual with the (merely) psychological, it should be noted, is also philosophically questionable, for reasons already suggested by Frege.

16. This could be what Sosa has in mind when he sets out the requirement that philosophical intuition stem from 'virtue' or 'competence'. I suspect it is not. But, if this is not what he has in mind, I'm not sure how the virtue or competence is supposed to be established without begging the question against those

only difference is that, in attending to the theorist's question, we do what we do all the time, and reflect upon it, in a more controlled way, in the face of theoretically significant cases; and this enables us to bring out and see more sharply features and dimensions of our concept that may get obscured in the hustle and bustle of everyday speech.[17]

From the perspective of the prevailing conception, this response to the calibration objection would seem compelling. But where would it leave us with respect to the cognitive diversity objection and the empirical findings that have been adduced in its support? If in answering the theorist's question people are doing nothing essentially different from what they do whenever they find or say of someone that she knows or does not know that such and such, how is it that such seemingly stark disagreements have emerged among those responding to the question? Williamson's answer is that some of us are just better than others in applying 'abstract concepts to complex examples' (2004, 150). He also thinks that people can get better at this, in much the same way that lawyers may become better at 'the application of very general concepts to specific cases' (2005a, 14). This, then, is how Williamson proposes to deal with empirical findings such as WNS's: if one group of respondents says 'knows' and the other says 'does not know' in the face of some case, then one group judges correctly and the other incorrectly.[18]

---

suspicious of the prevailing program. An advantage of Williamson's account is that it contains a ready answer to this kind of question.

17. See Goldman and Pust (1998, 183–191), and Jackson (1998, 31–32).

18. Two possibilities that Williamson does not consider are emphasized by Sosa (2007a, 102–103): first, that different people might differently imagine the case about which the theorist's question is asked and, second, that different people might understand in different ways the theorist's question itself. Where neither of those possibilities obtains, Sosa is happy to say, with Williamson, that one party is just right and the other just wrong (ibid., 102). As it stands, I find Sosa's appeal to the two possibilities uncompelling. Sosa, it seems to me, owes us some story about how a Gettier case, for example, may be imagined— in philosophically relevant respects—in different ways by different people, and how the question of whether the subject knows that such and such may, again

And who's to say whose judgment is correct? Philosophers? It sometimes seems that this is what Williamson proposes, on the grounds that not all competent speakers are 'good at philosophy' (2007, 40, 191). At other times, however, he acknowledges that philosophers often disagree among themselves about the correct answer to the theorist's question (2005a, 11), and points out that they are sometimes mistaken in their judgments precisely because they have an investment in some theory (2003, 253–254, 285).[19] But if laypeople tend to disagree in their answers to the theorist's question of whether some case is a case of x, and if the commitments that come with philosophical theorizing are arguably just as likely to distort one's judgment as they are likely to improve it, then who's to say whether some actual or hypothetical case is a case of x? Williamson may be relying on reflective equilibrium to help us decide which intuitions we should rely on and which we should explain away (see Williamson 2000, 33). But I agree with Stich (1988) that reflective equilibrium, however wide, will not help us here. If the history of philosophy has taught us anything, it is that no matter how wide the reflective equilibrium is with which one philosopher has satisfied himself, it is always possible for another philosopher to find it fundamentally misguided.

Here, however, is a reply to the cognitive diversity objection that Williamson doesn't offer but that someone who believes in

---

in philosophically relevant respects, be understood in different ways. What I do think is true, and this is something that neither Sosa nor Williamson considers, is that it is none too clear what understanding the theorist's question requires and how we can tell whether we really understand it or only *think* we understand it. Surely, the fact that the words in which it is couched are familiar to us, and the fact that we *feel* we understand it and even know how to answer it is quite compatible with our merely thinking that we understand it. This is something that Kant teaches us in the 'Transcendental Dialectic' of the first *Critique*; I will discuss this Kantian connection in the epilogue.

19. This is what Goldman and Pust (1998) have called 'theory contamination'. Compare Weatherson (2003), who argues that when our intuitions clash with an otherwise compelling theory, it is not clear that we should always give up or amend the theory, as opposed to simply taking the intuitions, however robust, to be wrong.

the prevailing conception and in its attendant research program *could* offer: *The cognitive diversity objection is a red herring, at least as far as what WNS call 'the descriptive project' (2001, 430)—the attempt to become clearer about our concepts—is concerned. Granted, people who are sufficiently different from each other in their basic sensibilities, practices, and metaphysical commitments will also be different from each other, more or less significantly and more or less pervasively, in their concepts. It would not be implausible to think of this as a conceptual truth. However, wouldn't it be enough of an achievement for philosophy if it could help us to become clearer just with respect to* our *concepts—the ones we share only with those sufficiently like us, be they the whole species or only part of it? After all, the understanding of philosophy as a form of pursuit of self-knowledge has arguably been with it, however inconsistently, since its inception. If the practice of constructing theories of our concept of propositional knowledge and testing them in the light of examples can help us become clearer about our concept of propositional knowledge, which WNS nowhere deny, then it is a practice worth pursuing. And as for Stich's question of why we should care about what this practice reveals about what is merely our concept, the answer to it is simple: because it is ours; and becoming clearer with respect to it is becoming clearer with respect to those features and dimensions of ourselves and of our world to which this concept is responsive and of which it is therefore revelatory.*[20]

This, it seems to me, would have been a compelling reply to the cognitive diversity objection to the prevailing research program, but only if we had reason to believe that the prevailing

---

20. Compare Grice: 'Even if my assumption that what goes for me goes for others is mistaken, it does not matter; my philosophical puzzles have arisen in connection with my use of E [some philosophically troubling expression], and my conceptual analysis will be of value to me (and to any others who may find that their use of E coincides with mine)' (1989, 175). Needless to say, Grice's notion of 'use', unlike Wittgenstein's, is purely representational. The data for his analyses are simply his intuitions about which cases E 'applies' to.

program was indeed leading us to clarity with respect to our concepts, and were it not for the fact that, in the experiments reported by WNS and others, 'disagreements' emerged not only among people who belong to different cultural or social groups, but also among people who belong to the 'same' group.[21] Indeed, as we all know, substantive disagreements as to the correct answer to the theorist's question have emerged even within the relatively homogeneous group of analytic philosophers.[22]

This suggests that the significance of the experiments reported by WNS and others may lie elsewhere from where it is commonly taken to lie. What ought to have struck us about the findings of those experiments is that people who presumably are able to smoothly and effectively employ 'know that' and its cognates in their everyday dealings with each other, and who by any reasonable criterion understand and mean these expressions in the same way,[23] nonetheless have come up with opposing

---

21. Nichols and Ulatowski (2007, 347) anticipate an answer along the above lines to the cognitive diversity objection, and then stress in response to it the significance of what they call 'intra-cultural differences' (353–354). See also Mallon et al. (2009) for the significance of intracultural variation to philosophical theories of reference.

22. Williamson wishes to downplay the 'levels of disagreement' among 'trained philosophers' (2007, 191), but I don't think that the facts would support him in this in all cases. 'Contextualists' and '(non-skeptical) Invariantists' are split, for example, on the question of whether (it would be true for John and Mary to say that) passenger Smith, in Cohen's (1999) 'Airport' example, knows that the flight has a layover in Chicago. And neither position lacks supporters. Williamson also wishes to downplay the extent to which (near) consensus among trained philosophers, where it exists, is due more to 'unquestioning conformity' (2007, 191) than to 'high intelligence' and 'advanced education' (112)—and so is more revelatory of the psychology and sociology of professional philosophy than of the truth of its theories. Here again it seems to me that a more careful examination of the empirical facts is called for. On this, see Cummins (1998, 116) and Weinberg, Nichols, and Stich (2001, 438).

23. They normally do not become puzzled by each other's employment of these expressions; they normally respond to the other's employment of these expressions in ways that the other does not find puzzling; they never, or hardly ever, have occasion to ask the other 'What do you mean by "know"?', or to protest 'This is not what "knowing" means!'; etc.

answers to the theorist's question. On the face of it, this suggests that answering the theorist's question is not continuous with the everyday employment of the words in question; the capacities that are sufficient for doing the latter well may not be those required for doing well the former—whatever exactly doing the former well might be.[24]

Williamson himself acknowledges, and even insists, that someone may be 'mistaken' in his 'application' of 'C' to some particular case or set of cases and yet 'have the concept C', provided that 'in conversation, he uses "C" appropriately, and responds appropriately when others use it' (2003, 253; 2007, 89ff.). Williamson accordingly maintains that philosophers who say of the subject in a Gettier case that she knows the proposition in question

> exhibit theoretical deviance, perhaps bad epistemological judgment, but not linguistic incompetence. Some are native speakers of English; other native speakers of English do not classify them as incompetent in English. By any reasonable criterion, they understand the word 'know' and possess the concept *know*. (2005a, 11–12; see also 2007, 216)

24. In responding to Weinberg's and Stich's objection that his armchair approach ignores the possibility, and significance, of cognitive diversity, Jackson (2001, 661) cites the fact that we can smoothly and effectively communicate—sometimes via letters, emails, or phone—with people 'we have never met' and whose background is 'very different from our own'. Jackson's response is helpful in bringing out a question that Weinberg and Stich fail to address, but it overlooks precisely the issue that I am pressing in this chapter. When a stranger emails Jackson and asks, say, 'Do you know at what time the departmental colloquium is today?', she is asking a question that may be, and normally will be, presumed to have a point. Responding to her will be easy and straightforward enough and not at all an instance of following one's intuition. But this is precisely because she is *not* simply inviting Jackson to 'classify himself and the timing of the colloquium with respect to knowledge', and to do so for no particular reason. Let Jackson understand the question as inviting him to do the latter, and all of a sudden all of the difficulties that have befuddled Western epistemologists—skepticism, for example—will begin to emerge, and the question will naturally seem to call for an exercising of intuition.

It appears that there is tension between the different views to which Williamson seems to be committed. If to (be able to) employ '*x*' (and its cognates) competently, and to respond competently to other people's employment of it, is to understand '*x*' and possess the concept of *x* (2003, 250), and if people who, by this criterion, possess the concept of *x*, and possess the same concept of *x*, nonetheless disagree in their application of '*x*' to the cases with which the theorist is presenting them, is this not reason to suspect that what they are invited by the theorist to do in the face of his examples is *not* continuous with their everyday employment of '*x*'? Williamson's answer seems to be that the examples with which the theorist presents us are 'complex', so that in applying our concept of *x* to them we step beyond the common basis that we share with other competent employers of '*x*', and differences in 'skills at applying abstract concepts to complex examples' emerge (2004, 150) that do not normally emerge in the course of everyday speech. The idea seems to be that philosophical thinking, while still somehow continuous with the rest of our thinking, takes us to regions of our concepts in which we rarely travel and that not just anyone can travel in without getting lost.

But how plausible is this reply? Perhaps Gettier cases are, in *some* sense, more complex than the sorts of cases in the face of which we normally and ordinarily employ 'know that' and its cognates. I will argue in the next two sections that for normal, everyday intents and purposes there is nothing complex about Gettier cases; they only come to seem complex when we attempt to apply our concept of propositional knowledge to them from a metaphysically external position, and apart from any of our normal intents and purposes. Leaving Gettier cases aside for a moment, consider, for example, Cohen's (1999) 'Airport' case. This case is surely as simple as any that one could hope to encounter in the everyday: some passenger's itinerary says that some flight has a layover in Chicago. And yet, while Williamson, along with other 'invariantists', is inclined to say (judges, intuits, or what have you) that the passenger in Cohen's example just knows that the flight has a layover in Chicago, irrespective of the context in which we consider his case (Williamson 2005c, 232), Cohen, along with other 'contextualists', is inclined to say that in some contexts of considering his case it would be false to say that he 'knows' this.[25] And yet, for all that, I suspect that if the invariantist and the contextualist found themselves facing together a situation of the sort Cohen describes in his example, they would be able to get along just fine with each other, as far as understanding what they each said (and meant) with their words was concerned.

Of course, understanding what the other says and means with her words does not mean agreeing with her every assertion or empirical judgment. This is precisely why it would be wrong-headed to object to the worry I've been pressing by appealing to the fact that we also do not always agree in our applications of 'know that' and its cognates *outside* of philosophy, in spite of the fact that we all presumably are competent employers of these words and possessors of the concepts they 'express'. Both Williamson (2004, 150; 2007, 192) and Sosa (1998, 2007a, 2007b) attempt to discount the threat to the prevailing program from the fact of disagreements on the correct answer to the theorist's question by appealing to the fact that we also do

25. Or consider another example. Hawthorne (2004) structures a whole book around what he calls 'the lottery epistemological puzzle'. The most compelling version of the puzzle requires that we be inclined to think, or say, that we know things about our future such as where we will spend the summer. Hawthorne chides Williamson for seeming to deny that we know such things (ibid., 3n7). But any number of philosophers have been happy to concede, and have even insisted, that we do not know such things as what will happen to us or what we will do in the future (see, for example, Feldman's (2007) critical study of Hawthorne's book). A clash of intuitions. If one of the two positions here is just wrong, then it is just wrong about a very significant region of our concept of propositional knowledge. And yet its proponents would most likely be no less competent in their employment of 'know that' and its cognates in that region than the proponents of the opposite position, and members of the two opposing parties can presumably nonetheless smoothly and effectively speak to and understand each other.

not always agree in our empirical judgments. But the two kinds of disagreement are altogether unlike each other. The former is part of normal practice; the latter reveals the anomalousness of the theorist's question.

Normally, if you say of someone (a politician, for example) that he knows something and I say he does not, what we disagree about are *the facts* or their significance, not the meaning of 'know(s) that'. We disagree about the case, but we are still in agreement *in* our use of 'know that' and cognates, and in our understanding of these words. In fact, it is precisely this underlying agreement that makes it possible for us to disagree on particular cases and to go about trying to settle our disagreements. This is precisely what does *not* happen when, in the context of theorizing about knowledge, you say in the face of some example 'knows' and I say 'does not know' (or, if I am a contextualist, 'It would be false for so and so to say "knows"'), where nothing but a philosophical theory of knowledge hangs on our answers. If the example is to do its intended theoretical work, there should be no disagreement among the respondents about the facts—we all are supposed to know all that any normal person would know about the case, once she has read its author's description of it. If there is genuine disagreement between us here, it seems that it would have to be about the meaning of our words.

Therefore, there is an important sense in which we *do no work* with our words—we are not *using* them—when we pronounce on the theorist's question. But neither are we pronouncing on how the words in question *ought to be used,* or reminding ourselves of how they ordinarily and normally *are used* in various contexts, which is what we do when we consider, with Austin, 'what we should say when, and so why and what we should mean by it' (1979, 181). Perhaps this suspension of all interest in the case, this setting aside of the question of its significance, whether actual or imagined, is what Williamson means to register when he says that in answering the theorist's question we exercise our capacity for judgment 'off-line'. But I do not think he aptly appreciates the difference this makes. In the next two sections I will argue that the capacity to understand and competently answer everyday questions is essentially the capacity to see and properly respond to what may be called their point—the particular human interest or set of interests they express. And I will also argue that the theorist's question has no point, *in the relevant sense*; it invites us to apply our words to some given case apart from *any* non-purely-theoretical interest that anyone might have in that case. Whereas the point of an everyday question guides us in answering it and in assessing our own and other people's answers, this guidance is lacking when the theorist invites us to answer his question. The prevailing conception of language would have us suppose this lack to be a (theoretical) virtue. My aim in what follows is to show that, at least in the case of 'know that' and its cognates, that supposition is mistaken.

2. What Is It Like to Encounter a Gettier Case?

I have said that we may grant Williamson, at least for the sake of argument, that we may encounter or fairly easily imagine ourselves encountering cases of the sorts that philosophers have imagined for us in their examples. Where he goes wrong is in presupposing that in encountering such cases outside of philosophy we may need to answer, and actually do regularly answer, questions that are not essentially different from the question that the theorist is inviting us (and herself) to answer with respect to her examples.

Let me make my contention clear before I turn to argue for it: the *words* that express the theorist's question may well be the same, or more or less the same, as the words that express questions to which we do attend, and which we do need to answer, in the course of everyday life. But what the theorist's question *comes to* is fundamentally different from what the everyday questions come to, or may come to.[26] In particular, what

---

26. Throughout his defense of the prevailing program, Williamson takes it for granted that we can understand a question just on the basis of our familiarity

answering the theorist's question involves and requires is fundamentally different from what answering the everyday questions involves and requires. Thus, the continuity that Williamson is taking for granted, between everyday judgments and whatever it is that we are invited to do when we are invited to answer the theorist's question—that continuity does not exist. This does not mean that our answers to the theorist's question are revelatory of nothing, or of nothing potentially interesting. But it does suggest that what they reveal is not what proponents of the prevailing program have taken them to reveal.

Consider the Gettier-type case that WNS used in their 'cognitive diversity' experiment (2001, 443). It is formally very similar to the case that Williamson says he brought about, and it seems to come as close as possible, and certainly closer than Gettier's (1963) original two cases, to being a case of the sort that we might actually encounter in the course of everyday life:

> Bob has a friend, Jill, who has driven a Buick for many years. Bob therefore thinks that Jill drives an American car.[27] He is not aware, however, that her Buick has recently

---

with (the meaning of) the words that make it up and our knowledge of syntax (cf. *The Philosophy of Philosophy*, 39). For example, he takes it for granted that 'Was Mars always either dry or not dry?' is a question *about Mars* that someone who would 'like to know the history of Mars' might wish to answer (ibid., 24). But, as Bauer (unpublished manuscript) argues, it is doubtful that anyone truly interested in the history of Mars would ever attend to Williamson's question *as Williamson and other theorists of vagueness think of it*. And should a question arise in the course of an investigation of the history of Mars that might be expressed with roughly the same words, the attempt to answer it would take an altogether different form from that of philosophical theorizing about vagueness. The insistence that it would nonetheless be the same question, or that it would anyway have the same 'content' (ibid., 44), just because it would be expressed by means of more or less the same words, presupposes the conception of language that is part of the target of this book.

27. As Jackson notes (2001, 662), it is not clear, given how Weinberg, Nichols, and Stich phrase the example, whether Bob comes to think that Jill drives an American car by inference from the false (but 'justified') belief that she still drives her Buick (which is how Weinberg et al. intend the example to be

been stolen, and he is also not aware that Jill has replaced it with a Pontiac, which is a different kind of American car. Does Bob really know that Jill drives an American car, or does he only believe it?

The philosopher who holds the prevailing conception of language and is committed to its attendant research program assumes that the question that we are here invited to answer is one that, as competent employers of 'know that' and its cognates, we ought in principle to be able to answer, and answer correctly, and for the simple reason that the 'capacity' for answering this question correctly is also required for the competent employment of these expressions in everyday life. I will now argue that neither our everyday employment of 'know that' and its cognates nor anything else, with the exception of theorizing within the prevailing philosophical paradigm, ever requires that we answer the kind of question that we are here invited to answer.[28]

Suppose we 'encountered' the above case in the course of our everyday experience. Why should we need or care to know, or tell, whether Bob (really) *knows* that Jill is driving an American

---

understood), or by inference from the true belief that she's driven an American car for many years (so that if she for some reason no longer owns the Buick, she must have replaced it with another American car).

28. The argument that follows bears a certain affinity to the argument in Kaplan (1985). Kaplan seems to assume with the traditionalist, however, that the representationalist or 'descriptivist' question of whether (it would be true to say that) so and so knows that such and such is always in order—in the sense that it has a correct answer—and contents himself with arguing, very compellingly, that in everyday, nonphilosophical contexts, *nothing will hang* on the correct answer to it. In his more recent work (2008 and forthcoming), Kaplan continues to assume that the question is always in order, and argues only that the correct answer to it would be context-sensitive. In chapters 4 and 5, I explain why I do not find contextualist-but-still-representationalist accounts of knowledge such as Kaplan's satisfying. I fully agree with Kaplan that philosophical accounts of our concept of *x* should take their bearing from the ordinary and normal practice of employing '*x*' (see Kaplan 1991). But his view of the ordinary and normal practice seems to me metaphysically tainted.

car (or only believes it)? On what occasion, other than philosophical theorizing, might we actually (need to) attend to the
above question as the theorist thinks of it? I consider different
lines of answer, and I reply to them in turn:

> 1. *Someone who knows that such and such is in a position to
> assure others that such and such, and whether or not some-
> one is in that position may sometimes matter a great deal.*[29]

That may well be true. But then the question is why we, or
anyone, should need or care to know whether or not Bob is
in such a position with respect to Jill's driving an American
car. After all, we the readers of the example and anyone who
knows about this case as much as we do already know, on the
basis of an assurance that in earthly matters only God could
provide, that Jill drives a Pontiac and hence an American
car.[30] We, and anyone who knows about this case as much
as we do, do not need an assurance from Bob on this matter.

> 2. *What about someone, call her Agent, who does not
> already know but for some reason needs to know whether
> Jill drives an American car? Agent might be told by Bob
> that she does, and might then wonder whether she should
> count on that assurance.*

29. See, for example, Craig (1999) and Schaffer (2006). I will argue in subsequent chapters that this is only one region of our concept of knowledge.

30. This, by the way, is one important difference that Williamson fails to
note between hypothetical cases and actual cases. Williamson tells us that he
has been to North Africa. But what if his telling us this is itself part of some
philosophical exercise? What if he mis-spoke or -wrote? If we really care about
whether he has been to North Africa, should we rely just on what he says?
By contrast, someone who is assured that such and such by the author of the
case has an assurance that is qualitatively, metaphysically, different from any
assurance that we might have with respect to actual cases. In general, the significance of the difference this makes to our relation to the case has not been
appreciated by philosophers who assure us that *p* in order to get us to reflect
upon what knowledge requires *beyond* the truth of a belief. I will return to this
issue in chapter 5.

To begin with, whatever question with respect to Bob we imagine Agent to need or want to answer here, it cannot plausibly be thought of as the question of whether someone *in a Gettier situation* knows, for, by hypothesis, Agent does not perceive herself to be facing a situation of this type. The situation in which *she* finds herself is rather the common situation in which one wishes to find out whether such and such, and receives an assurance from someone else that such and such. It would nonetheless be instructive to consider this case, and precisely because Agent's situation, as we are here imagining it, is so common.

There are, basically, only two possibilities: either Agent knows the basis on which Bob is offering his assurance and is capable of assessing this basis, or she does not. If she doesn't know Bob's basis and for some reason does not ask for it, or if she knows it but for some reason is unable to assess it, then even if she still asks herself whether Bob knows that (or whether) Jill drives an American car, her question is clearly *not* the question that the theorist is inviting us to answer. For the theorist is inviting us to say (judge, intuit, or what have you) whether Bob's evidence, as described in the example, is "good enough for knowing" that Jill drives an American car, given that she does.[31] By contrast, not only does Agent not possess the kind of assurance *we* have for taking it that Jill is driving an American car, but also, by hypothesis, she either does not know what evidence, if any, Bob has, or is not in a position to assess how good it is.

On the other hand, if Agent does know Bob's basis, and assuming that she does not doubt *its* truth—she takes it that Jill has indeed driven a Buick until quite recently; and if she also is (or anyway takes herself to be) capable of telling how good a reason this gives her for taking it that Jill currently drives an American car; then *that* becomes her question. In

---

31. Fantl and McGrath (2002: 67). For similar formulations of the theorist's question, see Stanley (2005: 88), and Bach (2005b: 62-3).

other words, the question she needs to (be able to) answer is whether the (presumed) *fact* that Jill was driving a Buick until at least quite recently gives her sufficient assurance that she is currently driving an American car. The theorist's question of whether *Bob* knows that Jill drives an American car, or whether he *knows* that she does—whatever exactly this question might come to here—is beside the point, as far as Agent is concerned. She has no reason to attend to it.[32]

As for the question Agent does have reason to attend to, it is altogether implausible to suppose that there is just *one* correct answer to it. People in situations such as Agent's need not always agree with each other about whether what they know or reasonably take for granted gives them *sufficient* assurance that some further state of affairs obtains. People with different temperaments, basic attitudes, past experiences, and so forth, would be likely to disagree with each other about such matters, and I see no reason to suppose that if they did, then, necessarily, at most only one of them would be saying something true, or correct. What fact, or set of facts, *sufficiently* ensures the obtaining of some other fact is not only a context-sensitive matter but, *within reason*, also a matter of opinion.

The theorist, I conclude, should either concede that the question that people in situations such as Agent's would need to ask themselves is just not her question, or else concede that her question, at least in cases of this type, is whether some set of facts sufficiently ensures the obtaining of some other fact. If she opted for the second possibility (and I don't think she would),[33] she would need to give up the assumption that her question has just one correct answer. She would also need to reconsider the significance of the answers to it that she is eliciting.

---

32. I argue this in far more detail in chapter 5.

33. Not least because this would mean that her question, in this case at least, does not essentially concern someone's mental state.

3. All right, go back to the situation of someone, let's call him Judge, who knows all that the reader of the example knows, and in particular knows that Jill drives a Pontiac and knows that, and why, Bob thinks she drives a Buick and hence an American car. And now imagine that Judge learns that Bob has assured Agent that Jill drives an American car. Judge may now wonder whether Bob was in a position to give Agent the assurance he gave. And to wonder about that *is precisely to wonder whether Bob knew that Jill drove an American car. To make the case more plausible, imagine that a great deal is at stake for Agent in whether or not Jill drives an American car; imagine that Judge knows this; imagine that Bob knows this as well; and imagine that Judge knows that Bob knows this.*

Judge's interest in this matter must not be imagined to be merely theoretical, or academic, for if it were, we would be begging our question. Presumably, then, he has reason to be concerned that, given what is at stake for Agent in finding out whether Jill drives an American car, Bob might have been too casual (uncaring, thoughtless, rash) in assuring Agent that she does. I leave aside the question of what reason exactly Judge might have for being concerned with this.[34]

Whatever his reason for concerning himself with this matter, Judge must put himself in *Bob's* position if he is to judge him competently. His question must therefore be asked from *Bob's* epistemic perspective. The things that Judge knows about the case but that Bob does not—including some of the facts that turn it into a Gettier case—are accordingly irrelevant to the question Judge needs to answer. This means, first of all, that Judge's question, just like Agent's, is not really the question of whether someone

---

34. Is he concerned, for example, about Bob's moral well-being, and worries in particular that he tends to be too casual when it comes to things that matter to other people? Or is it rather that he cares about Agent, and is therefore outraged by Bob's (alleged) casualness?

in a Gettier situation knows, and therefore is clearly not the theorist's intended question.

Even more pertinently, Judge's question is really whether, under the circumstances, Bob was *right* (reasonable, not thoughtless, or rash, or negligent, or silly, and so on) to assure Agent that Jill drove an American car.[35] And this question—once again like Agent's and unlike the theorist's intended question—is not one that has only one correct answer. When, how, and under what circumstances an assurance ought to, or may reasonably, be given, is not only a context sensitive matter, but also, within reason, a matter of opinion. Disagreement on such matters is not uncommon, and need not imply that at least one of the parties to it is wrong.

The theorist is likely to insist here that his question may still be raised about this case, regardless of whether it would make sense for Judge to raise it under the circumstances we are here imagining; and he would insist that to suppose otherwise is to have fallen prey to what Searle (1999, 141–146) has called 'the assertion fallacy'—to have come to confuse, that is, what it would make sense actually to *say* or even just *think* under some set of circumstances with what would be *true* (to say, or think). I will come back to this. For now, remember that our question at this point is only whether we would ever have occasion, outside of philosophical theorizing, to attend to the theorist's question. And what we have just seen is that people in situations such as Judge's wouldn't.

4. *But suppose it is Bob's* duty—*part of his job, for example*—*to make sure Jill drives an American car and to report to headquarters the moment she doesn't. Someone could then raise the question of whether Bob has been fulfilling*

---

35. I note that here, as in the previous scenario, it is going to matter a great deal whether Bob told Agent his basis, as people in his situation normally would have, either on their own accord or upon being asked "How do you know?".

his duty. And wouldn't that *question be the theorist's ques-*
tion of whether Bob really knows that Jill is driving an
American car or merely believes this?

No. The question would be whether Bob has been fulfilling
his duty. Given the latest developments in Jill's car situation,
and since by hypothesis Bob is not aware of those developments, there is good reason to think that Bob has neglected
his imagined duty. But the question of whether or not he has
would once again not be the theorist's intended question—
the purely semantic question of whether he *knows*.

5. *So far, we've focused on situations in which knowledge*
that such and such matters to us because it puts its possessor
in a position to assure others that such and such. Let's try a
different tack. It sometimes matters to us whether someone
knows that such and such not in the philosopher's sense of
having proper assurances for her true belief *that such and*
such, but simply in the sense of having learned *that such*
and such, where we ourselves take it for granted that such
and such. Perhaps we think that, for one reason or another,
she would be interested to learn that such and such if she
hadn't already. Or perhaps, if she already has learned that
such and such, there are certain things that we could, or
should, reasonably expect (of her), whereas if she has not
yet learned this, it would be unreasonable for us to expect
those things, and reasonable to expect other things.[36] *Or*
we might simply be curious to know—that is, to learn—
whether she has learned that such and such.

True, the question of whether someone knows that such
and such may sometimes just be the question of whether
he is in possession of some piece of information—a piece
of information that those who attend to the question take
themselves to already possess. In fact, it almost always is.[37]

36. In the next chapter, I discuss these sorts of situations in much more detail.
37. If you go back to the previous 'proposals' and my replies to them, you'll
see that while I did use 'know' and its cognates liberally in them, I used them in

But how could this help motivate, or make seem natural and appropriate, the theorist's question of whether Bob really knows that Jill drives an American car or only believes it? By hypothesis, Bob thinks that she is still driving a Buick, and hence an American car. He would therefore not be interested to learn that Jill drove an American car; nor is it clear how, conceptually speaking, he could learn *this*. What he might be interested to learn, and what is clearly possible for him to learn, is that Jill is no longer driving her old Buick and instead drives a Pontiac. This is something that, given his story as told, he clearly does not know. Notice, however, that 'knows' here contrasts not with 'only believes' or 'believes on grounds insufficient or inappropriate for knowing', as it does in the theorist's intended question, but with 'has not yet learned, or become aware'.

As for the question of what to expect of Bob, well, we know what he knows, what he does not yet know, and what he thinks—vis-à-vis the type of car Jill drives. His epistemic relation to the fact that Jill drives an American car is as clear as it can be:[38] We know about it all that will ever be known about it that would be pertinent to answering questions regarding what we ought to, or may reasonably,

---

the way, or sense, that we are now considering, not in the way or sense on which philosophers have tended to focus. Bach notes, as I do, the difference between what most commonly concerns us when we ask whether someone knows that such and such and what the epistemologist seeks to track in his question of whether some person's belief 'rises to the level of knowledge' (2005b, 62–63). For Bach, however, it is the latter that ought to concern epistemologists, and for him this means that much of our ordinary use of 'know that' and its cognates has no (obvious) bearing on how we ought to answer the theorist's question. By contrast, this chapter argues—following, in effect, Williamson—that if the theorist's question is not one to which we need to attend in the course of our everyday employment of the relevant words, then it is not clear what justifies the prevailing program in epistemology and other areas of philosophical inquiry.

38. Since Bob is a fictional character whose existence, presumably, is confined to WNS's example, there *is*, metaphysically speaking, nothing that *could* be learned about him beyond what is given to us in the example.

expect of Bob. Nothing therefore hangs, as far as answering *that* question goes, on what the ('correct') answer might be to the theorist's question of whether Bob *knows* that Jill is driving an American car, or only believes it; and there would therefore be no reason for anything like this latter question to arise in the sort of situations that we are here imagining.

3. Why 'Intuitions'?

It would be unreasonable for me to expect that considerations of the sort raised in the previous section would by themselves lead those committed to the prevailing research program to give it up. It is far more likely that such considerations would be dismissed as irrelevant on the grounds that they belong to the realm of 'pragmatics' and therefore have no bearing on the viability of the prevailing research program. Proponents of the prevailing program would most likely argue along the following lines: *What it would and would not make sense to say or ask under various circumstances is affected by factors other than, and therefore has no clear or straightforward bearing on, what questions may philosophically legitimately be asked and how they ought to be answered. Why can't the theorist just ask whether Bob knows or does not know that Jill drives an American car, and look for an answer to her question?*

But of course I do not say that the theorist can't ask her question. She can and she does. My aim is to bring out the anomalousness of her question and thereby to raise doubts about the presumed significance of the answers to it that she and others might give. We must keep in mind where exactly we are in the dialectic. In response to the objection that theories produced within the prevailing program rest on nothing but philosophers' intuitions, and that it is unclear what if anything those intuitions reveal or why we should care about whatever it is that they might reveal, Williamson has claimed that philosophers have relied not on anything aptly describable as 'intuitions' but rather on a capacity for 'applying concepts in judgment' to 'empirically encountered cases'—a capacity that, according to Williamson, we all exercise in our 'nonphilosophical thinking'. In claiming this, Williamson has given voice to a widely held conception of what the everyday employment of our words involves and requires. I have interpreted Williamson's claim to mean that the question the philosopher invites us to answer with respect to his examples is not essentially different from questions that we need to (be able to) answer in the course of everyday life, as part of the normal and ordinary employment of our words.[39]

In the previous section, however, we imagined someone "encountering"—each time from a different perspective and with an interest or concern of a different sort—an individual, Bob, whose relation to some proposition is of the Gettier type. I do not claim to have covered all of the different sorts of possible contexts of encounter, of course, but I do believe that I have presented a representative enough sample. In considering each of the different encounters, we saw that the question that the person encountering Bob would naturally ask herself—whether or not it may even aptly be put in terms of 'knowing'—is importantly different from the question that the theorist has wanted, and taken himself, to be asking. What answering the everyday

39. It has been suggested to me, on Williamson's behalf, that the *capacity* could be the same, even though what it is expected to accomplish in philosophy is fundamentally different from what it accomplishes in 'nonphilosophical' thinking. I do not know how capacities might plausibly be identified and individuated other than by what they are capacities *for*, but given my aims in this chapter, I'd be happy to drop the talk of capacities altogether. The point that matters for my purposes is that if there is not the sort of continuity that Williamson assumes between what we do with our words outside of philosophy and what we are invited to do with them when we are invited to answer the theorist's question, then there is good reason to worry about the soundness of the prevailing program, irrespective of what one chooses to say about the capacities involved in each case. In other words, my interpretation of Williamson captures not only what he quite clearly means in his talk of 'same capacity' but also what he *must* mean by this expression, if he is to offer a compelling response to Cummins's calibration objection.

question would normally involve and require, in each of the different cases, is nothing like what answering the theorist's question involves and requires.

And this is no accident. In particular, the fact that the case I considered was of the Gettier type played no essential role in my argument. There is good reason to suspect that no question that may naturally arise in the everyday would come to anything like the theorist's question. This really has nothing to do with the nature of the cases we encounter, inside and outside of philosophy. Williamson is perfectly right about this. It has everything to do, however, with the nature of the encounter. Whenever a question arises in the everyday that might seem to be the same or essentially the same as the theorist's purportedly purely semantic question, what competently answering it involves—and hence, in an important sense, what the question itself comes to—is inseparable from the *point* of the question. The point of the question guides us in answering it, and everyday questions that are competently raised have a point: they are expressive in some suitable way of some particular interest in the case.

Someone has given you an assurance and you wonder whether it is good enough; someone gave someone else an assurance and you wonder whether it was right for her to do so; someone was supposed to stay on top of something and you think he has neglected his duty; you think someone would be interested to learn that such and such, and you wonder whether she already has; someone could have been expected to do something if he had been aware of the fact that such and such, and you wonder whether you are justified in getting angry with him for not having done it; you're simply curious to find out whether someone is aware of the fact that such and such; and so on and so forth. In each of these situations a question arises that might seem no different from the theorist's question. But let anything that might seem like the theorist's question arise in a context where it has a point, and answering it—while it may sometimes be a difficult or delicate task—will normally not be the seemingly profound and befuddling task that answering the theorist's question is. Nor will answering it seem to be, or be, merely a matter of following our intuition.

But a point such as everyday questions normally have is precisely what the theorist's question lacks—and lacks not accidentally, but self-consciously and methodologically: this is what the separation of 'semantics' from 'pragmatics' has come to within the prevailing program. And this, I propose, is what gives rise to our sense that other than theory, which we know we are not supposed to heed, we have nothing but intuition to go on in trying to understand and answer the theorist's question. This is also what explains the fact that even fully competent speakers who by ordinary criteria agree in their understanding of 'knowing that' and share the concept of knowledge could nonetheless come up with contrasting answers to the theorist's question. All that normally and ordinarily guides us in understanding and answering everyday questions that concern empirically encountered cases has been methodologically removed—all but the case itself, and some familiar words to which we are invited to respond. And this is not at all what everyday 'nonphilosophical' speech and thinking involve and require.

The closest that we come in ordinary, 'nonphilosophical' discourse to being in the theorist's peculiar context and attending to something resembling her question is in situations in which disputes arise concerning *what we ought to call* some given case, or *how we ought to describe* it, where it is assumed that there is no real disagreement between the parties about the nature of the case itself. But even in those situations, a particular context of *significant* application is normally in place, or at least assumed or imagined. Indeed, if my argument in the previous section and in the following chapters is on the right track, then, at least in the case of 'know that' and its cognates, no determinate question *may* be raised about a case by means of those words apart from some such context.[40] And this means

---

40. If Travis (1989, 1991, 2000), Recanati (2004), and other 'contextualists' are correct in their claims about the pervasive 'context sensitivity' of language,

that the question asked in those ordinary contexts is *not* the theorist's question of whether the case is a case of *x simpliciter*. Rather, it is the question of whether we should call it '*x*' or describe it as *x given some actual or imagined constellation of interests ('intents and purposes')*. Though the focus in such contexts may be on the word, the question is still a question about its (proper) *use;* and the actual or imagined *significance* of the case must still be taken into consideration, if only implicitly, in determining what we should call it or how we should describe it.

The prevailing conception would have us suppose that none of this should matter, as far as the theorist's purposes go, that the case and the familiar words should suffice, that a clear enough question has nonetheless been raised by the theorist, and that as competent employers of 'know that' and its cognates we ought to be able to answer it. But while the prevailing conception is widely assumed and often insisted on, and while it *might* be harmless enough when it comes to *some* words, we have seen reason to suspect that as a *general* conception of language it may be importantly misguided. Why *must* our capacity to competently employ each and every one of our words presuppose a capacity just to apply this word to cases, apart from any particular interest and without doing anything else with the word beyond sheer application? Why *must* there be a purely semantic component to the understanding of every general term—a component that may theoretically be separated from all of the rest of what this understanding involves and requires, and that may fully be cashed in terms of 'reference' and 'truth-conditions'?

The widespread assumption that our understanding and employment of each of our generally 'referring' expressions has a semantic component that can be isolated and identified in terms of reference and truth-conditions may, in general, be supported either by conceptual considerations (having to do with

---

this would also be true of such perfectly humble predicates as 'is red', 'weighs 79 kilos', and 'is a philosopher'.

our everyday criteria for 'understanding a word' or 'knowing the meaning of a word', for example), or by empirical ones (having to do with what we need to presuppose in order to empirically explain our ability to learn and employ words as we do). I do not see that our relevant concepts lend any support to the insistence. Williamson himself acknowledges, as we have seen, that the normal criterion for 'understanding a word' or 'knowing the meaning of a word' is the ability to employ it competently in (a large enough variety of) everyday contexts. Now, does *that* ability presuppose an ability to apply the word to cases apart from any context of significant use? If my argument in the previous section and in following chapters is on the right track, then there is good reason to suspect that at least 'know that' and its cognates are actually *unfit* for such application: their competent application to cases is too tightly tied to the point of the application. And this seems to me to suggest that, *empirically* speaking, far from being necessary for explaining our ability to learn and employ words as we do, the above insistence actually leads to a distorted view of the very ability that needs to be explained.

It is important to see that I am not questioning, here or anywhere else in this book, every distinction that one might draw between what may be called 'semantics' and what may be called 'pragmatics'. I am questioning a very particular way of drawing that distinction, or trying to. If the distinction between semantics and pragmatics is the distinction between, for example, *what one would be saying,* or could reasonably be taken to be saying, in uttering some sentence in some particular context, and whether it would be 'appropriate' (pertinent, wise, not misleading, not bad manners, and so on) to say it under the circumstances, then I have no problem with it. If it is a distinction between *what one would be saying* if one were to utter some sentence in some context, and what one could reasonably be taken to *imply* or otherwise 'implicate' or 'convey' in (or by) saying it, then again I have no problem with it. Such distinctions may sometimes be worth drawing. My argument in the previous section, however, concerned precisely *what* question one would raise, or could reasonably be taken to have raised, in a given situation, in asking 'Does so and so know that such and such?' What I *am* questioning is the widespread assumption, which is presupposed throughout by Williamson, that the meaning of 'know', together with the meanings of the other words that make up that sentence, is enough for determining *that*.

Against Williamson's defense of the prevailing program, I argued that what the question of whether someone in Bob's situation knows the Gettier proposition would come to in 'nonphilosophical thinking' would be inseparable from the point of the question—from the particular interest in the case of which the question is expressive; and I accordingly argued that, at least in the case of 'know that' and its cognates, no question that might naturally arise in the everyday would be the theorist's question. There is nothing that we do outside philosophy that could aptly be described as simply 'classifying empirically encountered cases with respect to knowing', or as merely 'applying' 'know that' and cognates to cases—not if this classification or application is supposed to require nothing beyond familiarity with the cases and with the meaning of 'know'. If we had, or if philosophy were somehow to construct for us, a concept that enabled us to do *that,* that concept would not be our concept of propositional knowledge. Nor is it clear of what use such a concept would be. I will come back to these issues in the following chapters.

Williamson is right, I believe, in proposing that philosophers' descriptions of themselves as intuiting their answer to the theorist's question bespeak uneasiness on their part concerning their method of inquiry (2004, 119). But if my argument has been on the right track, this uneasiness is in place and ought not to be shrugged away by attributing it to misguided skepticism, as Williamson does (2004, 113–119; 2007: 220–246), for it registers the discontinuity between our everyday employment of the words under investigation and whatever it is that the theorist invites us to do with them in the face of his examples—a discontinuity that undermines the prevailing research program. If any skepticism is relevant here, it is skepticism concerning, not our everyday capacity for judgment—for that capacity, as we saw, is really out of play, or at least severely handicapped, when we attempt to answer the theorist's question—but the soundness of the prevailing research program and its suitability for elucidating our concepts.

A proponent of the prevailing program could still insist, on various theoretical grounds and despite all that we have seen, that there *must* be a purely semantic component of the sort envisioned within that program to our concept of *knowing that,* even if it is not related to our everyday understanding and employment of 'know that' and cognates in anything like the straightforward way that Williamson presupposes in his defense of the program. This purely semantic component, this proponent might argue, is what is supposed to get revealed in our intuitive answers to the theorist's question and what philosophical theories of knowledge (for example) are in the business of tracking.

However, even if we ever arrived at some sort of reflective equilibrium that accounted for at least most of *our* intuitive answers to the theorist's questions and satisfied at least us, we would still face versions of Stich's question of why we (or anyone else) should care about whatever it is that *our* intuitive answers to the theorist's question track, and Cummins's question of what justifies the assumption that these intuitive answers track whatever it is that they are supposed to track—knowledge, for example, or our concept of knowledge. While the invocation by philosophers of some sort of special faculty of philosophical intuition *calls for* such skeptical questions, Williamson's defense of the prevailing program has promised to answer them. Once this line of defense is given up, as I have argued it should be, it is not clear how these challenges to the prevailing program could be answered. If there is no connection of the sort Williamson supposes between what guides and informs our ordinary and normal employment of our words and whatever it is that inclines us to give this or that answer to the theorist's question, then there is a real worry, which should not simply be dismissed, that our answers to that question may in the end only be revelatory of how we—with or without philosophical training—are inclined to answer that question. And it is not (yet) clear what the significance of *that* might be.[41]

4. *Must* Philosophers Rely on Intuitions?

It might still be objected: *But surely you can't deny that we understand the theorist's question and, furthermore, are normally not in the dark when we give our answer to it?*

How can we tell whether we really understand the theorist's question or only *think* we understand it? To be sure, the words in which it is couched are usually perfectly familiar, and in a suitable context they could very well express a question that any competent speaker could reasonably be expected to understand. The rather peculiar context in which we attend to the theorist's question, however, is precisely not such a context. That the theorist's question is couched in familiar words that, if uttered in a suitable context, *would* express a question that makes perfect sense, may be the reason why we can easily enough be tempted to *think* we understand it.[42] But the criteria that ordinarily and normally guide us in distinguishing between someone's truly understanding a question and her merely thinking she understands it—namely, whether her answer is responsive to the particular interest that the question is most reasonably taken to express, whether her requests for

---

41. Compare Kaplan's complaint against Chisholm's theory of justification, and against theories of justification more generally that do not take their bearing from our actual practices: 'The extraordinary, methodologically inert sense of "justification" with which we have had to say Chisholm is concerned, is a sense of "justification" with which we can claim no familiarity. Commonsense tells us nothing of its nature. Reflection upon the canons of inquiry reveals nothing of its contours. The concept of justification, in this extraordinary sense, is a creation *ex nihilo*' (Kaplan 1991, 144).

42. See Wittgenstein 1969, remark 10.

clarification are reasonable or appropriate, what she goes on to say and do when her answer is challenged or misunderstood, and so forth—those criteria are inapplicable in the theorist's context, and inapplicable by design.

I am *not* saying that our answers to the theorist's question are merely arbitrary and reveal nothing about the concept under investigation. In all probability, our answers are affected, to some extent and in more or less traceable ways, by what we know in knowing how to competently employ and respond to other people's employment of (for example) 'know that' and its cognates in different kinds of contexts, hence by our knowledge of the meaning of these words, and hence by our concept of knowing that. It seems clear to me, for example, that the Gettier intuition is affected by considerations that do guide us in our competent employment of 'know that' and its cognates *in certain contexts* (but not in others), and in this way is revelatory of an aspect of our concept of propositional knowledge. In a context in which the possibility that Jill's Buick was stolen and replaced by a different car has become one that ought to be taken seriously (perhaps because it has turned out to be actual!), the fact that she was driving a Buick until quite recently would, by itself, be a poor basis indeed for claiming to know that she is currently driving an American car. It is this feature of our ordinary employment of 'know that' and its cognates to which 'relevant alternatives contextualists' have been responsive, and it is this feature, I propose, that can explain the relatively broad (though still not unanimous) endorsement that the Gettier intuition has enjoyed among both philosophers and nonphilosophers. In all 'Gettier cases', a possibility that if 'relevant' (and uneliminated) in some context would render the protagonist's basis for claiming to know inadequate in that context is revealed to the reader as actual and therefore 'relevant'.[43]

---

43. As we will see in the conclusion, that the actual is always relevant for 'relevant alternatives' contextualists such as Lewis and Travis has important bearing on their response to skepticism.

To show that contemporary 'contextualism' has not sufficiently broken away from the tradition to get us out of traditional difficulties will be the burden of chapters 4 and 5 as well as the conclusion. (By way of anticipation, note that I said nothing about truth and falsity in my description of the features of our ordinary and normal employment of 'know' that may account for the Gettier intuition.) For now I will just say that even though our intuitive answers to the theorist's question are likely to be affected by features of our ordinary and normal employment of the word in question and may *thereby* be revelatory of features of the meaning of that word, there is no telling in advance how far the theoretical context might at the same time distort what we know in knowing how to employ that word 'outside philosophy'. An underlying distortion, I have argued, is precisely the assumption that it *must always* be possible to separate the 'semantic' or 'referential' powers of words from their other powers. This assumption is *built into* the prevailing program (in both its traditional armchair version and its new experimental version) and into the rather special context in which we attend to the theorist's question. It encourages us to expect our words, or their meaning, to ensure the sense of the theorist's question. But this is something that, given the work that we ordinarily and normally do with these words and the conditions under which it may felicitously be done, there is no good reason to expect them to do. What Goldman and Pust have called 'theory contamination' (1998), I am suggesting, begins earlier, and goes deeper, than they suspect. And it doesn't only affect (professional) philosophers.[44]

And the question arises: if our answers to the theorist's question are revelatory of our concept of *knowing that* (for example)

---

44. Wittgenstein's notion of 'picture' is relevant here. Wittgensteinian pictures are prototheories, as it were. Similar to theories, they can interfere with our seeing aright the ordinary and normal functioning of our words. And we needn't be philosophers in order to form pictures for ourselves—for example, of the soul as separable from the body, or of the soul of the other as hidden behind, or inside, her body (see Wittgenstein 1963, 422–427).

only because and to the extent that they are affected by considerations that would be pertinent to the competent employment
of 'know that' and its cognates in different sorts of ordinary
contexts, why not forgo reliance on intuitive applications of the
words outside of practice and instead appeal directly, in the face
of this or that philosophical difficulty, to (our shared knowledge
of) what competently (reasonably, intelligibly) employing these
words, in different types of situations, would normally involve
and require? This proposal is likely to strike those who are theoretically inclined as woefully unsatisfactory. But for those of
us who find ourselves unconvinced by all of the recent attempts
to defend the prevailing program and who have come to suspect—not out of 'impatience with the long haul of technical
reflection', which is 'a form of shallowness' (Williamson 2007,
45), but precisely as result of serious reflection on this program's
rationale—that it might be inherently incapable of delivering on
its promises, showing that it has a viable alternative, however
theoretically nonambitious, may be all that is needed.

The alternative I am proposing is a form of OLP. To begin to
appreciate this alternative, consider our ordinary and normal
criterion for the possession of the concept of x: competently
employing 'x' (and its cognates) and competently responding to
other people's employment of it. As Williamson plausibly claims,
someone who competently employs (and responds to other people's employment of) 'x', in a sufficiently wide and potentially
open-ended range of contexts, knows what 'x' means and our
concept of x 'by any reasonable criterion'. 'Meaning', as Adri-
ane Moore usefully puts it, 'is a matter of how we carry on'
with a word (1985, 144).

And let us next, and this is perhaps the hardest part, not assume
that we can know in advance what distinctions it will be philosophically useful to draw among the many different things and
kinds of things that we know in knowing how to competently
carry on with 'x'. In particular, let us not assume that neat categories such as 'semantics' and 'pragmatics', or 'what's said' and
'what's merely suggested or implied', will always be useful to us

when we wish to elucidate some concept, nor that we can know in advance what exactly such categories, even where useful, will come to in each particular case. Indeed, let us, as much as we can, not commit ourselves to any assumption about what we know in knowing how to carry on competently with 'x', before some particular philosophical question or puzzle about x has arisen. Our aim, remember, is to elucidate some concept in the face of philosophical difficulty, to disentangle some particular conceptual tangle, not to come up with a general theory of language.

To be sure, distinctions exist that would suggest themselves as relevant for some particular philosophical question concerning x, or our concept of x. Many of those distinctions are ones that competent employers of 'x' ought to be able to make—for example, the distinction between saying something false and failing to say anything (clear), or the one between saying something and merely implying or suggesting it. There is nothing in my proposal that rules out the invocation of such distinctions, when it is called for. But we should let the particular question that we have about x—the particular puzzle or unclarity that we wish to alleviate—guide us in determining which distinctions it would be useful to invoke and how exactly they should be drawn. This would not make the distinctions we draw and appeal to ad hoc; it would only make it more likely that they are truly useful and do not get in the way of attaining clarity. For remember that at least very many philosophical difficulties— those surrounding the question of whether knowledge is justified true belief, for example—owe whatever sense and urgency they appear to have to theoretical assumptions.[45] They are not difficulties that naturally arise in the course of our everyday nontheoretical employment of our words.

45. One tends to forget that quite a lot of theorizing, whether explicit or implicit, has already taken place before one comes to understand 'belief' and 'justified belief' as philosophers understand them, and to think of knowledge as justified true belief—a precondition for taking Gettier's counterexamples to have the significance they have widely been taken to have.

Consider once again the theorist's question of whether Bob knows that Jill drives an American car. Philosophers working within the prevailing program have often insisted on the need to distinguish the 'pragmatic' question of whether, or under what circumstances, it would make sense to actually raise or try to answer the theorist's question, and the 'semantic' (or else 'metaphysical') question of what the correct answer to this question is. But note the very assumption that the theorist's question, as it stands, is clear enough to be answered correctly or incorrectly, and the further assumption that as competent speakers we ought in principle to know the correct answer to that question. These assumptions presuppose the distinction between pragmatics and semantics, as philosophers have tended to think of it. In section 2 I argued, by means of direct appeal to what I believe we know in knowing how to carry on competently with 'know that' and its cognates, that at least in the case of these expressions, what is typically thought of as belonging to semantics and what is typically thought of as belonging to pragmatics cannot be separated in the way that proponents of the prevailing program have assumed—not without distorting what we know in knowing how to employ these expressions, and hence not without distorting our concept of knowledge. All of this will be argued for in far greater detail in the following chapters.

In proposing that we replace theorizing on the basis of answers to the theorist's question with direct appeals to what we know in knowing how to competently employ our words, I do not mean that we should replace the prevailing program with an empirical investigation of how we in fact carry on with, for example, 'know that' and its cognates in different types of situations. As far as my proposal goes, we may remain in our armchairs. We only need to make sure, however, that we bring to them not only the world *of* which we speak and think, but also the world *in* which we speak and think. The question that I take to be relevant for the clarification of our concepts is not the empirical question of what words we tend to utter, generally or statistically speaking, in different types of circumstances.

Rather, the relevant question is which utterance(s) would *make sense* in some particular type of situation, what sense exactly that would be, and what would need to be in place, in the background as it were, for the utterance to have or make that sense. And this, I believe, is not a question that may aptly be called empirical. If we genuinely disagree in our answers to this question, it need not be the case that at most only one of us is right, nor is it even clear what 'being right (or wrong)' in one's answer to this question might mean.[46]

But isn't this appeal to what does and does not make sense and to what sense some utterance would most reasonably be taken to have in some particular context—and precisely because it is not an empirical appeal—yet another form of reliance on intuition, and a rather dogmatic form of such reliance at that?[47]

Consider my argument in section 2 of this chapter, for example, or my responses to the prevailing arguments against OLP in chapter 2. These exemplify the sort of philosophical practice I propose as a replacement for the prevailing program. And say, if you will, that I was relying on intuition in my arguments. Remember, however, that by now I have already said what truth I think there is in philosophers' description of themselves and others as *intuiting* their answers to the theorist's question. What

46. A recurrent complaint against ordinary language philosophers is that their appeal to ordinary, nonphilosophical discourse could only be empirical, and that, as such, it is woefully unscientific (see Fodor and Katz 1971). That this complaint is misguided has most compellingly been argued by Cavell. In 'Aesthetic Problems of Modern Philosophy' (in Cavell 1969), Cavell likens the ordinary language philosopher's appeal to an aesthetic judgment, as characterized by Kant in his *Critique of Judgment*. In both cases there is a distinct form of apparent dogmatism, the justification for which is that it bespeaks an insistence on the possibility of making ourselves intelligible to others (as well as to ourselves). In the opening pages of Cavell 1979, he similarly speaks of the ordinary language philosopher's appeal as constituting 'a claim to community [that] is always a search for the basis upon which it can or has been established' (20).

47. Defenders of the prevailing practice recurrently argue that those who object to it are themselves relying on intuition in their objection, or anyway on nothing more solid than what those engaged in the prevailing practice have relied upon. See Pust (2001, 251), Williamson (2004, n11), and Sosa (2007a).

is important is that I was not, in *that* sense, relying on intuition in my arguments. The appeal to what question it would make sense to attend to in different types of situations and, more broadly, to what making sense by means of our words in different types of situations involves and requires, is not the same as the appeal to what concept, or term, applies to what (sort of) case apart from any context of significant use. In particular, the first is an appeal to what we *must,* conceptually, on some level already know insofar as we are competent employers of the expression in question. For our competence just *is* our knowledge of the sorts of things OLP appeals to. By contrast, the second appeal is to something that, given what the competent employment of our words normally involves and requires, there is no good reason to suppose we know.

Still, it is easy enough to imagine versions of both the calibration objection and the cognitive diversity objection arising with respect to the practice you recommend.

Here is my answer to the calibration objection as it might arise with respect to the philosophical practice I recommend: The practice I recommend consists essentially in reminding ourselves of things that we must already know, in knowing how to carry on competently with our words. If we didn't already know these things and know them together—if we weren't already calibrated, as it were—we wouldn't be able to speak to and understand each other in the ways that we do.

And here is my answer to the cognitive diversity objection as it might arise with respect to the practice I recommend: It *might* indeed emerge that there are genuine disagreements among us when it comes to the sorts of questions that I propose as replacements to the theorist's question. I suspect, though, that there are fewer such disagreements than we might be inclined to suppose, and that many apparent disagreements would be revealed as merely apparent upon further conversation between the parties and by means of successful diagnosis. My reason for thus suspecting is that we can and do speak to and understand even people with whom we have substantial disagreements—be they philosophical, moral, political, religious, or other sorts of deep disagreements. This is at least true when it comes to 'know that' and its cognates and many other philosophically contentious expressions. (Remember that to disagree about this or that matter is not yet to disagree about—or, perhaps better, *in*—what our words mean.) However, if it should turn out that there are certain substantive disagreements among us with respect to the questions that I propose we ask, this would not undermine my proposed alternative to the prevailing program. Rather, it would indicate that we fundamentally disagree in our sense of what makes (or has) sense, of what sense (if any) different things make, and of how they make that sense. To the extent that we do disagree thus fundamentally, we will not have the same concepts, and our conflicting answers to the questions that I recommend we ask would faithfully reflect that. This is in contrast with our conflicting answers to the theorist's question, which, as Williamson himself contends, reflect no such thing.

But hasn't it already been shown, and in so many cases, that the ordinary language philosopher's direct appeal to ordinary and normal practice as a way of becoming clearer with respect to our concepts suffers from the lack of any underlying systematic theory? In particular, hasn't it been shown that ordinary language philosophers everywhere confuse meaning and use?

As I said at the end of chapter 2, though objections to OLP sometime proceed from the assumption that a systematic theory of language must inform our inquiries into particular concepts, I do not know that it has ever been shown that ordinary language philosophers have ever gone astray because their inquiry is not informed by such a theory. In particular, we have seen that those who charge ordinary language philosophers with failing to note the distinction between 'meaning' and 'use' tend to presuppose the very conception of (word or sentence) meaning that OLP questions. No doubt, particular attempts to become clearer about this or that concept by way of considering ordinary and normal discourse may be confused, partial, beside the point, plain wrong, or otherwise flawed in any number of ways.

But I do not think it has ever been shown that the best way to avoid such failures is to arm oneself with a systematic theory of language. As I have argued in this chapter, all too often it is actually theoretical commitments that lead us astray, and in the most fundamental ways. When that happens, OLP may be precisely what we need.

But OLP is only concerned with words, or concepts, whereas many philosophical questions and difficulties concern not merely words or the concepts they embody but things themselves. What philosophers have primarily wished to understand is, for example, knowledge, not 'knowledge' or our concept of knowledge.[48]

Part of what I am questioning in this book is the assumption that when it comes to knowledge, or to any of many other phenomena that have occupied and befuddled philosophers for millennia, it is possible to investigate and become clearer about the phenomenon, in a distinctly *philosophical* (as opposed to empirical) manner, other than by investigating the concept that delineates it and picks it out, as that concept manifests itself in ordinary and normal discourse. Using Kantian terminology, we might say that philosophers have wanted to think of themselves as (capable of) investigating not phenomena—as these make their appearance in a world structured by human capacities, needs, concerns, and interests, and become articulated in human discourse—but things as they are in themselves. However, that philosophers have often *thought* of their difficulties as rooted in the nature of things as *contrasted* with our concepts of them is, of course, no evidence at all against OLP's understanding of the nature of philosophical difficulty.

On the other hand, it is a serious mistake to suppose that conceptual difficulties are not at the same time difficulties with seeing our *world* aright. 'We forget', Cavell writes, 'that we learn language and learn the world *together,* that they become elaborated and distorted together, and in the same places' (1979,

48. See Soames (2003a, 286, 292), Sosa (2007a, 2007b), and Williamson (2007, 10–47).

19). Becoming clearer about a concept *is* becoming clearer about those elements or dimensions of our world that get articulated and come to light in it, or by it. In urging us not to suppose that the meaning of a word is separable from its ordinary and normal use, OLP—far from calling on us to concern ourselves *merely* with words, or concepts—is urging us to attend to all that needs to be in place for the use of this or that word, in general or on a particular occasion, to be at all possible. Thus Austin describes himself as doing 'linguistic *phenomenology*' (1979, 182) and says that what in the last resort he is trying to elucidate is 'the total speech act in the total speech situation' (1999, 148); and Wittgenstein says that our agreement in the language we use is 'agreement in form of life' (1963, 241; see also 19).

Far from focusing on mere words and leaving the world aside, OLP's procedures are precisely designed to bring a world lost through philosophical theorizing back into view—but again, not just the world we speak and think *of*, but also the world we speak and think *in*. If you go back to my argument in section 2 of this chapter, you'll see that it no more concerned our concept of knowledge than it concerned the human needs and interests, and more broadly the human and worldly *conditions,* against the background of which 'know' and its cognates have acquired their specific powers and significance. Somewhat ironically, it is actually the attempt to investigate things as they are in themselves that ultimately leaves us with mere words. Or rather, it leaves us with words and pictures—such as the picture of knowledge as a super-strong connection between a mind and a fact—that are supposed to, but cannot, ensure their sense.

CHAPTER 4

Contextualism and
the Burden of Knowledge

IN THE INTRODUCTION TO THIS BOOK, I spoke of the wide-spread belief that OLP has somehow been refuted, or anyway seriously undermined. I then argued in chapters 1 and 2 that this belief is unjustified: those who dismiss OLP have not enti-tled themselves to that dismissal. This does not mean that OLP is not dead. I think it currently is dead and has been dead for a while—at least for the mainstream of analytic philosophy. The aim of this book is to show that OLP's death was untimely and, in particular, that contemporary analytic philosophy has suf-fered as result of its failure to acknowledge and take seriously OLP's perspective and its critique of the tradition.

In chapter 3, we began to see this. The difficulties encountered by the prevailing program, I argued, are rooted in the assumption that it ought to be possible for us to become clearer about our words and the concepts they embody simply by asking ourselves to which (sorts of) cases they do and do not 'apply', while setting aside the question of what work they have been fitted for by the history of their employment. That this assumption is bound to lead to the sorts of difficulties encountered by those pursuing the prevailing program is, in a way, OLP's most basic insight.

The aim of this and the next chapter (chapter 5) is to further dispel the rumor that OLP has justly been dismissed, and to further press the relevance of its perspective to contemporary analytic philosophy, by way of dispelling another rumor—the rumor, namely, that the position known in contemporary analytic philosophy as 'contextualism' constitutes some sort of clear and straightforward continuation of the work of either Austin or Wittgenstein or both.[1] OLP's perspective, I will ultimately argue, fully anticipates whatever truth there is in contemporary contextualism. But the contextualist is still wedded to the representationalist conception of language that informs the prevailing program, and this leads him to misconstrue the truth in his own position. Contemporary contextualism is a move in the right direction—not least because it is often offered as a response to internal difficulties encountered by those pursuing the prevailing program. But without a deeper change in our philosophical orientation, that move is bound to leave us too close to the source of our difficulties.

1. Stage Setting: Contextualism, Anti-Contextualism, and the Theoretical Question of Truth and Falsity

As thought of within the mainstream of contemporary analytic philosophy, contextualism with respect to some word is the position according to which the contribution made by that word to

---

1. The only philosopher I know of for whom the idea of a link between contextualism on the one hand and Austin and Wittgenstein on the other proceeds from a serious and sustained interpretation of these two philosophers' texts—an interpretation, as will emerge, with which I ultimately disagree—is Charles Travis. His most detailed attempt to link his version of contextualism to Wittgenstein is presented in Travis (1989); see also Travis (2006). His most detailed argument for the link to Austin, in the case of knowledge, is presented in Travis (2005); see also Travis (1997). Others who have proposed that Wittgenstein and Austin just were contextualists or at any rate were the forefathers of contextualism—in addition to DeRose, who I discuss in the text—are Recanati (2004, 84, 141ff.), Brady and Pritchard (2005, 162), and Cappelen and Lepore (2005, 5).

the 'truth-conditions' of sentences of which it is a part depends not on its 'meaning' alone but also on the particular context in which it is uttered or otherwise used. Some words—such as 'I', 'you', 'here', or 'this'—are 'context-sensitive' in very obvious ways in the contribution they make to the truth-conditions of sentences of which they are part, so contextualism with respect to them would not be an interesting position.[2] Contextualism becomes interesting when it concerns words that have traditionally been thought to be context-*in*sensitive, or 'invariant', in their 'semantic' contribution to sentences. It becomes even more interesting when it proposes that the realization that certain words are semantically context-sensitive could shed light on, and even dissolve, traditional philosophical difficulties.

It is possible to be—and many in contemporary analytic philosophy are—contextualists with respect to some (nonobvious) word(s) but not others.[3] Contextualists with respect to 'know that' and its cognates maintain that the truth-conditions of 'knowledge ascriptions' depend not alone on the meaning of 'know' (and the other words that make them up) but also on the context in which they are made. Thus, they maintain that an utterance of 'N knows that such and such (at t)'—where 'N' names some particular person and 'such and such' refers to some particular (purported) fact (or 'expresses' a particular 'proposition')—may be true in one context and false in another.

There are two respects in which contemporary contextualism might be thought to continue the work of OLP as exemplified, however differently, in the writings of Wittgenstein and Austin. First of all, there is the contextualist's *thesis*. There are passages in both Wittgenstein and Austin in which they urge us not to

2. They are also context-sensitive in nonobvious ways, but I will not argue for this here.

3. Cappelen and Lepore (2005) argue that all contextualists should be *radical* contextualists—contextualists with respect to every general term—if they are to be faithful to the line of reasoning that has led them to become contextualists with respect to any term that does not belong to the list of *obviously* context-sensitive terms, such as indexicals and demonstratives.

suppose that we should be able to tell what, if anything, someone is saying by means of some particular form of words on the
basis of her words alone (see, for example, Wittgenstein 1963,
remark 117, and 1969, remark 248; Austin 1964, 41). I have
suggested that these passages are better seen not as advancing a
general theory of meaning but rather as alerting us, especially in
our capacity as philosophers, to the possibility that it may not
be clear what, if anything, we are saying, even when the words
we utter are perfectly familiar. But someone who is already
committed, as we shall see contextualists are, to the idea that
understanding an utterance or 'a sentence in context' is essentially a matter of knowing its 'truth-conditions', and who furthermore ignores the philosophical context in which Austin's
and (especially) Wittgenstein's urging takes place, would almost
be bound to interpret those passages as putting forth a general
version of the contextualist's thesis.

And then there is the contextualist's typical *form of argumentation.* The traditional 'anti-contextualist' theorist believes
that, with but few obvious exceptions, whether some word or
expression truly 'applies' to a case does not depend on the context of application. He therefore sees no problem in trying to
elucidate the meaning of a word by inviting himself and others directly to consider whether it applies to this or that case.
By contrast, the contextualist's thesis commits her to appealing
to intuitions about the application of the word to some case
within a certain context.[4] This has led contextualists to make
central use of examples of (purportedly) everyday discourse in
their arguments in a way that traditional theorists have not.
This form of appeal to ordinary and normal discourse might

4. There is actually quite a lack of clarity among contextualists (and anti-
contextualists) about what it means for a word to be 'in a context'. It is clear
what it would mean for a word to be *used* within a certain context, if 'use'
means what Wittgenstein means by it. But in contemporary analytic philosophy,
'use' has become a technical term that is close in meaning to the philosopher's
'apply'. And this, as I point out in the next note (n5), renders the intended relation between words and contexts quite obscure.

be thought to resemble the ordinary language philosopher's appeal to the ordinary and normal use(s) of our words. Thus, in a recent article, Keith DeRose, one of the leading proponents of contextualism with respect to 'know' and its cognates, presents his contextualist argument as 'largely an exercise in how to do ordinary language philosophy' (2005, 172).

The contextualist's way of linking 'semantics' and 'pragmatics', and his characteristic reliance in his argument on examples of everyday discourse might, not implausibly, be thought to constitute at least a step toward recognizing the truth of OLP. But there is an important sense in which the contextualist's particular way of breaking away from traditional commitments ends up reinforcing what is most deeply problematic about them. In challenging as he does the traditional separation of semantics from pragmatics, the contextualist is still committed to the traditional categories of 'semantics' and 'pragmatics' themselves, whereas OLP radically questions these categories and their philosophical usefulness. Contemporary contextualism may well be the closest that contemporary analytic philosophy has come to acknowledging the truth of OLP. But this only shows how far contemporary analytic philosophy is from truly acknowledging that truth.

Consider DeRose's anecdote about how his teacher, Rogers Albritton, responded to his early attempts to compose the sorts of examples to which contextualists have appealed in arguing for their position:

> [Albritton] ... objected, as near as I can remember, 'Nobody would really talk that way!'. I replied that it didn't matter whether people would talk that way. All I needed was that such a claim [a claim of the form 'N knows (or does not know) that p'] would be true, and that certainly was my intuition about the truth-value of the claim. He would have none of that, and answered, quite sternly, 'Look, if you're going to do ordinary language philosophy—and that's what you're doing here—you'd better do it right'.

> Albritton never explained to me why the examples should
> be constructed so that what's said is natural and appropri-
> ate, beyond insisting that that's how ordinary language phi-
> losophy should be done. (2005, 172)

Why is it important that the words that philosophers who
wish to become clearer about our concepts put in the mouths
of their protagonists be ones that actual human beings might
actually utter under the circumstances they invite us to imagine?
What could Albritton have in mind when he told DeRose that
he was, or that he ought to have been, doing ordinary language
philosophy, but that he was not doing it right? I will come to
DeRose's answer to these questions in a little while. My own
answer should be more or less expected by now: words are natural and in place ('appropriate') when we do some work with
them that is called for under the circumstances and for which
their history has fitted them; and there is no better way of gain-
ing clarity with respect to the concepts embodied by our words
than to consider the (different sorts of) work these words are fitted to do under various circumstances. A major source of philosophical difficulty is the idea that it ought to be possible for us
to get at and grasp the meanings of our words, or the concepts
they express, apart from a consideration of the work they are
fitted to do and of the conditions under which they can do it.
A related source of difficulty is the idea that it ought to be possible for us just to 'apply' any of our 'referring' words to cases,
even apart from doing any specific work with it, and that the
application would then always be felicitously assessable in terms
of truth and falsity, irrespective of what specific point, if any, it
had. These observations may be seen as the point of departure
for OLP and as the heart of its disagreement with the tradition.
And from this perspective, contemporary contextualism still
operates within the bounds of the tradition's way of thinking.

Several decades after the exchange recounted in DeRose's
anecdote, the examples appealed to by contextualists and anti-
contextualists alike still tend, as we shall see in this and in the

following chapter, to feature people uttering sentences that, upon reflection, it is hard to imagine anyone actually uttering under the circumstances described in those examples. When I say 'hard to imagine anyone uttering', I do not just mean that people do not, or mostly do not—as a matter of empirical fact—talk that way. I mean, rather, that it is hard to see to what use the protagonists could possibly be putting the words that are put in their mouths—what work they could possibly be doing, or meaning to do, with them. Not less importantly, in cases where one could hear or interpret the protagonists' utterances in such a way that they would actually be using the words that are put in their mouths, the theoretical discussion tends to proceed without regard for the question of what use exactly that would be and what (else) we would need to imagine about the circumstances of the utterance if we were to truly imagine the words as having been put to that use.

And this is symptomatic of the fact that both sides of the debate still take it, as DeRose did back then, that it doesn't really matter how, if at all, the words that they put in the mouths or minds of their protagonists are being used under the circumstances they describe—what work is being done by means of them.[5] What matters for both sides of the debate is *whether the*

---

5. Schaffer's (2006) argument for contextualism is revealing in this respect. He simply invites the reader, just as is done in the prevailing program, to intuit whether the subject in his examples knows or does not know some fact. The only difference from the prevailing program is that he manipulates the reader's 'context' by sometimes raising 'alternatives' and sometimes not, by inviting the reader to imagine herself in some particular situation, etc. But the intuitions he elicits are directly about the subject and whether he knows, not about the truth-value of ascriptions of knowledge to him within various contexts.

Of course, there are many participants in the debate who wish to believe that the Wittgensteinian question of use can be bypassed altogether by insisting, as, for example, Hawthorne does, that 'a sentence can be true at a context even if it is not asserted at a context', or that 'a sentence may serve as a vehicle of belief at a time, even if it is not asserted' (2004, 83). See also Neta (2003, 10n33). It is hard to see what 'context' might mean here, given that it evidently *cannot* mean 'whatever one must take into account in order to see what specific *use* someone has *actually* made of his words'. Normally, when we speak of 'so and so's *words are true or false.* Both parties assume that *that* question is always in order—in the simple sense that it can be answered correctly or incorrectly—and that the correct answer to it will tell us something important about our concept of knowledge, and about knowledge.

The traditionalist ('invariantist', 'anti-contextualist') philosopher assumes that our concept of *knowing that* is such that, with respect to any pair of person S and fact (or proposition) referable to by 'such and such', one may simply and directly ask, without incurring philosophical risk, whether S knows that such and such (at t); and he further assumes that the 'correct' answer to that question would be so for all people and at all times. In opposition, the contextualist has insisted that the correct answer to the traditionalist's question is going to depend on the context in which it is being asked or answered. The traditionalist's question thus receives a 'semantic ascent' in the hands of the contextualist and becomes 'Would it be true for so and so, situated as he or she is, to say of S, "She knows that such and such (at t)"?'.

The contextualist question constitutes only an amendment to the traditionalist's question, not a rejection of it. The traditionalist will find the contextualist's semantic ascent *unnecessary*, because, for him, if (and only if) the protagonist knows, then *in any and every context* it would be true to say of her 'She knows', and if (and only if) she doesn't know, then *in any and every context* it would be false to say of her 'She knows'. But other than regarding it as unnecessarily cumbersome, the

---

context (or situation)', what we refer to by means of this expression depends on the context (situation, circumstances) in which *we* speak. It is therefore not the case that for every person there is, at every moment, *the* situation, or context, he is in. (This suggests, among other things, that Hawthorne's (2004) and Stanley's (2005) 'subject-sensitive invariantism', thought through, boils down to the very contextualism with which it is meant to compete.) And it is equally hard to see what it might mean for words to *be at* a context—to see in what their presence at this or that context is supposed to consist—when no one, real or imagined, actually uses them.

traditionalist will have no problem with the contextualist's version of his question.

From OLP's perspective, the difference between the traditionalist's original question and the contextualist's version of it does not make enough of a difference. Therefore, except for where I indicate otherwise, I will henceforth use 'the theorist's question' to refer to both the traditionalist's question and to that question in its contextualist version.

The contextualist shares with the traditionalist ('anti-contextualist') the same basic idea that I have identified as underlying Williamson's defense of the prevailing program. That idea, recall, as applied to our concept of propositional knowledge, goes something like this: *The basic thing we do with 'know that' and its cognates is to 'apply' the concept of* knowing that, *or 'ascribe' the relation of* knowing that *to pairs of person and fact (or proposition). Put otherwise, the basic role of 'know that' and its cognates is to enable us to* represent, *'describe', people as knowing this or that. (Witness here DeRose's glossing what we do by means of 'knowledge-attributing (and knowledge-denying) sentences' [2005: 172] as 'describing situations' [174].) In thus representing people as knowing this or that, we could of course also be performing any of many 'illocutionary' acts, but what act we perform does not affect the identity of our representation* qua representation *and cannot make it philosophically unwise or misleading for us to take what we've produced* as a representation *and to raise the question of truth and falsity about it. To find out what 'knowing that' means, or names, or refers to, we should look for the conditions under which people may truly be represented as knowing this or that—the conditions under which 'know that' or one of its cognates may truly apply to them.*

The contextualist's invitation to ask ourselves of supposedly everyday 'assertoric' utterances featuring 'know that' or one of its cognates whether what is said in them is true or false is, in effect, an invitation to perform a secondary, parasitic act of judgment. We are invited to see, that is, whether (the concept of) 'knowing that', with its 'truth-conditions' presumably fixed or determined by the 'knowledge ascriber's' context, applies to the person and fact in question.[6] *Our* (parasitic) application of 'know that' or one of its cognates is essentially done outside of ordinary and normal practice and commits us, at most, to nothing but a purely theoretical stand. Both the traditionalist and the contextualist assume that there is no problem with *that*.[7] In this chapter and in the next, I will question this assumption.

DeRose's own answer to the question of why it matters whether the protagonists in philosophers' examples speak naturally and appropriately is that natural and appropriate 'assertoric' utterances are normally true (2005, 172)—and it is the 'truth-value' of the utterance that interests the contextualist. Consider, by contrast, Austin's remark in a famous—many would surely say infamous—footnote to 'A Plea for Excuses'. Having said that ordinary language—as it reveals itself in an examination of 'what we should say when, and so why and what we should mean by it' (1979, 181)—should provide 'the first word' for philosophy, Austin goes on to implore his reader to 'forget, for once and for a while, that other curious question "Is it true?"' (ibid., 185). DeRose, having just congratulated Austin for being contextualism's 'granddaddy', cites Austin's footnote and says that he finds it 'troubling' (2002, 196).[8] It is clear why he should find this footnote troubling: contemporary 'contextualism' is *essentially* a theory about the truth-conditions of utterances of 'declarative' ('assertoric', 'indicative') sentences. DeRose further notes that the footnote is consistent with Austin's writings on epistemological matters in which he 'avoid[s] issues of whether

6. The contextualist, in other words, is inviting us to say whether we *agree* with the protagonist. However, the felicitous performance of the speech-act of agreeing with someone requires a suitable context, and it is not clear that every 'serious and literal' utterance by a character in a philosophical example of an indicative sentence featuring 'know' or one of its cognates creates such a context.

7. Cavell has most aptly described the underlying assumption here as the assumption, or fantasy, that it ought to be possible for us 'to speak without the commitments speech exacts' (1979, 215).

8. Grice (1989, 13) also complains about Austin's footnote.

our epistemological claims (especially claims about what is and is not known) are true or false' (2002, 196).

And this is true. In 'Other Minds', Austin says such things as the following:

> If you say 'That's not enough' [to challenge a knowledge claim by way of challenging the basis given as its support], then you must have in mind some more or less definite lack. . . . If there is no definite lack, which you are at least prepared to specify on being pressed, then it's silly (outrageous) just to go on saying 'That's not enough'. (1979, 84)

He also says that what's enough is a matter of what is 'within reason', and depends on 'present intents and purposes' (1979, 84). One could see in these passages of Austin's all of the main ingredients of contemporary contextualism about 'knowing that', except that he seems content to speak in terms of when we would be 'right' to say we know (ibid., 98), or 'justified' in saying this (101), or in terms of what would or would not be 'silly' or 'outrageous' or 'within reason' to say. He never asks when it would be *true* to say of someone who has claimed to know that there is a goldfinch in the garden, 'He knows there's a goldfinch in the garden'. He never says that if the knowledge-claimer has said enough for all intents and purposes to support his claim, then he just *knows,* or at any rate has claimed something *true.* Why doesn't he? Both the contextualist and the anti-contextualist are bound to find this feature of Austin's practice unjustified and unmotivated, if not simply perverse. But beyond arguing that 'I know' is more akin, in its functioning and force, to 'I promise' than we tend to realize, and that, therefore, to suppose that it is a 'descriptive phrase' is to have fallen prey to 'the descriptive fallacy' (ibid., 98–103), Austin himself does preciously little to disarm such a response. The rest of this book may be seen as an extended argument on Austin's behalf for why philosophers interested in becoming clearer about our concept of *knowing that* should forget, for once and for a while, the *theorist's* question of truth and falsity (as contrasted with questions of truth and falsity that may naturally arise within suitable contexts as part of ordinary and normal practice).

There is a sense in which the argument of this and the following chapter complements that of chapter 3. There I started with a person 'encountering' a Gettier case under particular circumstances and asked what question(s) it would make sense for such a person to ask and attempt to answer. In what follows, I will start with the words that contextualists and anti-contextualists have put in the mouths of their protagonists, and I will ask how (if at all), given the circumstances as described by the authors of the examples, these words might reasonably be understood.

It will turn out that pressing (their versions of) the theorist's question with respect to their protagonists' words has blinded both contextualists and anti-contextualists to the way these words actually function, or could actually function, in the imagined conversations. And it will further turn out that the theorist's question plays no role in the ordinary and normal functioning of the words. In other words, competent employers of 'know (that)' and its cognates never have to attend to, let alone answer, the theorist's question—in either its traditional or 'contextualized' version. And this means that the contextualist amendment to the prevailing program is insufficient for saving it from versions of both Cummins's and Stich's skeptical worries. There is still good reason to worry that our intuitive answers to the theorist's question, even in its contextualist version, at best only track a philosophical construct; and it is far from clear what relation that construct might have to our concept of knowledge (or to knowledge, for that matter), or what significance it might have.

2. Travis's 'Milk in the Refrigerator' Example and Knowledge as a Liability

I begin with one of the examples Charles Travis employs to support his claim that the semantics of knowledge ascriptions and denials is 'context (or occasion) sensitive'.[9] More specifically, Travis contends that for an utterance of the form 'N (I, you, she, etc.) know(s) that such and such' to be true, only the 'real doubts' as to such and such's obtaining need to be 'discharged' for N, where what counts as 'real' (as opposed to 'mere') doubt is going to depend on the circumstances in which the utterance is made and be, in this sense, context-sensitive.[10] Replace Travis's 'real' with 'relevant', his 'doubts' with 'alternatives' or 'defeaters', and his 'being discharged for N' with something like 'eliminated by N's evidence (or experience)', and you essentially get what is known as the 'relevant alternatives' version of contextualism with respect to knowledge, as advocated, for example, by David Lewis, Michael Williams and, more recently, by Jonathan Schaffer and Michael Blome-Tillmann.[11] With Williamson, I take the 'relevant alternatives' form of contextualism with respect to propositional knowledge to be the most plausible and compelling, as well as the most prevalent form of that

9. As I already noted, Travis's contextualism is unique in that it takes its bearing from a serious and thorough interpretation of Austin and Wittgenstein. While I find Travis's interpretation too representationalist or descriptivist to capture the radicality of Austin's and Wittgenstein's break with the tradition, there are many moments in which I find his thoughts very congenial. I focus in much more detail on Travis's contextualism as an interpretation of Wittgenstein and Austin in Baz (2008). For the purposes of this book, I mostly ignore Travis's differences from other contextualists.

10. This is a brief summary of Travis's account of the semantics of knowledge ascriptions in Travis (1989, 151–187; see, in particular, 159, 165, and 170). I set aside the thorny question of what exactly it means for a doubt (or alternative) to be discharged (or eliminated) for one. In Travis (2005), we get an account that, so far as I can tell, is formally the same. It's just that this time he does not speak in terms of conceivable doubts that should be divided into mere and real doubts; rather, he talks in terms of a distinction between ways for P to be false that count as things that *might be* and ways for P to be false that do not so count. Again the claim is that the determination of what might be is occasion-sensitive.

11. See Lewis (1996), Williams (2001), Schaffer (2004, 2005, 2006), and Blome-Tillmann (2009). Williams, I should note, mostly focuses on justification, rather than on knowledge. This, I believe, has to do with his 'epistemological anti-realism', which, as I observe later in the text, places him closer to the perspective of OLP than other contextualists.

position.[12] Indeed, for reasons that will emerge in the next chapter, I think this version of contextualism contains an important grain of truth (but, regrettably, too much 'truth').

Travis's example reads as follows:

> Hugo, engrossed in the paper, says, 'I need some milk for my coffee'. Odile replies, 'You know where the milk is'. Suddenly defensive, Hugo replies: 'Well, I don't really *know* that, do I? Perhaps the cat broke into the refrigerator, or there was just now a very stealthy milk thief, or it evaporated or suddenly congealed'.[13]

Upon considering this little story, we are expected to find that Hugo's reply 'fails to count against Odile's words'. Under these circumstances, Travis says, Hugo's reply 'does not even tend to show that Hugo does not know where the milk is'.[14] This and similar examples are supposed to support Travis's contention that 'N know(s) that such and such' only requires, in order to be true, that N will have discharged all of the real doubts as to such and such's obtaining, and not the merely conceivable doubts— where the distinction between real and mere doubts is occasion-sensitive. This is what we are supposed to realize about 'the cognitive achievement' that is required for knowledge.[15] Hugo's response fails to count against Odile's ascription of knowledge to him, because the doubts he supposedly expresses happen to be mere doubts on that occasion and, therefore, incapable of undermining Odile's ascription of knowledge to him (on the most natural way of imagining the circumstances, of course; we

12. '[Although] different contextualists offer different context shifting mechanisms . . . most of them make some play with the idea of change in the contextual relevance of various possibilities of error' (Williamson 2005b: 97). Schaffer (2005) raises objections to other forms of contextualism with respect to propositional knowledge.

13. Travis (1989, 156).

14. Ibid.

15. Ibid., 173.

could imagine them to be real, if we stretched our imagination a bit).

But how exactly are we to imagine Odile's meaning of her words? What is she doing when she says 'You know where the milk is'? And what could Hugo possibly be doing in responding to her as he does? For the traditionalist, such questions are altogether beside the point. His question is simply: Does Hugo, as he stands (or sits), *know* that the milk is in the refrigerator? That Odile said what she said and how she meant (or could possibly have meant) her words is simply irrelevant as far as the traditionalist is concerned, and neither is it relevant what Hugo is imagined to have said in his response to her words. But in light of what I said in the previous section, I want to suggest that the contextualist too has no real use for the particular way in which Odile meant her words, and for how, if at all, Hugo meant his response. For the contextualist, the question is just this: Would it be *true* to say with reference to Hugo, as he stands, 'He knows that the milk is in the refrigerator'?— a question that the traditionalist will find unnecessarily cumbersome, but otherwise unobjectionable. The basic difference between the two positions is just that for the contextualist, as opposed to the traditional philosopher, it matters who is imagined to do the saying (or thinking) and under what circumstances. Pace both positions, I will argue that it does matter how Odile and Hugo are imagined to mean their words, and that it even matters for the very thing that both the contextualist and the traditionalist are interested in: what 'know that' and its cognates mean (or might mean) and when, or under what conditions, someone counts (or ought to count) as knowing that such and such.

The most natural way of imagining Travis's example, it seems to me, is to hear Odile as *rebuking* Hugo for his laziness, or chauvinism, or both.[16] If this is how we hear her words, then it

16. Or we could imagine her to be encouraging Hugo to regain his trust in his faculties, say after a serious head injury. I will not discuss here this way of

matters very little that she chose words of the form 'N know(s) that such and such' to make her point. What she says to him is, in effect, that if he wants milk, he should get some himself. The problem with Hugo's 'response' would then seem to be, not that the 'doubts' he 'raises' are irrelevant (or mere doubts), but rather that the occasion is not one for raising doubts. He has missed altogether the point of her words, or else has attempted a very lame joke.

Of course, this is likely to impress neither the traditional philosopher nor the contextualist; for both of them, it would seem to only touch upon the *'merely* pragmatic' dimension of the exchange. Both the traditional philosopher and the contextualist would say: *Look, Odile said of Hugo—whatever else she said or meant to be saying—that he knew where the milk was, or that it was in the refrigerator. (Perhaps, as you just said, she said that as a way of saying that he has no epistemic excuse for not getting the milk himself, and thereby implying that he has no other excuse either.) Hugo denies her ascription of knowledge to him and supports his denial by citing various conceivable doubts, or alternatives to the milk being in the refrigerator. And now the question is just this: Given that the doubts he raises, and many conceivable others, are ones that he has not ruled out and that he is not in a position to rule out, does he or doesn't he know what Odile says he knows?*

As I said, for both the traditional philosopher and the contextualist, this last question would always make perfect sense, and would always have a correct answer. The difference is just this: the traditional philosopher takes it that there is essentially only one correct answer to this question[17]—either 'Yes'

---

hearing Travis's example. Thought through, however, it would also show the limitations of the contextualist's account.

17. This is assuming, of course, that we ask about Hugo as he is *at some particular moment in time.* I disregard, again, the possibility of 'borderline' cases. It seems to me neither here nor there when it comes to the disagreement between contextualists and anti-contextualists. So far as I can see, both positions can accommodate borderline cases.

or 'No'—and that this one answer would be correct regardless of the circumstances under which it was given; for the contextualist, by contrast, the correct answer to this question would be sometimes 'Yes', sometimes 'No', and sometimes 'The question is not determinate enough to be answered either correctly or incorrectly', depending on the circumstances under which the question was raised, and answered. The traditional philosopher, Travis argues, owes us a story about how we are to tell, occasion-*in*sensitively, which of the countless conceivable doubts that are clearly undischarged for Hugo must be discharged, and which ones need not be discharged, if he is to know what Odile claims he knows. And according to Travis, there is just no principled and plausible way of drawing the distinction context-insensitively: requiring that *all* conceivable doubts as to such and such's obtaining be discharged, if it is to be known that such and such, would lead to skepticism (as Travis thinks of it); requiring none of those doubts to be discharged would make knowledge uninterestingly easy to attain. Either alternative would make the concept of propositional knowledge useless and hence empty, Travis claims.[18]

Go back to Odile's words, however, and to the idea that she means them as a rebuke. Imagining her words in this way points to a generally neglected region of our concept of knowledge,[19] one in which knowledge is a kind of liability, sometimes even a burden, and is the basis not for deference and respect, but for reproach, accusation, and blame. Philosophers have almost

18. See Travis (1989, 168; 1991, 245; 1997, 97–98). 'Subject-sensitive invariantists' such as Fantl and McGrath (2002), Hawthorne (2004), and Stanley (2005) would argue against Travis that he has missed their anti-contextualist way of drawing the distinction between relevant and irrelevant alternatives.

19. I say 'points to' because, as I said, it's not even clear that Odile, in Travis's example, is at all concerned with Hugo's *knowledge* of where the milk is. In considering what I go on to argue in the text, the reader is invited to substitute a clearer example, such as charging an executive with having known that her company was in trouble, or that she wouldn't be able to keep a promise. I chose to stick with Travis's example.

invariably thought of knowledge as some sort of achievement that *entitles* us to certain things.[20] Consequently, they have tended to speak of utterances of the form 'I know that such and such' as knowledge *claims*. But knowledge thought of as a kind of liability is not something to be claimed, but rather is something to admit, confess, or acknowledge; and in the second and third person it is something more aptly said to be imputed, rather than, say, attributed.[21]

This region of our concept of propositional knowledge is, arguably, at least as central to it as the region that has predominated in the tradition, and it is quite thought provoking, I think, to find that it has been virtually ignored by contextualists and anti-contextualists, skeptics and anti-skeptics, alike.[22] Imagine

20. Thus, for example, Williamson has argued that only knowing that such and such entitles us to assert that such and such (2000: 238–269); see also DeRose (2002). Fantl and McGrath (2002) argue that knowing that such and such rationally entitles us to 'act as if such and such'. And Hawthorne and Stanly (2008) argue—less plausibly to my mind—that *only* knowing that such and such entitles us to use the proposition *that such and such* as a reason for action.

21. Consider in this connection Williams, who, having listed all of the kinds of problems philosophers have had in trying to understand knowledge, or our concept of knowledge, goes on to say that 'the problems just sketched are significant only if knowledge is worth having' (2001, 2). Of course, the traditional problems Williams lists have themselves been shaped, to a large extent, by the assumption that knowledge is naturally desirable. But can't one be interested in becoming clearer about our concept of knowledge not because knowledge is (necessarily) worth having, but rather because 'know' and its cognates, hence our concept of knowledge, play various significant roles in the human form of life—because, so to speak, *they* are worth having?

22. I know of only two exceptions. The first is Warnock (1983). Warnock, however, takes the fact that 'assertoric' sentences featuring 'know' and its cognates are used in the performance of a great variety of speech-acts—including those of charging someone with having known something and of admitting or confessing to have known something—as an indication that we should distinguish between the question of 'what to know something is, what "knowing" means' (49) and the question of 'whether possession of a given item of putative knowledge is, on this or that occasion, claimed or disclosed, admitted or avowed, presupposed or advertised . . .' (ibid.). He is thus relying, together with Searle, Grice, Soames, Williamson, and many others, on the very notion of word (and sentence) meaning that this book is questioning. The other exception

what the history of the philosophical treatment of skepticism would have looked like if skepticism had been thought of, not as denying us the knowledge that we would ordinarily claim or wish to claim for ourselves, but rather as aiming to disburden us of knowledge that it is difficult or shameful or painful to possess. Even Austin, for all of his sensitivity to the nuances of human speech, writes of knowledge in 'Other Minds' as the sort of thing that one would naturally claim or wish to claim for oneself. His comparison of 'I know' and 'I promise' would not work if the former were taken as the expression of acknowledgement, for example. ('I know he is angry with me; I just haven't had the time to speak with him about what happened'.) It might be said in Austin's defense that he was responding to the tradition, and therefore justified in focusing on the tradition's favored use of 'I know'.

But why is any of this relevant to an understanding of our concept of propositional knowledge? After all, anything that we possess, or might possess, could conceivably become a liability or a burden. Why should knowledge be any different? And why should any of this be of interest to someone who wishes to find out what knowledge, or the possession of knowledge, is, or what 'know' means? The answer is that unlike, say, a piece of furniture, a piece of knowledge is not something whose nature, and whose possession by someone, can philosophically safely be determined regardless of the specific point of the determination. When, for example, you *charge* me with knowing (or having known) that such and such, then, normally, what conceivable doubts (or alternatives) there are with respect to such and such's

---

is Hanfling, who notes, in the context of arguing for a form of 'relevant alternatives' account of knowledge, that 'In some cases . . . the possession of knowledge is a matter of *admission* rather than claim or entitlement' (2000, 122). What Hanfling fails to note is that these cases actually belong to what he calls 'commenting situations' (96–97)—situations in which the obtaining of such and such is not in question. In such cases, I am about to argue, the question of relevant alternatives is beside the point and semantically inert.

obtaining, and which of them is real (or relevant), and whether I have discharged (or eliminated) all of the real ones, would be altogether beside the point. If, for example, you charge me with having known that the milk was in the refrigerator and complain that I therefore had no excuse for not getting it myself, then it would be uncomprehending ('outrageous') for me to say, for example, that for all I knew the milk might have been on the counter, unless I *actually believed* that it might be on the counter and unless *this* was at least part of the reason why I did not get up to get it myself.

It might be replied, on behalf of Travis and other relevant alternatives contextualists: *The milk's being on the counter, for example, is clearly an alternative to its being in the refrigerator. Further, in the situation envisioned that alternative has been made real, or relevant to your knowledge (or lack of knowledge) that it was in the refrigerator, by your actually believing that it might be on the counter. And this alternative was clearly (we can suppose) an alternative to the milk's being in the refrigerator that was undischarged for you at the time.*

The problem with this defense of the contextualist's account is that there is no reason to think that *this* way of making alternatives to such and such's obtaining real or relevant has anything to do with the context-sensitivity of knowledge ascriptions as the contextualist thinks of it. If I really did believe that the milk might be on the counter, then I did not know that it was in the refrigerator, and this has nothing to do with the relevance or irrelevance of any alternatives to its being in the refrigerator or with the question of which of the relevant alternatives were eliminated or discharged for me at the time. If you find my belief unjustified, then you can charge me with *that,* and say, perhaps, that I *should have known* the milk was in the refrigerator, but you cannot—no one can—rightfully charge me with having known that it was.

It might further be argued on behalf of the contextualist: *But of course none of the above is relevant to the contextualist*

account of the context-sensitivity of knowledge, or for that
matter to anyone's account of the context-sensitivity or -insen-
sitivity of knowledge. Everybody agrees that for anyone to be a
candidate for knowing that such and such, that person has got,
first of all, to take it ('believe', in philosophers' jargon) that such
and such. If she takes it that not such and such, or is unsure
whether such and such, or at any rate is just not taking it that
such and such, then she cannot know that such and such, and
this has nothing to do with the alternatives to such and such
that may or may not be discharged for her. The occasion-sensi-
tivity of knowing that such and such, as contextualists think of
it, only comes into play when we consider people who take it
that such and such (see Travis 1989, 160n17).

But where does this leave us? You say—*charge*—that I
knew the milk was in the refrigerator. Now either I did not
take it that it was or I did.[23] If I did not (because, say, I actually thought it might be on the counter), then, regardless of
the context of assessment, I did not know (though perhaps I
should have known) that it was in the refrigerator. If, on the
other hand, I took (and still take) it that the milk was in the
refrigerator when I asked you to get me some, and you charge
me with having known this, then the philosopher's question
of whether all 'real' or 'relevant' doubts about our being out
of milk have been discharged or eliminated is beside the point
as far as you and I are concerned. If I were to try to defend
myself by 'raising' *any* conceivable doubt, as Hugo does in Travis's example, then my words would fail to count against yours
because I would not be in a position to mean them as raising a
doubt and, therefore, would not *be* raising a doubt by means of
them, not because I would be raising a doubt that was unreal

23. I actually believe that this is a false dichotomy. I am using the dichotomy
between taking it that such and such and not taking it that such and such heuristically here. As with many of our concepts—as, for example, with 'knowing
that' or 'acting voluntarily' (Austin 1979, 190)—the concept of 'taking it that
such and such' only felicitously applies, either positively or negatively, to a person
and a fact, under certain conditions and when the application has some point.

or irrelevant.[24] It is still knowledge we are talking about—my (alleged) knowledge that the milk is in the refrigerator. But the question of which doubts or alternatives to its being there are relevant and which of the relevant ones have been discharged or eliminated, as Travis and other contextualists think of it, is out of place in our context, and is therefore irrelevant to an understanding of your knowledge 'ascription' to me. Nor would a third-party witness to our exchange need to attend to this question in order to understand your accusation.

In situations in which someone is charged with knowing (or having known) that such and such, the question on which the relevant alternatives contextualist account is supposed to bear does not normally arise. This is not a linguistic accident. It is a function of our interest in what goes by the name of 'knowledge' in situations of this sort. Situations of this sort are a subset of a wider set of situations in which, while it does matter to the conversants that, or whether, someone actually knows, or knew, that such and such, they themselves *already* take it that such and such—there is no doubt in their mind as to its obtaining and they therefore are not looking for anyone's assurance of it.[25] In asking whether the other knows, or in taking it that she does, they therefore are not normally concerned with whether 'her assurances are good enough' (Travis 1989, 177), or with whether 'her evidence is [or was] good enough to know' (Fantl and McGrath 2002, 67; see also Stanley 2005, 88), or with whether her belief that such and such (or her otherwise taking it that such and such) 'rises to the level of knowledge' (Bach 2005, 62–63). And this means that the question to which both contextualists and anti-contextualists have proposed competing answers is just not a question to which competent employ-

24. Of course I could try lying to you. I could falsely deny having taken it that the milk was in the refrigerator. But then, and supposing that you believe my lie, we are back with our first disjunct, as far as our 'conversational score' is concerned.

25. These are the sorts of situations that Hanfling calls 'commenting situations' (2000, 96ff.).

ers of 'know that' and its cognates would (need to) attend in situations of this sort.[26]

Here it might be objected: *But does not all this just show that we need to distinguish between knowledge ('knowledge') as it concerns us in the everyday and knowledge (knowledge) as philosophers think of it?*[27] *Why should it matter for a philosophical reflection on what knowledge is, and requires, that for both the imputer of knowledge and the person charged with knowing some fact, the question of which doubts as to the obtaining of that fact are relevant and whether all of the relevant doubts have been discharged is beside the point? This question may still be raised. Indeed, this is precisely the question that philosophers ought to raise and think about if they wish to find out whether (it would be true to say that) Hugo, for example,* knows *that the milk is in the refrigerator. As far as the truth-conditions, or value, of utterances featuring 'know' and its cognates are concerned, it is simply of no consequence that this is not a question that people in contexts such as that of Odile and Hugo would need to attend to and, indeed, that it would make no sense for people in such contexts to attend to this question.*

We were bound to arrive at this moment of conflict all along. I am hoping, though, that some of what we saw on the way has put us in a position to begin to look at the conflict with fresh eyes.

---

26. Anticipating the objection that sometimes—for example, in the sorts of contexts discussed in the text—we ascribe knowledge to people where no doubt is 'in the offing', Travis responds that even in those cases we could imagine a context in which some doubt *would* have been alive for the person said to know with respect to what he is said to know (1989, 157–158). This response seems to me forced, and not in line with Travis's overall Wittgensteinian position, for it proposes to explicate the sense of an utterance made in a context of one kind by imaginatively placing it—that is, the words—in a context of another kind.

27. The latter is what Wittgenstein would call 'knowledge with a metaphysical emphasis' (1969, remark 482).

3. Taking Stock

For the traditionalist, words acquire their meaning by coming to refer to 'items in the world', as we saw Williamson putting it; and the items are supposed to be there anyway, waiting to be referred to by the words, their identity and presence unaffected by the context in which the referring takes place. But why assume that knowing is such an item, and that it is only by virtue of referring to such an item that 'know' and its cognates have the meaning they have? Why can't at least some of our words—'know' and its cognates, for example—have their meaning not, or anyway not first and foremost, by virtue of referring to items of a certain kind, but rather by virtue of being employed by us, in different ways, under different circumstances, for different intents and purposes? Why can't our knowledge of their meaning just be a matter of our knowing how to employ them competently and how to respond competently to other people's employment of them? I am not proposing that these words refer to *nothing* in the world. My proposal, rather, is that what they refer to when competently employed is inseparable from the work they do, and may only be seen aright through an appreciation of that work.

An important aspect of this proposal is that it brings out the ways in which the world implicates itself in human speech and bears on its rationality (intelligibility, appropriateness) other than by *being represented*.[28] And this, in turn, suggests a radical

28. That there are ways for words to stand in various rationally assessable relations to the world that are not ones of representing it is something that Austin (1999) brings out in his elaboration of the conditions of the felicitous performance of speech-acts. It is also, I believe, a point that Wittgenstein symbolizes, as it were, early on in *Philosophical Investigations,* when he proposes that it would be most natural, and least confusing, to reckon the color samples that 'the builders' A and B use in their communication 'among the instruments of their language' (1963, remark 16). Part of what enables the builders to form representations of what they want and what there is are things (the color samples) that are part of their world and yet are not themselves *being represented*.

response to skepticism about 'the external world'. For it suggests that the felicitous adoption and expression of *any* cognitive attitude or stand, including that of wondering about the existence of 'the external world', presupposes, in the background, the existence of the world. It presupposes, in other words, a rationally assessable relation to the world that is not one of representing it in either speech or thought. I'll come back to this 'phenomenologist' response to skepticism in the final pages of the epilogue.

Now, for the contextualist, knowledge can no longer be thought of as an item in the world that is there anyway, independently from the context in which the question of its presence arises. Michael Williams puts this point by saying that his version of contextualism stands in opposition to 'epistemological realism' (2001, 170–172)—not, I would add (echoing Kant), to epistemological *empirical* realism, but to epistemological *transcendental* realism. In other words, for the contextualist, knowledge can no longer be thought of as a 'thing in itself'— (a) something whose presence does not depend on our ways of establishing, indicating, or otherwise minding, its presence. In this respect, contextualism does constitute an important departure from the traditional conception (and picture) of knowledge. For the contextualist, knowledge is something that may appear and disappear, as it were, depending on the context in which we attend to the question of its presence.

But the contextualist is still committed to the idea that *when* knowledge appears, it always appears in the same guise, as it were, and under the same essential conditions. And he still thinks, with the traditionalist, of the meaning of 'know' and its cognates in terms of reference to some very particular

---

For an insightful elaboration of this point, see Brandom (1994, 632, 715n28). More recently, Brandom has usefully put the basic point this way: 'Feedback-governed practices [including linguistic ones] are "thick", in the sense of essentially involving objects, events, and worldly states of affairs. Bits of the world are *incorporated* in such practices . . ' (2008, 178).

item—albeit an item whose presence depends in part on the context in which it is being considered. But why, having gone *this* far from the traditionalist's picture, assume *that?* Why assume with the traditionalist that 'know' and its cognates *first* refer, and only *thereby* become usable in different ways? In assuming this, the contextualist is still thinking within the bounds of the traditional picture of language. I am trying to show that this picture has been hurting us in two ways. First, the picture has given rise to a question—the theorist's question—that has entangled philosophers in irresolvable disputes and which, but for that picture, would not have presented itself as a question that *must* have a correct answer. And second, rather than illuminating ordinary and normal discourse and the world that comes to light in it, the picture has blinded us to them.

So far we have seen this: First, the contextualist's 'relevant alternatives' account of our concept of 'knowing that' essentially just adds context-sensitivity to the tradition's understanding of knowing that such and such as a cognitive achievement that places one in a position to legitimately dismiss alternatives to such and such. Second, the account is unfaithful to at least one central region of our everyday employment of 'know that' and its cognates—namely, accusatory 'charging' of knowledge. It presents as essential to the applicability of the concept a question that, in applying the concept in such contexts, we simply do not and need not ask. It thereby encourages a distorted picture of what is at issue when knowing that such and such is at issue in such contexts.

Had Lewis considered the possibility that knowledge might be a liability with which we might be charged, as opposed to some sort of achievement that we would naturally wish to claim for ourselves, I cannot imagine that he would have maintained that simply mentioning or considering an alternative to p is enough to make it relevant and so something that must be eliminated if p is to be known.[29] He would have seen right away that if this were

29. Lewis (1996, 559).

generally true, then it would be far too easy to disown a painful, or shameful, or otherwise unwanted piece of knowledge.[30] And had Schaffer attended more carefully to ordinary and normal practice, he would not have said that 'the social role of knowledge ascriptions is to identify people who can help us answer our questions'.[31] If 'knowledge ascription' means anything (clear), then Odile can surely be said to be ascribing knowledge to Hugo in Travis's example. But she does not need him to answer any question (except perhaps the question of why it does not occur to him that he should get the milk himself). She takes it for granted that the milk is in the refrigerator, and does not need Hugo to assure her, let alone inform her, of that. This is why she has no need to attend to the question of whether he has good enough assurances as to the milk's being in the refrigerator. The mechanism of 'context-sensitive relevant alternatives'—just like any other metaphysical account of knowledge—may still somehow be applied to their exchange from the outside (as in the anticipated objection at the end of section 2). But it plays no role within it and is therefore semantically idle. In the next chapter, we will turn to a different region of our concept of propositional knowledge that is closer to the tradition's preoccupations, and we will see that there too the theorist's question, in both its traditionalist and contextualist versions, has been leading us astray.

30. Of course, I am not the only one who finds this part of Lewis's account objectionable. But it is telling, again, that the routine objection to this part of Lewis's account is that it makes it all too easy for someone else ('the skeptic') to rob us of knowledge that we supposedly possess.

31. Schaffer (2006, 100). See also Craig (1999), who, while claiming to be breaking away from the confines of the traditional analysis of knowledge, has from the perspective of this book stayed within those confines.

CHAPTER 5

Contextualism, Anti-Contextualism, and Knowing as Being in a Position to Give Assurance

I**N 'A PLEA FOR EXCUSES'**, Austin says something that bears on what we saw in the previous chapter and on what we will see in this chapter. He speaks of our words as 'invoking models' and then cautions:

> It must be remembered that there is no necessity whatsoever that the various models used in creating our vocabulary, primitive or recent, should all fit together neatly as parts into one single, total model or scheme of, for example, the doing of actions [substitute here: knowing that such and such]. It is possible, and indeed highly likely, that our assortment of models will include some, or many, that are overlapping, conflicting, or more generally simply *disparate*. (1979, 203)

The models Austin talks about, I take it, have emerged and evolved naturally and organically as, prompted by needs and interests that have themselves evolved over time, we have had to put our linguistic resources to work under shifting and increasingly complex conditions. The present use of some of our words may not be essentially different from their or their ancestors' primitive use, and in this sense invokes models not essentially different from the primitive ones. But the use of other words has evolved in such ways that it is now best seen as invoking several different models that are connected to each other and to some primitive *ur*-model in complicated and intricate ways. 'Know' and its cognates, I am proposing, belong to the latter group of words.

This suggests a serious problem with the theorist's procedure of inviting competent speakers to 'intuit' whether (it would be true for so and so to say that) one of the protagonists of some 'example' knows that such and such—a procedure that has been absolutely central to theorizing about knowledge within analytic philosophy. What the theorist in effect invites us to do is apply a word whose competent application requires different things under different models, but to do so *apart from any particular model*. Part of the reason why our intuitive answers to the theorist's questions tend to be 'unsystematic'[1] may therefore be that, in answering them, we are pulled by disparate and possibly conflicting models.

The application of Austin's notion of 'models' to the argument of this book should be taken with a grain of salt, however. My talk, after Austin, of our words as 'invoking models' is meant to do no more than bring out something about their ordinary and normal employment—namely, that it is less homogeneous and more entangled than we tend to think. Wittgenstein makes the same basic point with respect to other words, and connects it to the creation, and overcoming, of philosophical difficulties:

> The criteria we accept for 'fitting', 'being able to', 'understanding', are much more complicated than might appear at first sight. That is, the game with these words, their employment in the linguistic intercourse that is carried on by their means, is more involved (entangled, *verwickelter*)—the role

1. See Gendler and Hawthorne (2005).

of these words in our language other—than we are tempted to think.

(This role is what we need to understand in order to resolve philosophical paradoxes.) (1963, remark 182)

In chapter 4, I argued that the picture of *knowing that such and such* as a naturally desirable mental state—a special 'cognitive achievement' that is arrived at by eliminating alternatives to such and such and puts one in (the best possible) position of authority with respect to such and such's obtaining—has blinded both traditionalists and contextualists to the actual functioning of 'know (that)' and cognates in at least one central region of their employment.

For traditional theorists, this may not seem to be a problem. From the traditional perspective, it is not clear why a theory of *knowledge* should do justice to or take into account the ordinary and normal functioning of 'know' and its cognates in nonphilosophical discourse. The contextualist, on the other hand, advertises his account as more than a merely theoretical solution to merely theoretical difficulties regarding a theoretically constructed concept of 'knowledge'. He advertises it as a true account of *our* concept of propositional knowledge as it manifests itself in the functioning of 'know' and cognates in nonphilosophical discourse. Accordingly he claims that 'the best grounds for accepting contextualism concerning knowledge attribution come from how knowledge-attributing (and knowledge-denying) sentences are used in ordinary, non-philosophical talk' (DeRose 2005, 172; see also 2002, 168). For this reason, the findings of the previous chapter ought to at least give the contextualist pause, for they suggest that his appeal to ordinary, nonphilosophical talk has been halfhearted and theoretically biased.

It might be thought that at most I have shown the contextualist's (and anti-contextualist's) account of knowledge to be *partial,* as opposed to wrong or distorted. The theorist who thinks of knowing that such and such as essentially requiring the elimination of doubts or alternatives to the obtaining of such and such has admittedly been focusing on only one region of our concept of knowledge, the objection would go, but surely, knowing that such and such does sometimes, and perhaps centrally, matter to us because the knower that such and such is in a position to assure us that such and such, where being in that position *is* a matter of having eliminated all (relevant) doubts or alternatives to such and such's obtaining. Isn't it only natural that the philosopher, whose business, presumably, is to look for things of which she can assure herself and others, would be primarily interested in this region or aspect of our concept of knowing that?[2]

However, *has* the theorist—whether contextualist or anti-contextualist—given us a faithful account of even that region of our concept of propositional knowledge that would seem closest to his preoccupations? I will argue that he has not. Whereas in situations of the sort discussed in the previous chapter the question of the truth or falsity of 'knowledge ascriptions' may arise naturally, albeit not in the way, or form, envisioned by the theorist, in situations of the sort we will now consider, the question of truth and falsity does not naturally arise at all. In pressing that question in the face of examples of situations of this second sort, both contextualists and anti-contextualists have set themselves in pursuit of a philosophical chimera.

My argument for this conclusion will progress dialectically with reference to three different examples that have appeared in the literature: DeRose's 'Bank' example, Stewart Cohen's 'Airport' example, and one of Jason Stanley's variations on DeRose's 'Bank' example. All three examples portray two people in a

---

2. Williams argues that knowledge matters because 'our most cherished views can be challenged' (2001, 5). But in contexts in which someone is accused of having known that such and such, knowledge matters not because it secures someone's views against challenges, but because it places an obligation on the knower to act in the light of such and such.

situation in which they need to decide how to act, where what decision would better serve their interests depends crucially on whether such and such obtains. In response to DeRose's example, I will argue that people in such situations have no need to answer the theorist's question with respect to an 'informant'— who in DeRose's example happens to be one of them—who tells them that such and such, and tells them how he knows this. (If they do not know on what basis the informant claims to know, then they most definitely are not in a position to answer the theorist's question.) In response to Cohen's example, I will argue that people in such situations have no need to answer the theorist's question with respect to themselves either. I will then briefly recapitulate these two arguments in response to Stanley's example. My criticism of all three examples is essentially the same and I could, in principle, have developed my argument with reference to just one of them. My main reason for discussing all three is to make clear that the target of my argument is a general and pervasive mistake, rather than the particular way in which a particular example was presented by its author.

1. DeRose's 'Bank' Example

I start with DeRose's well-known 'Bank' example (1992, 913). The example features two cases. In both cases, it is Friday and DeRose and his wife are driving by the bank with paychecks that they would like to deposit. In the one case, nothing bad would happen if they waited and deposited their checks on Monday—though, in general, they prefer to deposit their paychecks as soon as possible. In the other case, it is very important that the checks be deposited before Monday. In both cases, the lines inside the bank are long and DeRose therefore suggests that they drive straight home and come back the next morning to deposit their paychecks. In the first case, DeRose's wife raises the worry that the bank won't be open on Saturday, because 'lots of banks are closed on Saturdays', and DeRose describes himself as replying, 'No, I know it'll open. I was there two weeks ago on Saturday. It's open until noon'. In the second case, DeRose similarly proposes that they go home and come back Saturday morning, and similarly tells his wife that he was at the bank two weeks earlier and 'discovered' that it was open on Saturdays until noon. This time, however, his wife, after reminding him of how important it is that they deposit the checks before Monday, says, 'Banks do change their hours. Do you know that the bank will be open tomorrow?' DeRose then describes himself as 'remaining as confident as before' that the bank will be open on Saturday,[3] but as nonetheless saying, 'Well, no. I'd better go in and make sure'. We are supposed to find, or 'intuit', that in the first case DeRose is 'saying something true' when he says, 'No, I know it'll open', and that in the second case he is again 'saying something true', this time when he says, 'Well, no' (1992, 914).

In both stories, DeRose the protagonist (henceforth DeRose$_p$) comes to say—in response to his wife's raising the worry that, like many other banks, the bank might be closed on Satur-day—'No, I know it'll open'. I presume he means to reassure her (and/or to protest against her insinuation that he may have been thoughtless or irresponsible in proposing that they leave and come back the next morning). He then goes on to tell her the basis upon which he claims to know—the sort of thing one would normally give as an answer to the question 'How do you know?'. Is his basis adequate for supporting his claim to know? His basis would have been more fitting, and his claim itself would have been more natural—especially given his wife's rather *specific* concern—had his claim been 'I know it is open (on Saturdays)' rather than 'I know it *will* open (tomorrow)', for the latter is quite naturally heard as a claim to know more than what his basis is fit to support.[4] However, if we interpret

---

3. If he had not so remained, the intended lesson would have been undermined.
4. The most natural way of hearing his 'I know it'll open', it seems to me, is as an expression of conviction, as opposed to a claim to knowledge as philosophers have tended to think of it. This connects with the way in which

DeRose$_p$'s claim in the light of the specific worry to which it is, or had better be, responsive—the worry, namely, that the bank may not be open the next morning because it may be one of those banks that are closed on Saturdays—then it seems that the basis he offers for it would, under normal circumstances, be perfectly adequate.

Setting the matter of the adequacy of his basis aside for a moment, it is important to note that what matters at this point for DeRose$_p$ and his wife is not whether his knowledge claim was true or false. What matters, as far as they are concerned, is, presumably, whether (it would be reasonable for them to act on the assumption that) the bank will be open the next morning. (There is a tendency, which I address in the next section, to conflate these two questions.) And since DeRose$_p$ can anyway offer no more assurance with respect to the bank's opening the next morning (and no more solid basis to support his knowledge claim) than what may be derived from *the fact* that he was there two weeks before on a Saturday and saw that it was open until noon, and since *that* fact is anyway not in question between them, the question of whether *he* knows, or whether he said something true in saying he knew that the bank would be open—that question is beside the point as far as DeRose$_p$ and his wife are concerned.

Already there are a couple of related lessons that are beginning to emerge, not generally about *every* utterance of the form 'N knows that such and such', but about utterances of the form 'I know that such and such' that are meant to reassure someone else that such and such obtains. The first lesson is that a knowledge claim will not normally be more solid than the basis upon which it is made can make it; and this is something that competent users of 'know that' and its cognates will know. The second, and crucial, lesson is that in cases of the sort that

---

DeRose has both his protagonists shift their focus back and forth, and rather unnaturally it seems to me, between what seems to be a *general* concern that the bank won't open the next day, for whatever reason, and rather *specific* doubts.

DeRose broaches in his pair of bank stories and on which both contextualists and anti-contextualists have tended to focus—cases, that is, in which the participants need to decide on the basis of the information they possess how, under the circumstances, their practical interests would best be served—the normal effect, and point, of telling someone the basis upon which you claim to know is precisely that it makes the question of whether *you* know, or whether you *know,* moot.

The two points I just made suggest why it is quite odd, or forced, for DeRose$_p$'s wife—having raised the concern that the bank may not be open on Saturday, having heard back from her husband that two weeks earlier it was, and having gone on to challenge her husband's basis by reminding him that banks change their hours—to say, 'Do you know the bank will be open tomorrow?'. One way to make sense of her utterance would be to hear it as an invitation to her husband to ask himself whether he is *sure* that the bank will be open the next morning.[5] If this is how she means her words, she is not really talking about or 'referring' to *knowledge* as the theorist has wished to conceive of it, and her utterance is therefore not a candidate for the kind of assessment DeRose intends his reader to perform. However, if we do not hear her words that way, it is hard to avoid the impression that she is being what you might call 'philosophical' with her husband: trying to get him to concede the skeptical thesis that at least when it comes to matters such as whether the bank will open the next day, *no* evidence they may possess would be good enough for *knowing.* And if *this* is how the wife is meaning her words, then, despite DeRose's express intentions, the conversation is not 'nonphilosophical' and cannot in

---

5. As Peter Hylton pointed out to me, it would be far more natural for someone in the wife's situation to say, 'Are you *sure* that the bank will be open tomorrow?', rather than 'Do you *know* . . ?' The fact that 'Are you sure?' is more natural in such situations than 'Do you know?' is not a linguistic accident. As far as the wife is concerned, her husband's 'I know . . ,' *after* he has given her his basis, could anyway have no more force than 'I am sure . . ' I will return to this in the next section.

good faith be invoked as evidence in adjudicating philosophical disputes concerning who may truly be said to know what and under what conditions.

But let us suppose, for the sake of our assessment of the contextualist (and anti-contextualist) argument, that this is not a merely philosophical exercise on the part of the wife. Let us suppose, that is, that she is genuinely concerned that the bank might have changed its hours since her husband's visit two weeks earlier. He offered her his basis, and she has genuinely found it unsatisfying, and found it unsatisfying for *that* reason. The problem is that if this is what we suppose, then it is hard to see what her point could be in uttering her 'Do you *know* . . . ?' She and her husband may argue about how reasonable it is to worry that the bank might have changed its hours since his visit two weeks earlier. To competently claim to know that it has not, which is *not* what DeRose$_p$ has done, one would need a basis which, presumably, neither of them, as they stand, has got. Any competent speaker would know that merely having been to the bank two weeks earlier and having found it open then is no basis for claiming to know that it has not changed its hours since then.

'Relevant alternatives' contextualists may take all this in stride and say: *Look, if they don't know that the bank has not changed its hours, then it would seem that they cannot, on the basis of their evidence, know that it will be open the next day, which is, after all, what DeRose$_p$ has originally claimed. Further, similar doubts can be raised with respect to at least very many of the things that we normally would claim to know on the basis of evidence that we possess. Therefore, the only way to avoid the skeptical conclusion in such cases (and, in particular, the conclusion that DeRose$_p$'s original claim was false) is to insist that only some doubts or alternatives—ways for* p *to turn out false in spite of all that one knows or reasonably takes for granted—are relevant to the truth of some particular knowledge claim, in a given context. In DeRose's pair of bank stories, what changes between the first case and the second*

case is the raising not of the stakes, but rather of an alterna-
tive which, either simply because it has been raised (as Lewis
suggests), or because one of the participants has actually found
it plausible enough to worry about under the circumstances,
has been made relevant, and thereby has become an alternative
that would need to be ruled out if the claim to knowledge is to
be true. The reason that the wife's question strikes one as glib
is that, in (genuinely) raising her doubt, *she has made it so that*
the correct answer to her question is 'No'. Thus, she has made
it so that her question could only be rhetorical.

This contextualist account is responsive to something real. It seems to me undeniable that, normally and ordinarily, the determination of what someone has committed herself to in uttering a sentence featuring 'know that' or one of its cognates (and quite possibly also in uttering any other sentence) depends not only on the words themselves but also on features of the context in which the sentence is uttered. The problem, of course, is that this truism is something that anti-contextualists have had no problem accommodating; they have simply accounted for it at the level of what is 'pragmatically conveyed' rather than at the level of what is 'strictly' and 'literally' 'semantically expressed'.[6] Opting for this type of account has committed them to claiming, rather dogmatically it seems to me, that, for example, DeRose just does, or does not, know—context-*in*sensitively—that the bank will be open the next morning.[7] But since they themselves are comfortable with the commitment, or anyway take it to

---

6. See Rysiew (2001, 2007), and Black (2005).

7. Rysiew, for example, offers a 'non-skeptical invariantist relevant alternatives' account of knowledge, where the relevant alternatives—those that must be eliminated by the putative knower (or by her experience, or evidence, or what have you), in order for her to know—are supposed to be fixed, context-*in*sensitively, by 'what we (normal) humans *take to be* the likely counter-possibilities to what the subject is said to know' (2001, 488). But, as he himself acknowledges (ibid., 489), Rysiew offers us no reason to suppose that when it comes to the question of the relevance of alternatives, there is indeed the kind of context-insensitive and pervasive agreement between us that his account presupposes.

be inescapable, it is hard to see what could possibly settle this debate, in its present terms.

There is, however, an assumption that both sides share— namely, the assumption that whenever someone utters a sentence of an 'indicative form', and thereby says something clear and determinate enough for all intents and purposes, the question 'Did she say something true or something false?' is always in order, in the simple sense that there is a correct answer to it. And it is further assumed by both parties that the correct answer to the question, or anyway some suitable collection of such answers suitably arranged, would tell us something important or even fundamental about the concepts 'expressed'. This pair of assumptions is most deeply entrenched—a truism, even, when seen from the perspective of the prevailing philosophical paradigm. If it can successfully be thrown into question, it may turn out that contextualism, as currently advocated, is not the only principled, nondogmatic alternative to skepticism.[8]

So far, I have argued that as far as DeRose$_p$ and his wife are concerned, the theorist's question is beside the point; they know what information they possess, and what they need to decide is how (it would be most reasonable for them) to act in its light. They may disagree about *that,* but to present their disagreement as one about whether DeRose$_p$ (says something true in saying he) knows that the bank will be open is to misconstrue the situation. The concept of propositional knowledge has done what it could for this couple. If she thinks they ought to check further and he thinks that would be a waste of their time, neither of them need be guilty of a false application of the concept of propositional knowledge to DeRose$_p$ and the proposition that the bank will be open the next morning (or that it is open on Saturdays). Whether (it would be true for either DeRose$_p$ or his wife to say that) DeRose$_p$ in front of the bank really does, or

8. The claim that contextualism is the only principled, nondogmatic response to skepticism is central to Travis's argument for contextualism with respect to 'knowing that such and such' (see 1989, 168, and 1991, 245).

really does not, *know* that the bank will be open the next morning is a question that DeRose the theorist is forcing onto the situation, in part by having his protagonists speak unnaturally, or not fully naturally, and in part by encouraging us to suppose that however exactly, if at all, they are using their words, it should always be possible for *us,* so long as their words are of an indicative form and are uttered literally and seriously, to assess their words in terms of truth and falsity.

2. Cohen's 'Airport' Example

To show that the theorist's question, in either its traditionalist or contextualist version, ought not be asked with respect to the sorts of situations we are here discussing, and what the philosophical price of forcing that question is likely to be, will require more evidence than we have so far accumulated. So let us consider another example: Stewart Cohen's 'Airport' example (1999, 58). Mary and John are at the airport and are about to fly from Los Angeles to New York; but on account of a business meeting, it is 'very important' for them that their flight have a layover in Chicago. They 'overhear someone asking a passenger Smith if he knows whether the flight stops in Chicago'. They (presumably) see Smith looking at his itinerary and hear him reply, 'Yes I know—it does stop in Chicago'. But Mary still has her doubts; she worries that the itinerary is 'unreliable', that it may 'contain a misprint', and also that 'they could have changed their schedule at the last minute'. Mary and John are then described by Cohen as 'agreeing that Smith doesn't really know that the plane will stop in Chicago'. They decide to check further with the airline agent.

Passenger Smith's 'Yes, I know' in this story is more or less natural or anyway not clearly unnatural; but it is natural precisely because, or insofar as, it means something like 'Yes, I happen to have the information you're asking for', or 'Yes, my itinerary contains the information you need'. His 'Yes I know', uttered as he is looking at his itinerary, is most reasonably understood as a signal that he has found or identified the relevant information on his itinerary. Only prior commitment to the assumption that 'know that' and its cognates have a 'semantic content' that is separable from the different types of work they ordinarily and normally do for us would lead one to insist that this is something that Smith is merely *implicating* with his 'I know' while strictly and literally saying something else. Give up the commitment, and talk of 'implicature' would seem forced and unmotivated in this case.

To say of Smith, as Cohen does (1999, 58), that he *claims* to know that the flight has a layover in Chicago, would be to stretch our concept of claiming very thin: he is not so much *claiming to know* that the flight has a layover in Chicago as simply *letting the other know that he knows* (in the sense of having the desired information). After all, he might just as well have shown the itinerary to the other person and pointed out the relevant information on it.[9] As with DeRose's example, and here even more clearly, Smith's knowledge 'claim' is a 'claim' to know no more than what may be gathered from (familiarity with) *the fact* that his itinerary says that the flight has a layover in Chicago. And here again, since there is no question about the basis upon which he made his 'claim' (he does have the itinerary, and the itinerary does say that the flight has a layover in Chicago), the question of whether he *knows,* or whether *he* knows, is once again altogether beside the point. This is why Cohen's description of Mary and John as 'agreeing that Smith doesn't really know' is forced.

Like DeRose, Cohen makes his protagonists 'answer' a question that does not naturally arise in situations such as theirs. Why should it matter to Mary and John whether Smith *knows,* or whether *Smith* knows? The situation is perfectly clear: some passenger's itinerary contains an answer to their question of whether the flight has a layover in Chicago. What they need to decide is

9. I thank Dan Dennett for this way of pressing the point.

whether (they ought) to rely on that answer,[10] and people with different temperaments, sensitivities, attitudes, past experiences, etc., are likely to disagree on such matters. To present their disagreement as a disagreement about whether their informant knows that the flight has a layover in Chicago is to force the issue.

It might be objected: *Look, you may be right that for those who received, from or through someone, a piece of evidence pertinent to—either strongly or weakly indicative of—the obtaining of such and such, the question of whether their informant knows that such and such is a question to which, at least in the sort of situations you've discussed, they have no reason to attend. But isn't the question to which presumably they are required to attend—the question, namely, of whether, given what they have learned, it would be reasonable for them to act on the assumption that such and such—just the question of whether they know that such and such?[11] Don't John and Mary, for example, need to make sure they* know *that their flight has a layover in Chicago? And if so, don't they need to answer the theorist's question with respect to themselves and the proposition that the flight has a layover in Chicago?*

Let us think for a moment about this idea of answering the theorist's question with respect to oneself. To begin with, taking it that such and such, let alone deciding to act on the assumption that such and such, is not the same as taking ourselves to know that such and such, or deciding that we do. The question to which we regularly need to attend in the sort of situations we have been discussing is whether such and such, not whether we *know* that such and such.[12] What John and Mary need to do before proceeding to the gate is make sure that the flight has

10. How they have allowed themselves to come to a situation in which this is all they have got to go on in making such an important decision at such a late juncture is something with which, I am sure, they will want to reckon, once the whole thing is over.

11. This, if I understand, is what Hawthorne and Stanley (2008) propose.

12. Here I am in agreement with Stephen Schiffer's (2007) objection to Stanley's (2005) theory of how knowledge is related to practical reasoning and interests.

a layover in Chicago—not make sure *they know* that it does. And, from a first-person perspective, making sure that the flight has a layover in Chicago just means inquiring until one finds that one's evidence sufficiently ensures that the flight has a layover in Chicago, which is not the same as answering the theorist's question with respect to oneself.[13] I will shortly turn to discuss what happens when we conflate the two.

As agents in the world, as opposed to readers of philosophers' examples, we never can have the sort of assurance with respect to such and such that the philosopher is giving his readers in order to get them to see, and say, what is needed for knowledge *beyond* the truth of a belief. The philosopher's assurance, coming as it does from the author of the example, is as good as an assurance from God would be for agents in the world. But as agents in the world, at least in the sorts of situations that we are here discussing, we must act on assurances that are not just quantitatively but qualitatively different from an assurance from God. This means that we can be, and therefore need be, no more than *reasonable* in what we choose to do on the basis of what we know or reasonably take for granted. To expect anything more of us would be unreasonable.

To see the significance of this to the argument of this chapter, let us assume, for the sake of argument and as far as we can, that what John and Mary need to decide is whether they know that their flight has a layover in Chicago—whether the information contained in Smith's itinerary, together with everything else they know or reasonably take for granted, is good enough for *knowing* that it does. After all, if they disagreed with each

---

13. For this reason, the 'make sure we know that such and such' construction, though sometimes used in order to emphasize the delicacy of the matter ('Let's make sure we know he did it, before we get angry with him') or its importance ('Let's make sure we know that the flight has a layover in Chicago, before we get on it'), does not normally refer to anything other than making sure that such and such. Compare Kaplan, who argues that, from a first-person perspective, 'determining whether you believe *p* with justification and determining whether you know that *p* come to the same thing' (1985, 355).

other about what they ought to do next, John *might* express his position by saying, 'Come on, Mary, we (you) already know that the flight has a layover in Chicago', and she *might* then respond by saying, 'No, John, we (I) don't know that yet'. Now, if they chose to express themselves in this way, in the circumstances Cohen describes, which one of them would be 'speaking truth'? What would be the 'score' between them when it comes to truth and falsity?[14]

If you are a relevant alternatives contextualist such as, perhaps, Lewis, you might think that the doubts (in the sense of 'possible ways for p to turn out false, despite everything they know') Mary raises—either simply by virtue of having been raised, or by virtue of being of genuine concern to one of the participants—have become relevant, and ought therefore to be 'eliminated' by the couple, if they are to truly count, in the context of their conversation, as knowing that the flight has a layover in Chicago. Mary speaks the truth and John speaks falsely. If you are a relevant alternatives contextualist such as, perhaps, Travis, you might think that raising alternatives to p is not enough to make them relevant, not even if one of the participants happens to be genuinely concerned about them, and you might then concur with John, and take him to be speaking the truth and Mary to be speaking falsely. If you are a relevant alternatives contextualist such as, perhaps, Schaffer, you might find that both parties speak the truth: 'We know that the flight has a layover in Chicago' requires one thing in order to be true as uttered by John, and another thing as uttered by Mary—in *his* mouth it does not require making sure that there was no misprint, say, or that the flight schedule has not changed at the last minute, but in her mouth it does. Which of the above versions of contextualism would give us the correct score?

As far as John and Mary are concerned, *nothing* hangs on how we, or they, or anyone, would choose to answer this question. Upon hearing the first contextualist description of the

14. See Lewis (1979).

situation, Mary *might* feel vindicated. But John might quite reasonably say, 'All right, if this is what "knowing that the flight has a layover in Chicago" requires in order to truly apply to us in our context, then I suppose I am saying something false when I say that we know the flight has a layover in Chicago. Forget "knowledge", then. I still think that Mary's doubts are unreasonable and that we should proceed to the gate without delay'. Upon hearing the second contextualist description of the situation, John *might* feel vindicated. But Mary might quite reasonably say, 'All right, if in our context "knowing that the flight has a layover in Chicago" does not require, in order to truly apply to us, that we rule out or eliminate my doubts, then I suppose I am saying something false when I say that we don't know that the flight has a layover in Chicago. Forget "knowledge", then. I still think we should inquire further and make sure that the flight has a layover in Chicago'. In response to the third contextualist description of the situation, John and Mary might very well say, 'All right, so each of us is saying something true. That's very good to know. But you haven't helped us one bit, for the real question is what we ought to do next. And we are genuinely disagreeing about *that* (forget "knowledge")'.[15]

My point is this: *if* we thought that John and Mary (and people in situations similar to theirs) were addressing the theorist's question and offering conflicting answers to it, and also thought that the question had a correct answer—whether context-sensitive or not—then it seems that we would be committed

---

15. Williamson chides what he takes to be the contextualist resolution of disagreements—'You speak the truth, and you too, who seem to say the opposite, speak the truth'—for being 'glib and shallow' (2005b, 103). Williamson would rather be an 'invariantist' and say that one of the two parties 'misjudges'—i.e., is saying something false (ibid., 105). (Note that the case I'm envisioning in the text is one in which the disagreement arises *within* what Williamson would call 'the agent's context' [ibid, 104].) What I argue in the text is that to say of either John or Mary that s/he was saying something false would be no less unfaithful to the nature of the disagreement between them than to say that they both were speaking the truth.

to saying either that both parties were saying something true (correct) or that at least one party was saying something false (incorrect). It seems to me that this is not a commitment that, as philosophers, we should welcome. For as far as the parties to such disputes would be concerned, any such assessment of their disagreement would be what you might (derogatorily) call *merely* semantic—it would not be clear what significance it had, as far as they were concerned. The correct answer to the theorist's question, which was supposed to be all-important on account of the practical significance of knowing (or not knowing) that such and such, has turned out to have no practical significance at all for those who employ the concept in such situations.[16] *If* we had a concept—call it 'the philosopher's concept of knowledge'—that somehow sponsored one and only one correct answer to the theorist's question in such situations, it would be of no use to us in such situations. Nor would it be *our* concept of knowledge.

There is, however, one other contextualist way of settling the score between John and Mary that I have not yet considered. DeRose (2004) has proposed that in contexts in which each of the two parties stubbornly holds on to his or her 'standards', they may bring about a situation in which neither of them speaks truly and neither of them speaks falsely. DeRose proposes that in such a case, the conversational scoreboard *partially* 'explodes' and, as a result, if their epistemic state falls in the 'gap' between her high standards and his low standards, both of their claims are deprived of truth value (ibid., 13–19). Applied to the case we have been focusing on, DeRose's proposal would be that, in the context they have helped to create by refusing to 'adjust to one another's score' (ibid., 13), John and Mary may neither truly be said to know nor truly be said not to know that the flight has a layover in Chicago.

---

16. Williamson (2005b) emphasizes the practical significance of propositional knowledge, and so do Fantl and McGrath (2002), Hawthorne (2004), and Stanley (2005).

To the extent that it registers the impertinence of the theorist's question of truth and falsity in the sorts of situations we are here imagining, DeRose's proposal for how to settle the score in such situations is welcome. The problem, however, is that it still insists on trying to understand such situations from the perspective of that question. In fact, it proposes that the question is still perfectly in place and that there is a straightforward answer to it even here: John's and Mary's utterances *lack* a truth-value because the contribution made by 'know' to their semantics is indeterminate; their utterances have been rendered semantically *defective* because they each refused to accept the other person's standards.

But of course, John's 'We know' and Mary's 'We do not know' only appear defective on a construal that has the couple engaging in a merely semantic dispute about whether or not 'know' applies to them and to their flight's having a layover in Chicago—a dispute in which they have no good reason to engage in the sort of situation we have been discussing. Their imagined utterances only appear defective, that is, if we insist on imagining them as moves in an idle dispute. Let the two imagined utterances be heard in such a way that they have a non-merely-theoretical point, and there will be nothing necessarily defective about them or about the imagined dispute. Heard this way, however, the imagined dispute between John and Mary could not aptly be assessed in terms of true and false applications of 'know'.

3. Stanley's 'Bank' Example

Consider one final example—one of Jason Stanley's variations on DeRose's 'Bank' example, which he employs in arguing for his anti-contextualist ('invariantist') account of propositional knowledge. This time, Hannah and her wife Sarah are the ones driving home on a Friday afternoon with paychecks that they would like to deposit. It is very important that they deposit the checks before Monday. In this variation, Hannah calls up Bill on her cell phone and asks him whether the bank will be open on Saturday. Bill replies, 'Well, I was there two weeks ago on a Saturday and it was open'. But after reporting the discussion to Sarah, Hannah 'concludes that, since banks do occasionally change their hours, "Bill doesn't really know that the bank will be open on Saturday"' (2005, 5).

This story is even more puzzling, humanly speaking, than the previous two stories we have discussed. Presumably, Hannah decided to call Bill because she thought he should, or would, or might know whether the bank would be open the following morning. If so, then the most natural way of hearing his answer, as Stanley describes it, is as being quite explicitly non-committal, as a *disclaimer*—something like, 'Well, all I can tell you (all I know) is that I was there two weeks ago on a Saturday and it was open'. Hannah looks for Bill's assurance, and he very clearly implies that he cannot give it. He certainly does not claim to know that the bank will be open the next morning. Not in Stanley's story, anyway. This makes Hannah's 'Bill doesn't really know that the bank will be open tomorrow' even more forced than either DeRose's wife's attending to the question of whether he knows, or John's and Mary's attending to the question of whether Smith knows. As his contextualist opponents do, Stanley has his protagonists come out with quite unnatural utterances and, same as them, he assumes that there is, regardless, a correct answer to the question of whether these utterances are true or false—an answer, moreover, that would reveal something important about knowledge.[17]

It might be objected: *Oh, but look, people do sometimes utter sentences of the sort that Stanley puts in Hannah's mouth, in order to challenge assertions that they deem unwarranted. All*

---

17. Of course, unlike his contextualist opponents, Stanley does not *need* to have his protagonists *say*, or even think, anything of the form 'N know(s) (does not know) that such and such'. As an anti-contextualist, his theory may be stated without making use of 'semantic ascent' (but see next note). His argument, nonetheless, does rely centrally on our intuitions about what it would be true for someone to say, if only as data for which his theory needs to account.

you need to do is tweak the example a little, and Hannah's 'Bill doesn't really know . . . ' would be perfectly natural. I must confess that I have found tweaking Stanley's example so as to make it a believable example of human speech quite a challenge. It is hard to reconcile Hannah's decision to call Bill (as opposed to calling the bank or getting out of the car and quickly inquiring inside), and the answer that he goes on to give her, with her 'Bill doesn't really know'. But I suppose that if we simplified things a little, by having Bill call Hannah just as she and Sarah are driving by the bank, under the circumstances Stanley describes, then something like the following conversation *might* ensue:

> Hannah: Oh hi, Bill. Listen, you might be able to help us. Do you happen to know whether the (so and so) bank is open on Saturday?
>
> Bill: Yes, as a matter of fact I do. It is open on Saturday. I was actually there only two weeks ago on a Saturday.
>
> Sarah (anxiously): Well, what does he say? It's almost five o'clock and the bank will be closed in a few minutes.
>
> Hannah (turning to Sarah): He says it is open on Saturday ['He claims to know . . .' would have been intolerably awkward here, it seems to me]. But he doesn't really know that it is. All he knows is that he was at the bank two weeks ago on a Saturday and it was open, and banks do change their hours, as we all know. Let's not take a chance. Let's just park the car and go in.

It seems to me that this is as natural as 'He [Bill] doesn't really know that the bank is open on Saturday' can get in Hannah's mouth under the sort of circumstances Stanley invites us to imagine. To my ear, it still sounds conspicuously, alarmingly academic. But let's go along with the theorist and ask: Is she saying something true or something false in uttering 'He doesn't really know that it is'? Stanley's own answer is that she is saying something false, but understandable: what she really wants, and ought, to say is that Bill's evidence is not good enough for knowing that the bank will be open on Saturday for someone in *her* (and Sarah's) situation; that the evidence is good enough for *him* to know that the bank will be open on Saturday, given *his* situation,[18] is not what concerns her at the moment, and this leads her to speak falsely (2005, 102). Most contextualists, I presume, would say that what Hannah says of Bill is true: given what knowing that the bank will be open on Saturday requires in *her* context, her 'Bill doesn't really know . . .' is just true— either he hasn't ruled out alternatives that in her context are relevant, or he hasn't met the standards of 'knowing that' when so much is at stake, or what have you.

My own proposal is that the question to which the contextualist and the anti-contextualist are proposing conflicting answers is one that neither Hannah and Sarah, nor Bill, nor a bystander they might invite to adjudicate between them, would need to (be able to) answer. If I were a bystander invited by Hannah to adjudicate the matter, I suppose I might say something like this:[19] 'Say what you will about Bill's knowledge vis-à-vis the bank's opening on Saturday, or about the truth or falsity of his knowledge "claim", as long as you don't confuse yourself. The situation, after all, is clear, and how you choose to describe it in terms of "knowledge" is not going to make it any clearer. What you now need is to *act,* one way or the other. The concept of propositional knowledge, however carefully you might attempt to apply it to yourself, or to Bill, and to the proposition that the bank will be open the next morning, will not answer for you the question of how you ought to act. Nor could philosophy provide us with a concept that would do that. If, having heard

18. Unless, I suppose, his situation happens to include an interest in Hannah's and Sarah's interests—and shouldn't it? This connects with a point I made earlier about the context-sensitivity of 'so and so's situation' and about how Hawthorne's and Stanley's 'Subject-Sensitive Invariantism', thought through, boils down to the contextualism with which it is meant to compete.

19. Of course, the following is not something that anyone would actually say in an ordinary, nonphilosophical situation. But then, in such a situation no bystander would ever be invited to adjudicate the kind of dispute I am here imagining for the sake of argument. The response I offer is, if you will, a philosophically informed ordinary response to a nonordinary question. I thank Steven Affeldt for pressing me to clarify this point.

from Bill that the bank was open two weeks ago on a Saturday, you find that you still worry, then, unless it is for some reason too hard or complicated for you to do so, go ahead and call the bank, or inquire inside, or else simply park the car and get in line. This would not be unreasonable under the circumstances. If, on the other hand, you find yourself sufficiently reassured that the bank will be open tomorrow, then take the chance that, for whatever reason, it will not, and go home. This too, it seems to me, would not be unreasonable'. And now I might also tell her what (I think) I would have done if I had been in her situation. But whatever I would have told her I would do, I do not see that I would thereby have provided her with my answer to the question of whether she said something true in uttering 'He doesn't really know'. . . .

4. The Theorist's Knowledge as a 'Beetle in the Box'

The point I have been pressing in this chapter also applies to situations in which the 'You don't *know* that such and such' reminder or rebuke *would be* appropriate. In such contexts too, what is normally at issue is not the other person's being or not being in some particular mental state, but rather her evidence, and what conduct—be it action or assertion—that evidence may or may not justify under the circumstances. And here too there is, within reason, room for disagreement in which neither side is wrong. It would seem, therefore—and here I come back to a point I first made in chapter 3 when I discussed possible 'encounters' with a Gettier case—that the theorist should either concede that the question that concerns us in such moments is just not his question, or else reconsider the nature of his question, beginning by giving up the assumption that it has one and only one correct answer and ending, perhaps, by giving up the assumption that the question may philosophically safely and fruitfully be asked as a 'purely semantic' question.

I presume that the theorist would take the former option. Suppose he did. Suppose he insisted, that is, that *if* what truly concerns us in the sort of contexts we have discussed in this chapter is not the other person's mental state but the question of what possible conduct of hers would be justified by her evidence, *then* it is not the other person's *knowledge* that truly concerns us in such contexts—notwithstanding our routine employment of 'know' and its cognates in them. I note first that such a response would conflict with the invocation of such contexts in the debate between contextualists and anti-contextualists with respect to knowledge.[20]

But the real problem with the response that we are not really speaking of *knowledge* in the sorts of contexts we have discussed is the assumption that there is something that 'knowledge' successfully refers to or means *in that very response*—something of which we may speak in other sorts of contexts and which is the true object of the theorist's inquiry. So far, we have seen no reason to suppose that there is any such thing. On the contrary, what we have seen thus far suggests that the theorist's 'knowledge' refers to a philosophical chimera—something that drops out of consideration as irrelevant whenever we ask for, and recognize, the particular point of this or that use of 'know' or one of its cognates.[21] The conclusion to draw from this is not that knowledge is nothing (real), or that 'know' and its cognates refer to nothing when competently employed. Rather, the conclusion to draw is that the existence and nature of instances of knowledge are not separable from the discourse in which those instances become articulated as significant in one way or

20. It would also conflict with the invocation of such contexts as evidence in support of the so-called 'knowledge norm of assertion' (Williamson 2000, 538–569; DeRose 2002) and the so-called 'knowledge norm of action' (Hawthorne and Stanley 2008).

21. Kaplan's (2003) critical study of Williamson (2000) is relevant here. Focusing mainly on an example that Williamson employs in arguing that knowledge that *p* sometimes plays an important causal-explanatory role that cannot be played by any other mental state, Kaplan argues that, at least in that example, the state of being 'resiliently confident' that *p* can do the same causal-explanatory work that knowing that *p* can do.

another. Knowledge, it might be helpful to say here, is whatever
we refer to (speak of, claim, invoke, deny having, etc.) when we
competently employ 'know' and its cognates. It is not a nothing.
But it is not a something either.

The theorist's question invites us to conceive of ourselves as
reliable detectors of instances of knowledge, or of true (or false)
utterances of sentences of the form 'So and so knows that such
and such'—instances on the basis of which theories of knowledge, or of the semantics of 'know that' and its cognates, may
be constructed. But if my argument thus far has been on the
right track, there is no good reason for conceiving of ourselves,
in our capacity as competent employers of 'know that' and its
cognates, as such detectors; nor is there good reason to assume
that there is anything of the envisioned sort for us to detect.

In fact, if the debate between contextualists and anti-contextualists has taught us anything, it is that we can rely neither
on competent speakers' intuitions about who knows what fact,
nor on competent speakers' intuitions about when it would be
true for so and so to say of someone that she knows some
fact, to identify for us indisputable instances of knowledge, or
for that matter indisputable instances of sentences of the form
'So and so knows that such and such' being true. Not only
do competent speakers turn out to disagree in their intuitions
here, but there is also good reason to suspect that their intuitions are easily affected by the very theories they are supposed
to ground,[22] by the way the examples (and counterexamples)
are presented, and possibly by other forces as well that are
even more alien to the cause of truth (such as suggestive ini-

---

22. This is what Goldman and Pust have called 'theory contamination'. Their
proposed solution to it is to look for 'informants who can provide *pre-theoreti-
cal* intuitions about the targets of philosophical analysis, rather than informants
who have a theoretical "stake" or "axe to grind"' (1998, 183). However, if the
argument of this book is right, then the very invitation to informants to answer
the theorist's question, with the attendant suggestion that there is a correct
answer to that question and that, as competent speakers, they ought to know
it—all this is already theoretically contaminated.

tiation and conformism).[23] So even before one takes into consideration the underdetermination of theories in general by what has already been accepted as their relevant and legitimate data, the prospects of reaching true and stable satisfaction in our theorizing about propositional knowledge—understood as identifiable apart from a consideration of the ways in which we use 'know that' and its cognates and of the conditions, and significance, of using these words in one way or another—look rather bleak.

The real worry, however, is that even if we did arrive at some sort of reflective equilibrium that accounted for at least most of *our* intuitive answers to the theorist's question and satisfied at least *us,* our original and real interest—that of becoming clearer about what we normally and ordinarily speak of (refer to, claim, invoke) when we employ 'know that' and its cognates—would still remain altogether unanswered. Put more bluntly, the real worry is that our theories would be faithful to nothing real, and irrelevant to anything with which we have reason to be concerned. And this means that contemporary contextualism has left us pretty much in the state in which it found us at the opening of chapter 4: namely, with no truly satisfying response to versions of Stich's and Cummins's objections to the prevailing research program in analytic philosophy.

Perhaps, then, it is time to consider a shift in orientation with respect to the age-old philosophical quest for an understanding of (our concept of) propositional knowledge, or of the meaning of 'knowing that'. Instead of asking first what propositional knowledge is, or what 'know that' and its cognates speak of, or require in order to be true, and moving from there (if we do) to the question of how 'know that' and its cognates may intelligibly (competently, reasonably) be used—assuming the first question to be answerable apart from a consideration of the second, and taking the correct answer to the second question

23. On this, see Cummins (1998, 116) and Weinberg, Nichols, and Stich (2001, 438).

to be constrained by the correct answer to the first—we should rather begin with the question of how 'know that' and its cognates may intelligibly be used, and normally are used, in different types of situations. This shift of orientation in philosophy is what OLP, as I understand it, is trying to effect. Should we allow it to take effect, we may find that the answer to the second question tells us all that we might reasonably have expected to find when we raised the first question. And we would not even have to give up the talk of truth and falsity. We would just need to keep it to its natural, appropriate places.

Conclusion:
Skepticism and the Dialectic
of (Semantically Pure)
'Knowledge'

THE TRADITIONALIST (anti-contextualist) and the contextualist have both been pressing in their inquiry a particular form of question—'Does N *know* that such and such?' or, alternatively, 'Would it be true for so and so to say "N (I, You, She . . .) *know(s)* that such and such"?' This form of question, I have argued, *as either the traditionalist or the contextualist thinks of it*, does not naturally belong in the very situations on which the two parties have tended to focus. More precisely, in the first sort of contexts we discussed, the question of whether (it would be true to say that) someone knows this or that does arise naturally, but *what it comes to* is importantly different from what both the traditionalist and the contextualist would have us expect; in the second sort of contexts, no such question naturally arises.

It might be objected: *But surely you can't deny that we do at least sometimes wish to know whether someone* knows *that such and such in the philosopher's sense of having proper assurances as to such and such. For example, the president tells us that a foreign country has weapons of mass destruction and we wish to know whether this is something he really does* know. *For if it is, then perhaps he is justified in taking the country to war, and perhaps would be wrong not to. But if he does not know this, then he certainly would not be justified in starting a war before more decisive evidence was gathered. This is also the sort of situation in which the 'You don't (he doesn't) really know this' rebuke or complaint—which appears unnaturally in Stanley's 'Bank' example—would be in place. We can imagine the president saying that some country has weapons of mass destruction, and an assistant then reminding him, or complaining to another staff member, that he doesn't really know this.*

I have not denied that questions that look or sound just like the theorist's question may naturally arise in nonphilosophical contexts. My overarching contention, rather, has been this: when competently raised, everyday questions concerning someone's knowledge of this or that have a point—they are expressive in one way or another of some particular interest in that person and his epistemic (or other) relation to such and such. In competently going about answering everyday questions, or trying to, and in assessing answers to them, we are beholden to their point and are guided by it. And no such point is present when we are invited by the philosopher to intuit whether the protagonist of his example knows, or whether it would be true for so and so to say of her, 'She knows'. All that ordinarily and normally guides us in answering everyday questions has been methodologically removed, and we are left with nothing but the fictional narrative and some familiar words to which we are invited to respond ('Does he or doesn't he know?', 'Did he say something true or something false in saying he knew?'). Whereas the understanding of words in everyday discourse is a matter of seeing through their meaning, as it were, to their point, in the philosophical context all we have is the meaning of the words. And that meaning alone—apart, that is, from a particular context of significant use—does not sufficiently *orient* us with respect to the case under consideration, especially when we expect it to ensure the sense of a purely representationalist or 'semantic' question that plays no role in the ordinary and normal employment of the word(s) in question. It is therefore no wonder that a seemingly everyday question has come to seem, and be, so bewildering and intractable in the hands of the theorist.

Go back to the president. What is it exactly that we wish to know about him? (Initially, I assume that the war has not yet taken place and that it has not yet been established beyond any reasonable doubt that the other country did not, in fact, have weapons of mass destruction.) Do we wish to know whether he has been lying to the people, or at any rate has grossly misrepresented the information he has? This is a good question, and we know, at least in principle, how one might go about trying to answer it. But it is clearly not the theorist's question. Do we wish to know whether the president has credible and strong enough indications—a good enough basis for his claim—that the other country has weapons of mass destruction, whether he is justified in telling us that it does? These are the sorts of questions on which Austin would have us focus, and they may be answered, and normally are answered, at the level of what competence and reasonableness require, without invoking the assessment in terms of true and false applications of 'know that'.

If the president's basis is inadequate (or nonexistent), then he definitely should not have told us that (he knew) the other country had weapons of mass destruction. He would also not be justified in going to war if the only (or main) reason for doing so is the alleged possession by that country of such weapons. An Austinian assessment could tell us this much; and, theoretical preoccupations aside, it is not clear what more could usefully be said regarding the president's epistemic relation to the alleged presence of weapons of mass destruction in the other country.

Imagine, on the other hand, that it turns out that the president actually does have credible indications that the other country has weapons of mass destruction: a top-secret letter was intercepted that details quantities and locations; one of our spies managed to get into one of the facilities and has reported seeing the weapons; one of their top scientists defected and told us; their leader was shown on national TV visiting a facility and openly bragging that his country possessed the weapons, etc. It would seem that the president has all of the evidence anyone could reasonably ask for under the circumstances and given present intents and purposes. The Austinian assessment has run its course, let us assume. There is still the question of whether the president would be justified (responsible, wise) in going to war, or perhaps even wrong (irresponsible, cowardly, foolish) not to do so; but surely, we should not expect a philosophical account of knowledge to answer *these* questions for us. What more could we philosophically usefully ask about the case and, in particular, about the president's epistemic relation to the presumed presence of weapons of mass destruction in the other country?

The envisaged answer here, coming, respectively, from the traditionalist and the contextualist, is that we may, and should, still ask this: Does the president *know*? Has he been saying something *true* in saying he '*knows*'? It is in pressing these questions for purely theoretical reasons and from a purely theoretical perspective that we open the door to all of the seemingly intractable problems with which contemporary theorizing about knowledge, and Western epistemology in general, have been plagued. For might not the seemingly solid evidence have been misinterpreted? Can we, or the president, trust the experts on this? Might not the evidence have been fabricated or misrepresented by people in the military who are eager to go to war, or by enemies of the current regime in the other country, or even, out of gross miscalculation or sheer lunacy, by the current regime itself?[1] In the case of more mundane claims (to know) that such and such, one usually does not have to stretch one's imagination nearly as far in order to come up with *hitherto* uneliminated ways in which such and such might fail to obtain, despite all that we know or reasonably take for granted. This inescapable and undeniable fact—that the world may sometimes outstrip our wildest imagination, not to mention our reasonable expectations—has forced the traditionalist to opt either for fallibilism (which seems untrue of our concept of 'knowing that') coupled with antiskepticism

1. See Lewis (1996, 549).

(which is bound to appear merely dogmatic and empty to the skeptic), or else for infallibilism and the skeptical conclusion to which it has seemed unavoidably to lead.[2]

Austin's way of handling such seemingly weighty matters will again seem to both the traditionalist and the contextualist to fudge over important distinctions. For, once again, he seems to suppose that these sorts of issues can fully be disposed of at the level of what competently carrying on with the words involves and requires—the level of what we ought and ought not to *say*:

> 'When you know you can't be wrong' is perfectly good sense. You are prohibited from saying 'I know it is so, but I may be wrong', just as you are prohibited from saying 'I promise I will, but I may fail'. If you are aware you may be mistaken, you ought not to say you know, just as, if you are aware you may break your word, you have no business to promise. But of course, being aware that you may be mistaken doesn't mean merely being aware that you are a fallible human being: it means that you have some concrete reason to suppose that you may be mistaken in this case. (1979, 98)

But, both the traditionalist and the contextualist are likely to protest, *isn't there more that needs to be said here? Beyond the question of what we ought and ought not to say—which may lead us to run together semantic and pragmatic considerations that ought to be carefully kept apart—isn't there the fundamental, purely semantic, question of truth and falsity? Indeed, isn't it the case that we ought not to say we know, if we are aware we may be mistaken, because if we did we would be saying something false?*

The contextualist wants not to evade these questions, as Austin seems to him to do, but rather to address them head-on. So he says, 'Better fallibilism than skepticism; but it would be better if we could dodge the choice' (Lewis 1996, 550). And he tells

---

2. For this way of putting the traditional choices, see Lewis (1996, 550).

us how we can do this: supposing that the other country does have weapons of mass destruction, we could infallibly know this if only we could somehow *semantically legitimately* (as opposed to merely pragmatically legitimately) disregard seemingly far-fetched scenarios such as the ones just mentioned. And he offers us the liberating formula: it may be that in the president's (or our) context, the above scenarios do not constitute *real* doubts, or *relevant* alternatives, and therefore needn't be discharged or eliminated by the president (or by 'his experience' or 'his evidence') in order for him to truly say he knows. Not only reasonableness, but *truth* itself, does not require that these possibilities be discharged or eliminated.

But what sort of nonskeptical infallibilism is this? For all we know, and however seemingly far-fetched, couldn't one of the above scenarios somehow turn out to be actual, and couldn't it further turn out that the president could not reasonably be faulted for having failed to suspect that things might so turn out? Simply to insist that this couldn't happen would seem merely dogmatic. If you agree with Austin's general approach, you could respond to this by saying something such as 'We would then not know what to say', or 'What would you have said [if you were in our place, or if you were the president and had the (purported) information he had]?' (See Austin 1979, 88).[3] For these are the sorts of things people do say in such situations: 'Who would have thought?!', 'How could he (or we) have known?!', 'Everything seemed to indicate . . .' After all, by hypothesis, we ourselves have found the president's basis satisfying and his claim justified.

---

3. The Austin quotations are taken from a context that's slightly different from the one I discuss. But I do not think I am unfaithful to their spirit in the use that I make of them here. Hanfling seems to me to share in the Austinian spirit recommended here when he says, after discussing a similar situation, and anticipating the traditional philosopher's insistence that in such a situation the person who gave the assurance that such and such has turned out not to have *known* that such and such: 'In this situation the word "know" is more trouble than it is worth' (2000, 100).

For the contextualist, however, this sort of response would not be good enough. For surely, semantically (or metaphysically) speaking, if one of those scenarios turned out to be actual, it would show that the president had not *known,* wouldn't it? However *justified* the president still would be in having said he knew, and however *unjustified* anyone would be who faulted him for having said it, he still would have said something false, wouldn't he? It is true, the contextualist would be happy to acknowledge, that normally we would not *say* to the knowledge-claimer, 'So you didn't really *know* that such and such (did you?)', when such and such has turned out not to obtain, *unless* we meant that he should not have *said* he knew—but this is a matter of mere pragmatics. It might be pointless, or bad manners, or moralistic, to say that the knowledge-claimer didn't know, when we ourselves had accepted his basis as good enough for all intents and purposes, but it would still be *true* to say this, the contextualist would insist. He therefore has looked for a theoretically more satisfying response to the challenge from "far-fetched" possibilities—a response that would account for the seemingly undeniable semantic fact that if any such possibility turned out to be actual, it would reveal that the president had said something false in saying he knew.

The first part of the contextualist response to the invocation of 'skeptical scenarios' would be put by Lewis roughly along the following lines: 'Now that *you* have raised the possibility of such outlandish scenarios, they have become relevant in *this* context, and so they must have been eliminated by the president, if, in *this* context—the context that you have now enacted—he is to truly be said to have known' (see Lewis 1996, 559). This, according to Lewis, is what makes knowledge elusive: do some epistemology (or be paranoiac), consider incredible scenarios, and you'll thereby make it so that there'll be very little you or others could truly be said to know—but only in those contexts that are sufficiently affected or shaped by *your* worries and concerns. Travis and most other contextualists would not be happy with this part of Lewis's response. Most contextualists would want to allow that alternatives may legitimately count as irrelevant—as '*mere* (as opposed to real) doubts'—even if they *are* attended to; perhaps on the ground that there is no good reason to attend to them (other than sheer philosophical playfulness, or thickheadedness).[4] Travis says that skepticism just is 'incorrect', both inside and outside the study (1989, 187).[5] For most other contextualists, skepticism is true in the study, but, *pace* Lewis, not because the mere 'attending' to a possibility automatically makes it relevant. Rather, the epistemologist's traditional concerns and the nature of her inquiry are supposed to somehow turn possibilities that outside the study would normally be irrelevant into relevant possibilities, or alternatives.

But now, what if no one raised (or considered, or unreasonably failed to consider) the possibility of any skeptical scenario in the original context in which the president's words were assessed, but it now turns out that the documents were in fact fabricated and that there were no weapons of mass destruction? Here Lewis and Travis give essentially the same answer. Lewis simply says that 'the possibility that actually obtains is never properly ignored' (1996, 554), and then adds that a possibility that 'saliently resembles actuality' may not properly be ignored either (557). Travis puts the idea this way:

4. Or on the ground that their negation is 'pragmatically presupposed' in the context of assessment (see Blome-Tillman 2009).

5. Travis's considered position is actually not that skepticism is incorrect, but that it is nonsensical—that the skeptic, in saying that we don't, or can't, know this or that, does not so much as succeed in saying something that may either be correct or incorrect (see Travis 1991). In this, as well as in other respects, Travis is closer to the OLP perspective developed in this book than other so-called contextualists. I agree with Travis that at least certain forms of skepticism make no sense; but not because the skeptic attempts to use 'know' in a context in which its semantics (truth-conditions) are indeterminate, which is how Travis would have it. Rather, I think that some of the skeptical possibilities—the ones that have been taken to support skepticism about 'the external world' (that I might be dreaming right now, for example, or a brain in a vat)—actually make no sense. I argue this in Baz (forthcoming).

If there are facts to make this a case of F's not obtaining, then for any claim that A knows that F (or, equivalently, any occasion for judging whether A knows that F), there are some facts which show some doubt to be real for that claim or on that occasion which A has not discharged'. (1989, 162; see also 173)

In this way, Lewis and Travis build the so-called 'factivity' of knowledge (if you know that such and such, then such and such) and its infallibility (if you know, you—somehow epistemically—can't be wrong) into their account of what makes alternatives (or doubts) relevant (or real). If you turn out to have been wrong in taking it (and asserting) that such and such, or (as in Gettier cases) turn out to have been right only by some sort of luck (the documents you justifiably relied upon were fabricated, but there were nonetheless weapons of mass destruction), then you simply did not know—context-*in*sensitively, I take it—and it would therefore have been false, in *any* context, to say of you that you knew. For all that, we may still 'know a lot' (Lewis 1996, 549) and, in many ordinary contexts, may truly be said to know many things.

It is not at all clear that this account would, or indeed should, satisfy the skeptic. For it seems to amount to the claim that, on the assumption that the 'relevant alternatives' theorist of knowledge—be he contextualist or non-contextualist—is right about the semantics of 'know' and its cognates, many of our everyday 'knowledge ascriptions' *may* be true, but we do not and cannot (truly be said to) *know* them to be true. Only God could (truly be said to) *know* that. For *we* do not and cannot (truly be said to) know that none of the skeptical alternatives that have not been ruled out by the putative knower (or by her evidence, or experience, or what have you) either is actual or resembles actuality too closely.[6] We therefore do not and cannot (truly be said

6. As I say in the preceding note (n5), I actually believe that some of the most popular skeptical 'possibilities'—that I might be a brain in a vat, for example, or

to) know that none of those unelimitated skeptical alternatives to such and such obtaining is relevant. But *that,* presumably, is something we must know in order to know that someone knows that such and such. The actual ruling out or elimination of all skeptical alternatives may not, perhaps, be needed for knowledge, but it is still needed for the knowledge of knowledge. The 'relevant alternatives' account of knowledge—in either its contextualist or non-contextualist version—is therefore bound to seem to the skeptic as, at best, a roundabout way of acknowledging the truth of his position.[7]

At the other end of the field, anti-skeptical anti-contextualists have also not found the contextualist account satisfying. Once you allow that over and above the question of what commitments we take upon ourselves, or may reasonably be taken to have taken upon ourselves, in 'assertorically' saying this or that in this or that context, there is *always* the further question of truth and falsity—you open the door for people to dismiss all of the contextualist's data on the grounds that they pertain to the level of 'speaker meaning', as opposed to 'sentence (or word) meaning'. Once it is allowed that the speech-act of answering the contextualist's question of truth and falsity is itself beholden to nothing but, well, *THE TRUTH,* and carries no commitments other than theoretical ones, it becomes hard to say what's wrong with a theory that tells us when 'know(s) that' truly applies, context-*in*sensitively, and then explains away seemingly recalcitrant intuitions by appealing to complex extra-semantic factors. The anti-contextualist will argue that contextualism too is not free of counterintuitive implications.[8]

---

dreaming—make no sense. Here I'm ignoring this issue and pressing my argument from within the perspective of current debates. My aim is to show that appeals to the context-sensitivity of 'know' are quite impotent in the face of traditional skeptical worries.

7. Compare Fogelin (2000). For a strong assertion of the skeptical position, see Unger (1975).

8. The literature is full of examples that purport to establish the counterintuitive commitments of either side to the debate. Witness here Hawthorne,

What has concerned me in this book is precisely the set of assumptions and the philosophical mindset that have led both contextualists and anti-contextualists to suppose that the most we could reasonably hope for in philosophy—by way of understanding our own concepts and, hence, the human world they articulate—is a theory that does *relatively* well by the light of our intuitions.

It is hard to see how the current state of affairs in the debate between contextualists and anti-contextualists with respect to knowledge can be described as anything but a stalemate—a stalemate that seems to me to bespeak a crisis of philosophical paradigm. The former have relied heavily on examples of supposedly everyday situations and utterances that were designed to elicit certain intuitions from us concerning whether it would be true for someone to say of someone, N, 'N knows that such and such'. The latter have either questioned or outright denied the intuitions, or their robustness;[9] or accepted them but then tried to explain them away by attributing them to various pragmatic or psychological—and so presumably semantically irrelevant—factors;[10] or accepted them but then tried to show that

---

who says, in the course of arguing that his 'subject-sensitive invariantist' (anti-contextualist) theory of knowledge is the most plausible account of the so-called 'lottery paradox', 'This is not to say, of course, that there are no counterintuitive consequences to this version of sensitive invariantism. As far as I can see, every candidate story about our puzzle has counterintuitive results' (2004, 162). On the contextualist side, Cohen similarly acknowledges, 'Inevitably the conflict between contextualism and [Subject Sensitive Invariantism] will come down to which view has greater intuitive costs. And no doubt contextualism does have intuitive costs, despite my best attempts to mitigate them' (2005, 207).

9. See Bach (2005b, 62).

10. For a trenchant 'invariantist' criticism of contextualism, one which questions the contextualist's general reliance on intuitions, and discounts the intuitions on which contextualists centrally rely as revelatory not of the truth-value of 'knowledge attributions' but rather of nothing more than 'our willingness to make [a knowledge attribution] and the audience's willingness to accept it', see Bach (2005b). Similar objections to the contextualist argument can be found in Feldman (1999), Rysiew (2001, 2007), Williamson (2005b), and Brown (2005).

they (can) support a theory other than contextualism;[11] or else have altogether denied the relevance of those intuitions, and indeed of anything having to do with how we (ought to) use our words, to the age-old philosophical quest for an understanding of *knowledge*.[12] Various other kinds of moves, on both sides, such as appeals to the theoretical advantages or disadvantages of either position,[13] or to ways in which 'know' and its cognates compare in their functioning to other words,[14] have been, at best, indecisive. I do not say that all of the arguments on both sides have been equally compelling, and it should be clear by now that I take the contextualist to be closer to the truth than the anti-contextualist. But I also think that it is not clear what could possibly bring this ongoing dispute, in its present terms,

11. Showing that the intuitions on which contextualists rely can be accounted for by a sophisticated invariantist who appeals to the difference between knowing a fact and knowing that you know it, and knowing that you know that you know it, and so on, and to the different types of utterance (and action) each of those warrants, is one of the aims of Williamson (2005b). For a different kind of sophisticated invariantist counterinterpretation of the contextualist's data, one that appeals to varying extra-epistemic features of the *putative knower's* context, see Hawthorne (2004) and Stanley (2005).

12. Sosa (2000) charges the contextualist position in epistemology with committing the fallacy of inferring an answer to a philosophical question from information about the correct use of the words in its formulation. Hazlett similarly argues—by appealing to examples that are supposed to show the 'non-factivity' of our ordinary concept of 'knowing that such and such'—that 'traditional epistemology and ordinary language epistemology . . . would both be best served by going their separate ways' (2010, 522). This sort of position leads us straight back, it seems to me, to the worries about the 'prevailing program' with which chapter 3 opened.

13. In particular, there has been quite a lot of controversy about how satisfying the contextualist's understanding and handling of skepticism—which contextualists have often presented as an attractive feature of their theory (cf. DeRose 1995; Cohen 1998, 1999)—really is. See, for example, Feldman (1999, 2001) and Wright (2005).

14. See Stanley (2004), and Ludlow's (2005) cautious and subtle response on behalf of contextualism to criticisms such as Stanley's. I must say, in light of the argument of this book, that I cannot see why 'know' and its cognates cannot be, to a significant extent, sui generis in their properties and behavior, even if not in their superficial grammar.

to an end. The dispute seems to have taken the form of a Kantian 'antinomy'.

The way out of the dispute, I have argued, is to give up the assumption that it ought to be possible for us just to apply our words to cases without doing any work with them in doing that, and the further assumption that the application should then always be assessable in terms of truth and falsity. I do not say, because I would not know how to prove, that this pair of assumptions will be philosophically dangerous in *every* case. I only say, and have endeavored to show, that it is noncompulsory and not as well motivated as its adherents have taken it to be; that it *can* be philosophically dangerous; and that in the case of theorizing about knowledge within the Western tradition, it has led theorists astray.

Philosophical problems about knowledge, Travis argues following Wittgenstein, arise when 'language goes on a holiday' (1991, 246). Travis is thinking primarily about skepticism here. I basically agree. Getting us to suppose that it ought to be possible for us just to apply 'know that' or one of its cognates to any pair of person and fact apart from any context of significant use has been the most important move in the skeptic's, but not just the skeptic's, conjuring trick. I have tried to show, however, that at least in the case of 'know that' and its cognates, the contextualist's semantic ascent is not enough for bringing the words of our philosophizing all the way back to the language-games that are their natural, 'original home' (Wittgenstein 1963, 116). It is, therefore, not enough for saving us from difficulties for which not the meaning of the word (or concept) under investigation is responsible, but a conception of language that encourages ill-founded expectations of what the meaning of a word *must* be, and do. If we are to find our way out of those difficulties, 'true' and 'false' will also need to be brought back to the language-games that are their original home.

Epilogue:
Ordinary Language Philosophy, Kant, and the Roots of Antinomial Thinking

SEVERAL KANTIAN THEMES have made their appearance in this book at various points, more or less explicitly. I think it would be useful to explore this philosophical connection a little more systematically and in detail. While various links between Kant and, especially, Wittgenstein (early and late) have been proposed in the literature over the years,[1] the connection I have in mind has not yet been explored, so far as I know, though it is insightfully suggested at various points in Cavell's work.[2] There are striking and deep affinities between Kant's work, especially in the 'Transcendental Dialectic' from the *Critique of Pure Reason,* and the work of OLP.[3] There are also important differences. Both the affinities and the differences, I believe, are worth thinking about.

1. See, for example, Williams (1981) and Stocker (2004).

2. See, for example, Cavell (1969, 64–65) and Cavell (1979, 239 and [without mentioning Kant explicitly] 226–227).

3. The affinity is clearest in the case of Kant's treatment of the first two Antinomies of *Pure Reason.* I will mostly focus on that part of the 'Dialectic', ignoring interesting complications that would be added to the comparison if other parts of the 'Transcendental Dialectic' were focused on.

For the ordinary language philosopher as presented in this book, as for Kant, the fact that a dispute about a concept that members of both parties are equal masters of could go on in the way that the dispute between contextualists and anti-contextualists with respect to knowledge has, without it even being clear what could possibly settle it, suggests that both parties have been offering competing answers to a question that 'rests on a groundless presupposition', as Kant puts it, rendering the answers themselves not false, but somehow 'empty of sense *(sinnleeres)*' (1998, A485/B513).[4] Kant says that to the 'rationalist' (who in the case of each antinomy propounds the 'thesis') and the 'empiricist' (who in each case propounds the 'anti-thesis'), 'nothing seems to be clearer than that since one of them asserts that [for example] the world has a beginning in time and the other that it has no beginning and is from eternity, one of the two must be in the right' (ibid., A501/B529). But then they find that

> there is no way of settling [their dispute] once for all and to the satisfaction of both sides, save by becoming convinced that the very fact of their being able so admirably to refute one another is evidence that they are really quarrelling about nothing, and that a certain transcendental illusion has mocked them with a reality where none is to be found. (Ibid.)

Accordingly, Kant describes his method in that part of the first *Critique* as that of 'provoking a conflict of assertions, not for the purpose of deciding in favor of one side or the other, but of investigating whether the object of controversy is not perhaps a mere deception *(ein bloßes Blendwerk)* which each vainly strives to grasp' (1998, A423/B451). This is not unlike what I have tried to show about the dispute between contextualists and anti-contextualists with respect to knowledge (that such and such).

4. Compare Ryle's attempts to show in *The Concept of Mind* that 'both idealism and materialism are answers to an improper question' (2000, 22).

Both the ordinary language philosopher and Kant see our philosophical difficulties as, at bottom, conceptual difficulties, as opposed to difficulties with our understanding or knowledge of some ('transcendental') object to which these concepts 'apply'. Both also believe that, because those difficulties are conceptual, it ought to be possible for us to resolve them—not once and for all, but in each particular case. As Kant puts it, 'The very concept which puts us in a position to ask the question must also qualify us to answer it, since, as in the case of right and wrong, the object is not to be met with outside the concept' (1998, A477/B505).

For reasons that will emerge later, what Kant means by 'concept' is not what the ordinary language philosopher means by it. Kant, I will later propose, is a 'representationalist' in a way that the ordinary language philosopher, as I have presented her, is not; and this affects what they each understand and mean by 'concept'. If we keep this important difference in mind, however, I believe we may aptly say that for the ordinary language philosopher too, the object of many a philosophical difficulty—knowledge, for example—is not to be met with outside our concept. Given what the ordinary language philosopher means by 'concept', this means that knowledge, for example, is not to be met with apart from the contexts, real or imagined, in which we might felicitously refer to (speak of, invoke, claim, admit or deny having, etc.) it by means of 'know' and its cognates (and 'knowledge' itself). To master the use of these words is to possess the concept of knowledge and know what knowledge is. And this means that unless there is still something *empirical* for us to find out about some given situation, it should be possible for us, as competent employers of 'know' and its cognates, to tell how our concept of knowledge ought to be applied to—or, better, *in*—that situation. There ought to be no mystery here. We distort our knowledge, however, and turn into mysteries both the meaning of 'know' and its cognates and the situations in which these words may be of use to us, by imagining that it should be possible for us to know *knowledge*—and *thereby,* presumably, the meaning of 'know' and its cognates—as 'a thing in itself': that is, apart from the different contexts, and ways, in which 'know' and its cognates might competently be used. Something similar happens to us, according to Kant, when we attempt to apply our concepts to the world apart from what he calls 'the conditions of sensibility'. I'll come back to this.

Wittgenstein famously speaks of a tendency to become 'captivated by pictures', especially when we 'do philosophy' (cf. 1963, remark 115). Wittgensteinian pictures function as prototheories, and not only professional philosophers are liable to become captivated by them.[5] In raising questions about the 'object' of our inquiry, in the course of 'doing philosophy', we forsake the criteria that ordinarily and normally guide us in applying our words to objects and instead rely, in effect, on a picture of the object that we have formed for ourselves to ensure the sense of our questions.

As we have seen, in the case of the dispute between contextualists and anti-contextualists with respect to knowledge, there are actually multiple and variously interrelated pictures in play. There is first of all a picture of knowledge as a mental state that somehow reaches all the way to the known fact and guarantees its obtaining, thereby putting the knower in the best possible position for assuring others that the fact obtains. Possible alternatives to that fact's obtaining, what Travis calls 'doubts', are pictured as somehow coming between a person's mind and the (purported) fact, thereby breaking the superstrong link between them that would constitute knowledge; these alternatives must therefore be eliminated for knowledge to be attained. (The philosophical power of skeptical scenarios—the possibility that we might, for all we know, be dreaming, for example—lies in the picturing of a situation in which we presumably are failing to

5. For a useful discussion of the Wittgenteinian notion of 'picture' and its philosophical significance, see Kuusela (2008, 35–38).

come in contact with what we have taken ourselves to know, but have no way of telling that we are thus failing.) These are all aspects of the picture of the 'item' to which 'know' and its cognates are supposed to 'refer' or 'apply'. The picture of our words as somehow attaching, like labels, to items in the world may thus be seen to underlie the contemporary debate between contextualists and anti-contextualists and, arguably, any number of other contemporary debates with respect to propositional knowledge. This picture is encouraged, in turn, by yet another picture: the representationalist ('descriptivist') picture of human speech as consisting, first and foremost, in the production of representations ('descriptions') of states of affairs, or, as Wittgenstein puts it, in the communication of thoughts (1963, remark 304).

In Kant's case, the illusory 'object of controversy' between rationalists and empiricists is the 'absolutely unconditioned totality of the synthesis of appearances' (1998, A481/B509). In other words, the 'object' in question is the empirical world as a whole, thought of as a 'thing in itself', to which our basic categories of experience are presumed to be applicable apart from the transcendental conditions of empirical inquiry and judgment. So far as I know, Kant nowhere speaks of us as tending to form for ourselves a picture of this 'object'. He does, however, speak of us as having an 'idea' of this object, and he describes us as forming for ourselves a 'presentation' *(Vorstellung)* of that idea. And then he says something that connects him in an interesting way to OLP. He says that the transcendental idea is such that 'its falsity can more easily be detected through study of its application *(Anwendung)* and consequences than in its presentation alone *(abgesonderten Vorstellung)*' (ibid., A485/B513).

Thus we may form for ourselves a picture of the empirical world as a thing in itself—to which our concepts are supposed to be applicable from the point of view of God, altogether apart from the conditions under which *we* would be applying them. In the world as it is in itself, we might suppose, things just do stand in the relation of cause and effect to one another, regardless of what would lead *us,* in a given context, to claim (or just take it, or for that matter challenge the claim or deny) that one thing is the cause of another. And similarly we might suppose that in the world as it is in itself things just do stand in the relation of part and whole to one another, again independently of the conditions under which it would make sense for *us* to claim (or take it, or then again deny, etc.) that one thing is part of another.

A way of putting the general lesson Kant drew from Hume's skepticism would be to say that we do not really know what it is we are supposing when we suppose our concepts to be applicable to things as they are in themselves. But it is not *obvious* that we do not really know this. On the contrary, it can easily seem to us as if we do. That we do not gets revealed when we try to do something with, or reason on the basis of, our supposition. This, I propose, is what Kant means when he says that the falsity of the idea of the empirical world as a thing in itself can more easily be detected through study of its application and consequences than in its presentation alone.

For example, we think that if things stand in the relation of cause and effect to one another, independently of the conditions under which we may find them so to stand, then it should make sense for us to ask whether causal chains are infinite, or else end in a cause that does not itself have a cause. Or we think that if things stand in the relation of part and whole to one another, independently of the conditions under which it would make sense for us to say, or even just find, that one thing is part of another, then it should make sense for us to ask whether *everything* in the world has proper parts of its own, or else some things do not and are in this sense 'absolutely simple' (cf. Wittgenstein 1963, remark 47). And it is then, as Kant tries to show with his antinomies, that we run into trouble. We rely on the picture to ensure the sense of our question, but when we attempt to answer our question, we find ourselves pulled in two opposite directions, and we do not know what could possibly prove one of them right and the other wrong. We are at a loss; we lose our grip on words such as 'part', 'simple', and 'cause', or 'beginning', 'limit', and 'necessary'—words that in their ordinary and normal employment give us no trouble at all. The picture, it turns out, cannot replace all that ordinarily and normally guides us in our use of these words.

Kant's idea that certain mental presentations or pictures may seem harmless when considered on their own, and that their inadequacy only betrays itself when we attempt to reason or otherwise proceed on their basis, is strikingly echoed in a series of remarks in Wittgenstein's *Philosophical Investigations*. Here is an excerpt:

> What am I believing in when I believe that men have souls? What am I believing in, when I believe that this substance has two carbon rings? In both cases there is a picture in the foreground, but the sense lies far in the background; that is, the application *(Anwendung)* of the picture is not easy to survey. (1963, 422)

> The picture is there. And I do not dispute its validity in particular cases.—Only I also want to understand the application of the picture. (423; see also 424)

> In numberless cases we exert ourselves to find a picture and once it is found the application as it were comes about of itself. In this case we already have a picture which forces itself on us at every turn,—but does not help us out of the difficulty, which now only begins. (425)

> A picture is conjured up which seems to fix the sense [of our expression] *unambiguously*. The actual use [of the expression], compared with that suggested by the picture, seems like something muddled. . . . In the actual use of the expression we make detours, we go by the side-roads. We see the highway before us, but of course we cannot use it, because it is permanently closed. (426)

There is nothing necessarily wrong with forming for our-selves a picture of the human soul as an entity or item separable from the human body; and under certain circumstances such a picture may even serve a good purpose (say, in helping us to maintain a sense of inner purity and strength in the face of severe physical hardships). But as the history of philosophy has shown, problems begin when we ask, for example, how the soul knows the body, or animates it, or whether it survives the death of the body, and rely on nothing but our words and the picture to ensure the sense of our question.

There is nothing confusing or mysterious about Socrates's words when he tells his fellow Athenians that they must not care for their body or their wealth as strongly as for the best possible state of their soul, or about Stephen Dedalus's words when he says that the soul has a slow and dark birth, more mysterious than the birth of the body. Why then do we become so bewildered and entangled when we ask, with Descartes, how exactly the soul relates to the body, or whether it is separate from the body and survives its death? Why is it that, when we try to think Descartes's thoughts through, it becomes altogether unclear what his 'soul' means or refers to, or indeed *could possibly* mean or refer to?

The answer I propose is this. In the case of both Socrates and Stephen Dedalus, *there is a point to the words* and we are able to see it. We understand their words because, or to the extent that, we are able to see their point—to see, in other words, how they are meaning their words. It is clear to us, or anyway clear enough, what each of them means by 'soul', but what each of them means by 'soul' is not separable from what he is (most reasonably taken to be) meaning to say, from the particular point he is (most reasonably taken to be) meaning to make. The soul they speak of is not a nothing, but it is not a some-thing either. We *may* also come to associate various pictures or images with their words; but insofar as we are able to see their point, these pictures and images will be secondary, and the point primary: the aptness or usefulness of those pictures and images would itself need to be assessed in light of the perceived point of the words.

By contrast, Descartes's 'soul' is doing, and is supposed to do, no work beyond the purported tracking and recording of THE TRUTH. What *he* means by 'soul' is supposed to be determined by the meaning of the word alone, with the aid of whatever ideas and images he and his audience might have come to associate with the word. Descartes, we might say, *must* rely on the soul to be a something (a 'substance', as he puts it)—a something whose nature and identity do not depend on whatever point he or anyone might make by means of 'soul'. If there is not some such independently identifiable thing, such that Descartes could simply name *it* 'soul', neither he nor we can truly understand, let alone intelligibly answer, his question of whether the soul survives the death of the body, for example. But, again, that we cannot understand it is not something that Descartes's question wears on its sleeve. Rather, it is something we *find*—either when we attempt to answer the question, or when we ask ourselves what exactly we are being asked, and do not *assume* that Descartes's words by themselves can provide us with the answer to that question. The falsity of the picture of the human soul as separable from the human body reveals itself not in its presentation alone, but in its application.

In the last of the remarks I quoted from him above, Wittgenstein contrasts the 'side-roads' we take in our everyday employment of a word with the 'highway' we see before us, but cannot use, when we 'do philosophy'. The highway, I take it, is the philosopher's pure 'application' of the word. Borrowing Robert Brandom's (2008) terminology, we might say that the philosopher's 'application' of a word requires no special *entitlement* (beyond that possessed by anyone familiar with the word who is 'doing philosophy') and is free of all of the *commitments* that would ordinarily and normally attach to its use. The traveler on the highway is beholden to nothing but theoretical considerations and his picture of the object of his inquiry. When Wittgenstein says that the highway is permanently closed, I take him to mean that it is permanently closed in any of the contexts in which we would, or might, *use* the word. It is closed in such contexts by definition, as it were: you cannot be traveling on the highway and doing work with the word(s) at the same time. Try to perform the theorist's pure application in any context in which a *use* of the word is called for—try raising, for example, in a context in which a CEO is charged with having known that her company was in trouble, the theorist's 'purely semantic' (or 'purely metaphysical') question of whether the CEO's (outright) belief that the company was in trouble rose to the level of *knowledge*; or try raising, in a context in which the history of Mars is under scientific investigation, the philosophical question of whether (it would be true to say that) Mars was ever neither dry nor not dry (see Williamson 2007, 24)—and you'll condemn yourself to incomprehensibility, and worse. Of course, nothing stops us from attempting to travel the highway when we 'do philosophy'. The highway is not exactly closed then. But, as I have been arguing in this book, given what traveling on the side-roads of everyday thinking and speech normally involves and requires, there is no reason to suppose that attempting to take the highway with our words would get us anywhere (worth getting to).

In attempting to characterize the basic difficulty we run ourselves into when we 'do philosophy', Kant and Wittgenstein use strikingly analogous metaphors. Kant likens the philosopher who imagines he could apply empirical concepts to an 'object' apart from any connection with sensible intuition to a light dove that, 'cutting through the air in free flight, and feeling its resistance, could come to form the idea that it would fly even better in an airless space' (1998, A5/B8). Wittgenstein, in turn, talks of the philosopher (in each of us) who expects to find underlying actual language 'the crystalline purity of logic', and who accordingly believes that in setting aside all that the everyday employment of our words actually involves and presupposes she would be able to arrive at a clear view of our concepts and their interrelations, and thus to find her way out of philosophical difficulties. Wittgenstein likens this philosopher to someone who has 'got on to slippery ice where there is no friction and so in a certain sense the conditions are ideal, [but who], just because of that, [is] unable to walk' (1963, remark 107). Adapting Kant's and Wittgenstein's images to the dispute between the contextualist and the anti-contextualist, we might say that both have attempted to take steps with, respectively, 'know' and its cognates and 'true' and 'false' apart from the resistance or friction of everyday speech situations and the commitments that taking a step with one's words in such situations would normally exact. Wishing to be able *just* to classify given cases with respect to the words in question and so, in a sense, to do *less* with those words than what would ordinarily and normally be done with them, they ended up, I argued, expecting something of those words that there is no good reason to expect of them. It is like expecting a bird's wings to enable it to fly in a vacuum.

By way of first approximation, Kant may be said to part ways with the ordinary language philosopher and to remain bound to the traditional framework by being what I've been calling 'a representationalist'. One thing this means is that what Kant has in mind when he speaks of the 'resistance' philosophers imagine they would do well without is importantly different from what Wittgenstein has in mind when he speaks of the necessary 'friction' of which philosophers craving the crystalline purity of logic have deprived themselves. As we already saw, for Kant the question of sense appears to boil down to the question of whether our words succeed in referring to an object, and reference to an object requires, according to him, sensible 'intuition'. The conditions of (making) sense are thus, according to Kant's story, the 'conditions of sensibility' (1998, A240/B300; see also A239/B298)—or so, at any rate, it would seem. He says, for example, that 'we can understand only that which brings with it, in intuition, something corresponding to our words' (A277/B333). Kant argues that in the case of the transcendental object—be it the empirical world as a whole, or, for that matter, the soul, or God—nothing corresponding to our idea (or word) is given to us in sensible intuition, and this is why our attempted application of empirical categories to "it" is illusory and doomed to frustration. 'The merely transcendental employment *(Gebrauch)* of the categories', Kant writes, 'is . . . really no employment at all, and has no determinate object' (A247/B304). For Kant, as for the ordinary language philosopher, philosophical problems arise when language goes on a holiday—when we imagine ourselves still to be employing our words even though the conditions for their felicitous employment are missing. But for Kant, as for many in contemporary analytic philosophy, and in contrast with OLP, employment or use is understood purely representationally—in terms of the pure application of a 'universal', or concept, to a 'particular'. For him, the basic unit of sense is what he calls 'judgment *(Urteil)*'—the mental act of 'subsuming an individual under a universal'—not a humanly (socially, historically) situated linguistic act whose sense depends, among other things, on its having a point.

The above contrast between Kant and the ordinary language philosopher is accurate enough as far as it goes, I believe. But the fuller story is more complicated. For no sooner has Kant asserted that the transcendental employment of a concept is really no employment at all than he is forced to acknowledge that the very concept of the transcendental object—and more precisely, the concept of 'thing in itself', or 'noumenon'—*does important work for him*. Far from being merely empty, that concept is actually *'necessary (nothwendig)'*, Kant says. Its function is 'to prevent sensible intuition from being extended to things in themselves, and thus to limit the objective validity of sensible cognition' (1998, A254/B310). Though it refers to no object, and so does not function representationally, 'noumenon' nonetheless has an important use, hence meaning, in Kant's text.

And then it turns out that there are actually any number of other words—for example, 'Soul', 'God', '(Transcendental) freedom', 'unconditioned condition'—that despite being 'singular substantives' refer, and according to Kant can refer, to no empirical object, but that nonetheless are far from being empty or meaningless. We understand these words, or anyway are expected by Kant to be able to understand them, even though they bring nothing in intuition that corresponds to them. These words express what Kant calls 'ideas', and these ideas, he says, are neither 'superfluous' nor 'void': 'For even if they cannot determine any object, they may yet, in a fundamental and unobservable *(unbemerkt)* fashion, be of service to the understanding as a canon for its extended and consistent employment' (1998, A329/B385). These ideas are also fundamentally important, according to Kant, in 'making the transition from concepts of nature to practical concepts' (A330/B386). And of course, Kantian practical concepts—moral goodness, moral duty, moral friendship or love, etc.—are also emphatically not empirical concepts. In short, at the end of the day, the bounds of sense (sensibility, empirical significance) are not, for Kant, the bounds of sense (intelligibility, linguistic significance).

If Kant had allowed the realization that the legitimate employment even of 'singular substantives' does not (always) require that they first come to refer to something in the world, or be connected with an intuition, to inform his argument in the 'Transcendental Analytic', his response to Hume would have been more satisfying. Some of the least compelling and most obscure moments in that part of the first *Critique* are due to Kant's still thinking of human experience as the encounter between an isolated, disembodied subject and a 'sensible manifold'—an encounter in which the former supposedly puts order and unity into the latter by subsuming (portions of) it under concepts.

Hume stared hard at his billiard balls hitting each other and could identify nothing corresponding to 'cause' or 'necessary connection' in his experience. From this he mostly concluded that we have no *reason* to believe that the billiard balls will behave in the future as they have hitherto behaved. At other moments, and in faithfulness to the empiricist picture of how words come by their meaning, his conclusion is that the term 'cause' (or 'necessary connection') has been used by us 'without meaning or idea' (1993, 13).[6] It is clear that Kant thought that in looking for the meaning of 'cause', and for what legitimizes our employment of it, Hume was looking in the wrong place. But for all of his talk of the categories as necessary for what he calls 'experience *(Erfahrung)*'—i.e., a world-constituting unified system of objective judgments—I do not think Kant ever quite comes to tell us where Hume ought to have looked, insofar as the meaning of 'cause' is concerned and the question of what, if anything, entitles us to use that word or to make judgments of causation.[7]

6. See also Hume (1993, 49). Brandom also notes that Hume's skepticism hovers—not altogether consistently, it seems to me—between being epistemic and being semantic (2008, 96).

7. Brandom offers a response to Hume's skepticism that he attributes to Kant (via Sellars). Brandom argues, following Kant and Sellars, that 'the ability to use ordinary empirical descriptive terms such as "green", "rigid", and "mass" already presupposes grasp of the kinds of properties and relations made explicit by modal vocabulary' (2008, 96–97). Brandom's conclusion, as against Hume, is that 'one cannot be in the position the atomist (for instance, empiricist) critic of modality professes to find himself in: having fully understood and mastered the use of *non*-modal vocabulary, but having thereby afforded himself no grip on the use of *modal* vocabulary, and no access to what it expresses' (2008, 98). My main difficulty with this response, as a response to *Hume*, is that Hume clearly does recognize and finds perfectly legitimate one sort of modal relation—namely, what he calls 'relations of ideas', so it is not clear to me that he would wish or need to deny Brandom's claim that 'their involvement in . . . counterfactually robust inferences is essential to the *contents* of ordinary empirical concepts' (2008, 98). Nor is it clear that, if Brandom's Kant and Sellars are right in claiming this, this undermines Hume's skepticism about induction, or causation. Take Hume's famous example of the connection between bread and nourishment, for example (Hume 1993, 21). I take Brandom's 'Kant-Sellars thesis' to apply to this case in the following way: *That bread nourishes us is part of our concept of bread, part of what we mean by "bread". After all, it would seem that not many empirical beliefs are more counterfactually robust for us than the belief that bread nourishes. Should anything that seemed for all the world to be bread, and even to share the origins of bread, fail to nourish us, it would just not count for us as bread—our concept of bread would just not apply to it.* Perhaps, but, if so, Hume might very well say that the necessary connection between bread and nourishment falls under his category of relations of ideas, and therefore outside the target of his skepticism. He more or less says this much when he speaks not of bread failing to nourish us, but of 'a body of such sensible qualities' (1993, 21). It

Following the argument of this book, I want to propose that where Hume ought to have looked, first and foremost, is in the ordinary and normal *practice* of employing 'cause' (and related words):[8] the different sorts of situations, within and without empirical science, in which we might competently ask for the cause (or effect) of something, or attribute a cause (or effect) to something; the different methods we employ for identifying causal relations and for testing causal hypotheses; the different sorts of causes we talk about, and what sorts of causes are felicitously attributable to what sorts of phenomena; the role that theory may (or may not) play in guiding our search for causal dependencies; the *significance* of asking for or attributing a cause to something in different sorts of contexts (scientific, legal, personal, religious, and so on); the ways in which different kinds of interests affect what would count in some given context as the cause of what; the different ways in which the attribution of a cause to something might be challenged, and the significance, in different sorts of situations, of different sorts of challenges; and so on and so forth. To be sure, consideration of these matters would not have provided Kant with a response to Hume's skepticism about causation or induction that would have satisfied the latter. Nothing short of a direct and explicit assurance from

---

seems to me more likely, however, that if something like that happened on a large enough scale, an investigation would be conducted, to discover what about that *bread* (or about our digestion system) has caused it not to nourish us (anymore). What *is* true is that the investigation would be conducted under the assumption that there *must* be an empirically establishable cause for this unexpected and unfortunate phenomenon. This is something that Kant saw well, and in this he put his finger on an important tenet of the way *we* (moderns) typically think and conduct ourselves. But, as I note in the text, his argument in the 'Second Analogy' for why we *must* proceed under this assumption, if we are to have a world that is not merely subjective, is deeply problematic.

8. An important first step in the direction recommended here is to be found in Mill (1963). But the definitive text, and a very fine exemplar of OLP as defended in this book, is Hart and Honoré (1985). I am grateful to George Smith for pressing the relevance of these two texts to the treatment of our concept of causation sketched and recommended here.

God, it would seem, could answer Hume's skeptical question *as Hume understood it*.[9] But if our question is the Kantian *quid juris* question of what *entitles* us to use 'cause' as we do, or *legitimizes* our use of that word, in spite of the fact that we have no access to God's blueprints for the world, or if the worry is that 'cause' might actually have no meaning, then I believe there is no better route to the relief of the philosophical perplexity than a consideration of our ordinary and normal employment of 'cause'. 'Cause', I am proposing, has no more and no less meaning than we (English) speakers have given it, by using it as we have; and we are, and should expect to be, no more and no less entitled to use it than we make ourselves by actually (succeeding in) making use of it—whether customarily or more or less creatively.

The *quid juris* question thus boils down to the *quid facti* question, when the latter is correctly understood. Or rather: the two questions are not in fact separable in the way Kant assumed.[10] No doubt, we can *utter words* without any entitlement, but to the extent that we succeed in *using* them, we must have already entitled ourselves—by the humble standards of ordinary discourse—to using them in that way. Craving instead some sort of metaphysical entitlement that only a philosophical argument would secure (an answer to Kant's *quid juris* question), philosophers have ended up distorting the very thing they were seeking to legitimize or secure in the first place (giving false account of the *facti*, as it were).

There is a moment in the 'Transcendental Analytic' in which the *practice* of empirical inquiry comes into view as the key to

9. Quine's conclusion that 'the Humean predicament is [still] the human predicament' (1969, 72) is, accordingly, quite right, but only as far as it goes. That Kant's account of causation is not designed and was never meant to refute Hume's skepticism is one of the central claims of Watkins (2005).

10. Compare Wittgenstein: 'Our mistake is to look for an explanation where we ought to look at what happens as a "proto-phenomenon (*Urphänomene)*". That is, where we ought to have said: *this language-game is played*' (1963, 654).

understanding our basic categories of experience. This happens in Kant's general introduction to the three 'Analogies of Experience'. In a mathematical analogy, Kant says, when the two members of one relation and one of the two members of the analogous relation are given, the missing member of the second relation is 'likewise given' (1998, A179/B222). Thus, if we are looking for a number that relates to 4 as 4 relates to 2, say, then it is 8 we're looking for. In empirical inquiry, by contrast, the analogy only gives us 'a rule for *seeking* the fourth member in experience' (ibid.). I understand Kant's point to be this: in looking for the cause (or effect) of something, we do not and cannot know ahead of inquiry the thing we are looking for, for it has not yet been determined; we only know—have a schema of—how it would have to *relate* to the thing or phenomenon whose cause (or effect) we are seeking, in order to count as its cause (or effect). 'An analogy of experience', Kant goes on to say, 'is only a rule according to which a unity of experience may arise from perception' (A180/B222). The analogy—the principle, for example, that everything that happens has a cause—'will not be valid of the objects (that is, of the appearances) *constitutively*, but merely *regulatively*' (ibid.). And this means that our concept of cause and effect (for instance) is valid of objects—applies to them, if you will—only insofar as it guides our empirical investigation of them. Paraphrasing Wittgenstein (1963, remark 560), the point could be made by saying that if you want to find out what 'cause' means—what it is for one thing to count as the cause of another—you should ask yourself what form(s) *looking for* the cause of something takes within the practice of empirical inquiry. You should ask, that is, what asking for the cause of something comes to in practice, how answers to that question may be challenged or assessed, how they may be supported, etc.

This 'use-oriented' approach to the elucidation (and legitimization) of our concept of cause is no more than glimpsed in the above cited passage from the 'Analytic'. Ultimately, Kant was still too wedded to a representationalist conception of the relation between the human mind and its world to fully recognize that approach as a live philosophical possibility. His insight here, as in several other places, goes beyond the framework within which he generally thinks. We might say that he some-times comes close to doing what, according to Heidegger, *not even Kant* could do: jump over his own philosophical shadow (see Heidegger 1967, 150). And in those moments, he comes even closer to OLP's perspective than he generally does.

This happens again in several moments of the 'Transcendental Dialectic'. In those moments, reason's demand for the 'uncon-ditioned' or 'absolute'—the demand that, when combined with the idea of the empirical world as a thing in itself, generates the antinomies—is presented not merely as the demand to tran-scend the conditions of sensibility, but also—even primarily—as the demand to transcend the *temporal unfolding* of empirical investigation, or, as Kant refers to it, 'the successive synthesis of the manifold of intuition' (1998, A417/B444). Later on he refers to it—to the natural home, as it were, of our transcendental cat-egories and empirical concepts—as 'the advance of experience *(Fortschritt der Erfahrung)*' or as 'empirical advance *(empirische Fortschritt)*' (ibid., A493/B521; see also A479/B507). In wishing to (be able to) apply our concepts of experience to the empirical world in its totality, he says, we forget that 'the empirical syn-thesis . . . is necessarily successive'; we forget that the empirical application of our concepts carries with it 'limitation through time' *(Einschränkung durch die Zeit)* (A500/B528).

It seems to me that the temporality Kant invokes here may not aptly be thought of as the temporality of his transcenden-tal 'schemas' (1998, A137/B176–A147/B187), even though it is quite clear that in his mind these two were somehow closely connected; for it is neither the temporality (succession) of our 'inner representations', nor that of their Kantian 'objects'—the objects, that is, of scientific inquiry. Rather, it is the temporality of our empirical inquiry itself. Put another way, it is neither the temporality of the representation, nor that of the represented, but rather that of the practice of represent*ing*, of *forming* rep-resentations. And, even though I do not think Kant quite saw this, let alone the significance of this, this temporality, while not being the mathematical-objective temporality of what Kant calls 'nature', is nonetheless essentially public, or intersubjective, as opposed to private or 'inner'.

If Kant had followed through with this line of thinking, which, again, is no more than glimpsed in the passages I quoted from him, I believe he would have come to recognize as deeply misguided the starting point of his argument in the 'Second Analogy'.[11] There Kant famously argues that if it were not for our application of the concept of cause and effect to what encounters us in experience, we would be stuck with a merely 'subjective succession of apprehension' with no 'relation to an object'. Kant takes the burden of his argument to be that of showing that

> we never, even in experience, ascribe succession (of an event, in which something appears which previously was not) to the object, and distinguish it from the subjective succession of our apprehension, except when there is an underlying rule which necessitates us to observe this order of perceptions rather than another; and indeed, that this necessity is really what first makes possible the representation of succession in the object. (1998, A196–197/B241–242)

The controlling picture here seems to me essentially Cartesian: a lonesome and disembodied mind facing a sea of 'merely inner' presentations *(Vorstellungen)* (see A197/B242) and having to somehow move beyond them to an objective, mind-independent world. But, *pace* Kant's argument in the 'Second Analogy', the temporality of empirical inquiry—the way in which questions and answers follow upon one another, for example, or in which a challenge follows upon the raising of a hypothesis, or the execution of an experiment follows upon its planning, or a

---

11. That Kant does justice to something in the 'Dialectic' which 'he seems to forget in the "Analytic"', is a judgment shared by Merleau-Ponty (1996, 304).

further experiment follows upon a failed or inconclusive one—
is neither causally determined nor merely subjective or inner. It
is what the phenomenologists have called 'intersubjective', and
they have charged Kant, and much of the tradition of Western
epistemology (and metaphysics), with having missed that level of
human relation to the world. I believe they were right. And of
course, the shared activity of empirical inquiry is only one example. The back and forth of an everyday conversation, or a song or
a piece of music, or a mother's calling 'I'm coming, I'm coming'
as she rushes to her crying child, would have done just as well as
a counterexample to Kant's argument in the 'Second Analogy'.
All these carry with them or invoke a temporality (succession)
that is neither merely subjective, or arbitrary, nor causally or
mechanically determined or constituted.[12] I think that in many
cases, this temporality may usefully be thought of as musical.

More pertinently still, given one of the main themes of this
book, if Kant had fully acknowledged the essentially shareable
practice of empirical inquiry as the natural home of our empirical

---

12. Watkins seems to me to betray apt uneasiness with the Kantian argument
he wishes to vindicate, when he writes:

> While claiming that relational categories can solve the problem of time-
> determination may sound extravagant and appear to be driven solely by
> architectonic considerations, reflection on commonsense examples (such
> as what is actually involved when we not only look at a clock, but also
> interpret it as indicating objective time) makes it increasingly plausible to
> think that our everyday practices depend on an object's properties and
> causal mechanisms, which is an informal take on what Kant is arguing.
> (2005, 190)

And then he adds in a footnote: 'The point is even more obvious if one takes
"experience" in the restrictive sense of scientific experience' (ibid.).

From the perspective of my argument in the text, Watkins begs the question
when he invokes the clock example, and does it even more obviously when he
proposes to restrict the discussion to scientific 'experience'. People told time
by the sun and by the changing of the seasons and by aging long before it even
occurred to them to look for causal-mechanistic explanations of these phenomena. And they could relate and agree on the progression of a conversation, for
example, or that of a piece of music or poetry, even though it does not readily
lend itself to such explanations.

concepts, he would have come to see that, to use Heidegger's famous words, the real scandal of philosophy is not that, prior to Kant's 'Refutation of Idealism', no proof of 'the existence of things outside us' had been given (Kant 1998, Bxxxix), but rather 'that such proofs are expected and attempted again and again' (Heidegger 1962, 249). For he would have come to see that the application of concepts, which alone according to him wins for us a shared world, itself takes place, and is only possible, in such a world.

Even if Kant had gone *that* far, he still would not have gone as far as OLP in breaking away from the tradition as epitomized in the works of Descartes and Leibnitz on the one hand and Locke and Hume on the other. For one thing, the ordinary language philosopher does not take it, as Kant did, that we can know in advance which of our words or concepts is liable to give us philosophical trouble, and in what specific ways. Nor does the ordinary language philosopher take it that the natural home of all of our philosophically troublesome words is that of empirical inquiry on the model of the natural sciences. But despite these differences, which are not insignificant, Kant's anticipation of OLP seems to me striking. Thinking of Kant as having anticipated OLP could help us see his achievement in an interesting and fruitful light. Thinking of OLP as having been anticipated by Kant, on the other hand, would perhaps make the radicality of its break from the tradition a little easier to swallow.

References

Acknowledgments

Index

References

Alexander, J., and J. Weinberg. 2007. 'Analytic Epistemology and Experimental Philosophy'. *Philosophy Compass* 2: 56–80.

Austin, J. 1964. *Sense and Sensibilia*. Oxford: Oxford University Press.

Austin, J. 1979. *Philosophical Papers*. New York: Oxford University Press.

Austin, J. 1999. *How to Do Things with Words*. Cambridge, MA: Harvard University Press.

Azzouni, J. 2007. *Tracking Reason*. New York: Oxford University Press.

Bach, K. 1994. 'Conversational Implicature'. *Mind and Language* 9: 124–162.

Bach, K. 2005a. 'Context *ex Machina*'. In Szabó, *Semantics versus Pragmatics*.

Bach, K. 2005b. 'The Emperor New "Knows"'. In *Contextualism in Philosophy*. P. Gerhard and P. Georg, eds. New York: Oxford University Press.

Baker, G. P. 2004. *Wittgenstein's Method,* Malden, MA: Blackwell Publishing.

Baker, G. P., and P. M. S. Hacker. 1992. *Analytical Commentary of the Philosophical Investigations*. Vols. 1 and 2. Malden, MA: Blackwell Publishing.

Bauer, N. 'What's to be Done with Austin?' Unpublished manuscript.

Baz, A. 2005. 'Kant's Principle of Purposiveness and the Missing Point of (Aesthetic) Judgments'. *Kantian Review* 10: 1–32.

Baz, A. 2008. 'The Reaches of Words'. *International Journal of Philosophical Studies* 16: 31–56.

Baz, A. Forthcoming. 'Responses to Skepticism—Standard and Nonstandard'. *International Journal for the Study of Skepticism*.

Bealer, G. 1998. 'Intuition and the Autonomy of Philosophy'. In DePaul and Ramsey, *Rethinking Intuition: The Psychology of Intuition and Its Role in Philosophical Inquiry*.

Black, T. 2005. 'Classic Invariantism, Relevance, and Warranted Assertability Maneuvers'. *Philosophical Quarterly* 55: 328–336.

Blome-Tillmann, M. 2009. 'Knowledge and Presuppositions'. *Mind* 118: 241–294.

Brady, M. S. and Pritchard, D. 2005. 'Epistemological Contextualism: Problems and Prospects'. *Philosophical Quarterly* 55: 161–171.

Brandom, R. 1994. *Making It Explicit*. Cambridge, MA: Harvard University Press.

Brandom, R. 2008. *Between Saying and Doing*. New York: Oxford University Press.

Brown, J. 2005. 'Adapt or Die: The Death of Invariantism?'. *Philosophical Quarterly* 55: 263–285.

Burge, T. 1992. 'Philosophy of Language and Mind: 1950–1990'. *Philosophical Review* 101: 3–51.

Cappelen, H., and E. Lepore. 2005. *Insensitive Semantics*. Malden, MA: Blackwell Publishing.

Cavell, S. 1969. *Must We Mean What We Say?* New York: Cambridge University Press.

Cavell, S. 1979. *The Claim of Reason*. New York: Oxford University Press.

Chomsky, N. 1995. 'Language and Nature', *Mind*, 104: 1–61.

Cohen, S. 1998. 'Contextualist Solutions to Epistemological Problems: Scepticism, Gettier, and the Lottery'. *Australasian Journal of Philosophy* 76: 289–306.

Cohen, S. 1999. 'Contextualism, Skepticism, and the Structure of Reasons'. *Philosophical Perspectives* 13: 57–89.

Cohen, S. 2005. 'Knowledge, Speaker and Subject'. *Philosophical Quarterly* 55: 199–212.

Conant, J. 1998. 'Wittgenstein on Meaning and Use'. *Philosophical Investigations* 21: 222–250.

Craig, E. 1999. *Knowledge and the State of Nature*. New York: Clarendon Press.

Cummins, R. 1998. 'Reflection on Reflective Equilibrium'. In DePaul and Ramsey, *Rethinking Intuition: The Psychology of Intuition and Its Role in Philosophical Inquiry.*

Davidson, D. 2001. *Inquiries into Truth and Interpretation*. New York: Oxford University Press.

Davidson, D. 2005. 'A Nice Derangement of Epitaphs'. In *Truth, Language and History: Philosophical Essays,* with introduction by Marcia Cavell. New York: Oxford University Press.

DePaul, M., and W. Ramsey, eds. 1998. *Rethinking Intuition: The Psychology of Intuition and Its Role in Philosophical Inquiry.* Oxford: Rowman and Littlefield.

DeRose, K. 1992. 'Contextualism and Knowledge Attributions'. *Philosophy and Phenomenological Research* 52: 913–929.

DeRose, K. 1995. 'Solving the Skeptical Problem'. *Philosophical Review* 104: 1–52.

DeRose, K. 2002. 'Assertion, Knowledge, and Context'. *Philosophical Review* 111: 167–203.

DeRose, K. 2004. 'Single Scoreboard Semantics'. *Philosophical Studies* 119: 1–21.

DeRose, K. 2005. 'The Ordinary Language Basis for Contextualism, and the New Invariantism'. *Philosophical Quarterly* 55: 172–198.

Dummett, M. 1993. 'What Does the Appeal to Use Do for a Theory of Meaning?' In *The Seas of Language*. New York: Oxford University Press.

Fantl, J., and M. McGrath. 2002. 'Evidence, Pragmatics, and Justification'. *Philosophical Review* 111: 67–94.

Feldman, R. 1999. 'Contextualism and Skepticism'. *Philosophical Perspectives* 13: 91–114.

Feldman, R. 2001. 'Skeptical Problems, Contextualist Solutions'. *Philosophical Studies* 103: 61–85.

Feldman, R. 2007. 'Critical Study: John Hawthorne, *Knowledge and Lotteries*'. *Philosophy and Phenomenological Research* 75: 211–226.

Field, H. 1972. 'Tarski's Theory of Truth'. *Journal of Philosophy* 69: 347–375.

Field, H. 2008. *Saving Truth from Paradox*. New York: Oxford University Press.

Fodor, J., and J. Katz. 1971. 'The Availability of What We Say'. In *Philosophy and Linguistics*. C. Lyas, ed. London: Macmillan.

Fogelin, R. 2000. 'Contextualism and Externalism: Trading in One Form of Skepticism for Another'. *Philosophical Issues* 10: 43–57.

Fox, C. 2010. 'Wittgenstein on Meaning and Meaning-Blindness'. In *Wittgenstein: Key Concepts*. K. D. Jolley, ed. Durham, UK: Acumen.

Frege, G. 1977. 'The Thought'. In *Logical Investigations*. P. Geach, trans., and P. Geach and R. Stoothoff, eds. Oxford: Blackwell Publishing.

Frege, G. 1999. *The Foundations of Arithmetic*. J. L. Austin, trans. Evanston, IL: Northwestern University Press.

Geach, P. 1960. 'Ascriptivism'. *Philosophical Review* 69: 221–225.

Geach, P. 1965. 'Assertion'. *Philosophical Review* 74: 449–465.

Gendler, T., and J. Hawthorne. 2005. 'The Real Guide to Fake Barns: A Catalogue of Gifts for Your Epistemic Enemies'. *Philosophical Studies* 124: 331–352.

Gettier, E. 1963. 'Is True Justified Belief Knowledge?' *Analysis* 23: 121–123.

Glock, H. J. 1996. 'Abusing Use'. *Dialectica* 50: 205–223.

Goldman, A., and J. Pust. 1998. 'Philosophical Theory and Intuitional Evidence'. In DePaul and Ramsey, *Rethinking Intuition: The Psychology of Intuition and Its Role in Philosophical Inquiry*.

Grice, P. 1989. *Studies in the Way of Words*. Cambridge, MA: Harvard University Press.

Grover, D. 1977. 'Inheritors and Paradox'. *Journal of Philosophy* 74: 590–604.

Grover, D., J. Camp, and N. D. Belnap. 1975. 'A Prosentential Theory of Truth'. *Philosophical Studies* 27: 73–124.

Hanfling, O. 2000. *Philosophy and Ordinary Language: The Bent and Genius of Our Tongue*. New York: Routledge.

Hardwig, J. 1991. 'The Role of Trust in Knowledge'. *Journal of Philosophy* 88: 693–708.

Hare, R. M. 1952. *The Language of Morals*. Oxford: Oxford University Press.

Hare, R. M. 1970. 'Meaning and Speech Acts'. *Philosophical Review* 79: 3–24.

Hart, H. L. A., and T. Honoré. 1985. *Causation and the Law*. 2nd ed. New York: Oxford University Press.

Hawthorne, J. 2004. *Knowledge and Lotteries*. New York: Oxford University Press.

Hawthorne, J., and J. Stanley.2008. 'Knowledge and Action'. *Journal of Philosophy* 105: 571–590.

Hazlett, A. 2009. 'Knowledge and Conversation'. *Philosophy and Phenomenological Research* 78: 591–620.

Hazlett, A. 2010. 'The Myth of Factive Verbs'. *Philosophy and Phenomenological Research* 80: 497–522.

Heidegger, M. 1962. *Being and Time*. J. Macquarrie and E. Robinson, trans. New York: Harper & Row.

Heidegger, M. 1967. *What Is a Thing?* W. B. Barton and V. Deutsch, trans. Chicago: Henry Regnery Company.

Hertzberg, L. 2001. 'The Sense Is Where You Find It'. In *Wittgenstein in America*. T. McCarthey and S. Stidd, eds. Oxford: Clarendon Press.

Horwich, P. 2005. *Reflections on Meaning*. New York: Oxford University Press.

Hume, D. 1993. *An Enquiry Concerning Human Understanding*. Indianapolis, IN: Hackett.

Jackendoff, R. 1997. *The Architecture of the Language Faculty*. Cambridge, MA: MIT Press.

Jackson, F. 1998. *From Metaphysics to Ethics*. New York: Oxford University Press.

Jackson, F. 2001. 'Responses'. *Philosophy and Phenomenological Research* 62: 653–664

Kant, I. 1998. *Critique of Pure Reason*. P. Guyer and A. Wood, eds. and trans. New York: Cambridge University Press.

Kant, I. 2000. *Critique of the Power of Judgment*. P. Guyer, ed., and P. Guyer and E. Mathews, trans. New York: Cambridge University Press.

Kaplan, M. 1985. 'It's Not What You Know that Counts'. *Journal of Philosophy* 82: 350–363.

Kaplan, M. 1991. 'Epistemology on Holiday'. *Journal of Philosophy* 88: 132–154.

Kaplan, M. 2003. 'Who Cares What You Know?' *Philosophical Quarterly* 53: 105–116.

Kaplan, M. 2008. 'Austin's Way with Skepticism'. In *The Oxford Handbook of Skepticism*. New York: Oxford University Press.

Kaplan, M. Forthcoming. 'Tales of the Unknown'. In *New Essays on the Philosophy of J. L. Austin*. R. Sørli and M. Gustafsson, eds. New York: Oxford University Press.

Knobe, J. 2003. 'Intentional Action and Side Effects in Ordinary Language'. *Analysis* 63: 190–193.

Knobe, J. 2006. 'The Concept of Intentional Action: A Case Study in the Use of Folk Psychology'. *Philosophical Studies* 130: 203–231. Reprinted in Knobe and Nichols, *Experimental Philosophy*.

Knobe, J., and S. Nichols, eds. 2008. *Experimental Philosophy*. New York: Oxford University Press.

Kölbel, M. 2008. '"True" as Ambiguous'. *Philosophy and Phenomenological Research* 77: 359–384.

Kripke, S. 1980. *Naming and Necessity*. Cambridge, MA: Harvard University Press.

Kukla, R., and M. Lance. 2009. *Yo! And Lo!* Cambridge, MA: Harvard University Press.

Kuusela, O. 2008. *The Struggle against Dogmatism: Wittgenstein and the Concept of Philosophy*. Cambridge, MA: Harvard University Press.

Lewis, D. 1979. 'Scorekeeping in a Language Game'. *Journal of Philosophical Logic* 8: 339–359.

Lewis, D. 1996. 'Elusive Knowledge'. *Australasian Journal of Philosophy* 74: 549–567.

Ludlow, P. 2005. 'Contextualism and the New Linguistic Turn in Epistemology'. In *Contextualism in Philosophy*. P. Gerhard and P. Georg, eds. New York: Oxford University Press.

Machery, E. 2008. 'The Folk Concept of Intentional Action: Philosophical and Experimental Issues'. *Mind & Language* 23: 165–189.

Machery, E. 2009. *Doing without Concepts,* New York: Oxford University Press.

Machery, E., R. Mallon, S. Nichols, and S. Stich. 2004. 'Semantics Cross-Cultural Style'. *Cognition* 92: B1–B12. Reprinted in Knobe and Nichols, *Experimental Philosophy*.

Mallon, R., E. Machery, S. Nichols, and S. Stich. 2009. 'Against Arguments from Reference'. *Philosophy and Phenomenological Research* 79: 332–356.

Melnyk, A. 2008. 'Conceptual and Linguistic Analysis: A Two-Step Program'. *Noûs* 42: 267–291.

Merleau-Ponty, M. 1996. *Phenomenology of Perception*. C. Smith, trans. New York: Routledge.

Mill, J. S. 1963. *A System of Logic, Ratiocinative and Inductive*. In the *Collected Works of John Stuart Mill*. J. M. Robson, ed. Toronto: University of Toronto Press.

Moore, A. 1985. 'Transcendental Idealism in Wittgenstein, and Theories of Meaning'. *Philosophical Quarterly* 35: 134–155.

Neta, R. 2003. 'Contextualism and the Problem of the External World'. *Philosophy and Phenomenological Research* 66: 1–31.

Nichols, S., and J. Ulatowski. 2007. 'Intuitions and Individual Differences: The Knobe Effect Revisited'. *Mind and Language* 22: 346–365.

Pietroski, P. 2005. 'Meaning before Truth'. In *Contextualism in Philosophy*. P. Gerhard and P. Georg, eds. New York: Oxford University Press.

Pust, J. 2001. 'Against Explanationist Skepticism Regarding Philosophical Intuitions'. *Philosophical Studies* 106: 227–258.

Quine, W. V. O. 1969. 'Epistemology Naturalized'. In *Ontological Relativity and Other Essays*. New York: Columbia University Press.

Quine, W. V. O. 1991. 'Two Dogmas in Retrospect'. *Canadian Journal of Philosophy* 21: 265–274.

Ramsey, F. 1927. 'Facts and Propositions'. *Aristotelian Society Supplementary Volume* 7: 153–170. Reprinted in *Philosophical Papers*. D. Mellor, ed. Cambridge, UK: Cambridge University Press.

Recanati, F. 2004. *Literal Meaning*. Cambridge, UK: Cambridge University Press.

Ryle, G. 1971. 'Use, Usage, and Meaning'. In *Philosophy and Linguistics*. C. Lyas, ed. London: McMillan and Co.

Ryle, G. 2000. *The Concept of Mind*. Chicago: University of Chicago Press.

Rysiew, P. 2001. 'The Context-Sensitivity of Knowledge Attributions'. *Noûs* 35: 477–514.

Rysiew, P. 2007. Speaking of Knowing. *Noûs* 41: 627–662.

Schaffer, J. 2004. 'From Contextualism to Contrastivism'. *Philosophical Studies* 119: 73–103.

Schaffer, J. 2005. 'What Shifts? Thresholds, Standards, or Alternatives?' In *Contextualism in Philosophy*. P. Gerhard and P. Georg, eds. New York: Oxford University Press.

Schaffer, J. 2006. 'The Irrelevance of the Subject: Against Subject Sensitive Invariantism'. *Philosophical Studies* 127: 87–107.

Schiffer, S. 1996. 'Contextualist Solutions to Scepticism'. *Proceedings of the Aristotelian Society* 96: 317–333.

Schiffer, S. 2007. 'Interest-Relative Invariantism'. *Philosophy and Phenomenological Research* 75: 188–195.

Searle, J. 1962. 'Meaning and Speech Acts'. *Philosophical Review* 71: 423-432.

Searle, J. 1978. 'Literal Meaning'. *Erkenntnis* 13: 207–224.

Searle, J. 1999. *Speech Acts*. New York: Cambridge University Press.

Searle, J. 2007. *Freedom and Neurobiology: Reflections on Free Will, Language, and Political Power*. New York: Columbia University Press.

Soames, S. 2003a. *Philosophical Analysis in the 20th Century, Volume 2: The Age of Meaning*. Princeton: Princeton University Press.

Soames, S. 2003b. 'Understanding Deflationism'. *Philosophical Perspectives* 17: 369–383.

Soames, S. 2005. 'Naming and Asserting'. In Szabó, *Semantics versus Pragmatics*.

Sosa, E. 1998. 'Minimal Intuition'. In DePaul and Ramsey, *Rethinking Intuition: The Psychology of Intuition and Its Role in Philosophical Inquiry*.

Sosa, E. 2000. 'Skepticism and Contextualism'. *Philosophical Issues* 10: 1–18.

Sosa, E. 2007a. 'Experimental Philosophy and Philosophical Intuitions'. *Philosophical Studies* 132: 99–107. Reprinted in Knobe and Nichols, *Experimental Philosophy*.

Sosa, E. 2007b. 'Intuitions: Their Nature and Epistemic Efficacy'. *Grazer Philosophische Studien* 74: 51–67.

Stanley, J. 2004. 'On The Linguistic Basis for Contextualism'. *Philosophical Studies* 119: 119–146.

Stanley, J. 2005. *Knowledge and Practical Interests*. New York: Oxford University Press.

Stanley, J. 2008. 'Philosophy of Language in the 20th Century'. In *Routledge Guide to 20th Century Philosophy*. M. Dermot, ed. New York: Routledge.

Stich, S. 1988. 'Reflective Equilibrium, Analytic Epistemology, and the Problem of Cognitive Diversity'. *Synthese* 74: 391–413.

Stocker, B. 2004. 'Transcendence and Contradiction in the *Tractatus*'. In *Post-Analytic Tractatus*. B. Stocker, ed. Burlington, Vermont: Ashgate.

Strawson, P. 1949. 'Truth'. *Analysis* 9: 83–97.

Strawson, P. 1950. 'Truth'. *Proceedings of the Aristotelian Society*. Supplementary vol. 24: 129–156.

Strawson, P. 1974. 'Freedom and Resentment'. In *Freedom and Resentment and other Essays*. London: Methuen.

Strawson, P. 1998. 'Reply to John Searle'. In *The Philosophy of P. F. Strawson*. E. H. Lewis, ed. LaSalle, IL: Open Court.

Szabó, Z., ed. 2005. *Semantics versus Pragmatics*. Oxford: Oxford University Press.

Tarski, A. 1944. 'The Semantic Conception of Truth and the Foundations of Semantics'. *Philosophy and Phenomenological Research* 4.

Travis, C. 1989. *The Uses of Sense*. Oxford: Oxford University Press.

Travis, C. 1991. 'Annals of Analysis'. *Mind* 100: 237–264.

Travis, C. 1997. 'Pragmatics'. In *A Companion to the Philosophy of Language*. B. Hale and C. Wright, eds. Oxford: Blackwell.

Travis, C. 2000. *Unshadowed Thought*. Cambridge, MA: Harvard University Press.

Travis, C. 2005. 'A Sense of Occasion', *Philosophical Quarterly*, 55: 286–314.

Travis, C. 2006. *Thought's Footing*. Oxford: Oxford University Press.

Unger, P. 1975. *Ignorance: A Case for Skepticism*. New York: Oxford University Press.

Warnock, G. J. 1983. 'Claims to Knowledge'. In *Morality and Language*. Totowa, NJ: Barnes and Noble.

Watkins, E. 2005. *Kant and the Metaphysics of Causation*. New York: Cambridge University Press.

Weatherson, B. 2003. 'What Good Are Counterexamples?' *Philosophical Studies* 115: 1–31.

Weinberg, J., and S. Stich. 2001. 'Jackson's Empirical Assumptions'. *Philosophy and Phenomenological Research* 62: 637–643. Reprinted in Knobe and Nichols, *Experimental Philosophy*.

Weinberg, J., S. Nichols, and S. Stich. 2001. 'Normativity and Epistemic Intuitions'. *Philosophical Topics* 29: 429–459.

Williams, B. 1981. 'Wittgenstein and Idealism'. In *Moral Luck*. New York: Cambridge University Press.

Williams, M. 1999. 'Meaning and Deflationary Truth'. *Journal of Philosophy* 96: 545–564.

Williams, M. 2001. *Problems of Knowledge*. New York: Oxford University Press.

Williams, M. 2004. 'Context, Meaning, and Truth'. *Philosophical Studies* 117: 107–129.

Williamson, T. 1994. *Vagueness*. London: Routledge.

Williamson, T. 2000. *Knowledge and Its Limits*. New York: Oxford University Press.

Williamson, T. 2003. 'Blind Reasoning'. *Supplement to the Proceedings of the Aristotelian Society* 77: 249–293.

Williamson, T. 2004. 'Philosophical "Intuitions" and Skepticism about Judgment'. *Dialectica* 58: 109–153.

Williamson, T. 2005a. 'Armchair Philosophy, Metaphysical Modality, and Counterfactual Thinking'. *Proceedings of the Aristotelian Society* 105: 1–23.

Williamson, T. 2005b. 'Knowledge, Context, and the Agent's Point of View'. In *Contextualism in Philosophy*. P. Gerhard and P. Georg, eds. New York: Oxford University Press.

Williamson, T. 2005c. 'Contextualism, Subject-Sensitive Invariantism and Knowledge of Knowledge'. *Philosophical Quarterly* 55: 213–235.

Williamson, T. 2007. *The Philosophy of Philosophy*. Oxford: Blackwell Publishing.

Wittgenstein, L. 1958. *The Blue and Brown Books*. Oxford: Blackwell Publishing.

Wittgenstein, L. 1963. *Philosophical Investigations*. G. E. M. Anscombe, trans. Oxford: Basil Blackwell.

Wittgenstein, L. 1969. *On Certainty*. G. E. M. Anscombe and G. H. von Wright, eds., and Denis Paul and G. E. M. Anscombe, trans. New York: Harper and Row.

Wittgenstein, L. 1978. *Philosophical Grammar*. A. Kenny and R. Rhees, trans. Berkeley: University of California Press.

Wittgenstein, L. 1981. *Zettel*, G. E. M. Anscombe and G. H. von Wright, eds., G. E. M. Anscombe, trans. Oxford: Blackwell.

Wright, C. 2005. 'Contextualism and Scepticism: Even-Handedness, Factivity, and Surreptitiously Raising Standards'. *Philosophical Quarterly* 55: 236–262.

Acknowledgments

A version of section 2 of chapter 2 was published in the *Canadian Journal of Philosophy* under the title 'Geach's "Refutation" of Austin Revisited' (2010).

Portions of section 2 of chapter 4 and of the conclusion are part of a paper entitled 'Knowing Knowing (That Such and Such)', which was published in *New Essays on the Philosophy of J. L. Austin* (2011), Richard Sørly and Martin Gustafsson, eds., New York: Oxford University Press.

Portions of chapter 5 were published in the *European Journal of Philosophy* (2009) under the title 'Who Knows?'

Portions of chapter 3 will appear in a forthcoming article in the *Journal of Philosophy*.

Index